Gold Mining
in
North Carolina

D1568244

Gold Mining
in
North Carolina

A Bicentennial History

Richard F. Knapp
Brent D. Glass

NEW HANOVER COUNTY
PUBLIC LIBRARY
201 CHESTNUT STREET
WILMINGTON, NC 28401

Division of Archives and History
North Carolina Department of Cultural Resources
Raleigh

North Carolina Department of Cultural Resources
Betty Ray McCain
Secretary
Elizabeth F. Buford
Deputy Secretary

Division of Archives and History
Jeffrey J. Crow
Director
Larry G. Misenheimer
Deputy Director

North Carolina Historical Commission
William S. Powell (2001)
Chairman
Alan D. Watson (2003)
Vice-Chairman

Millie M. Barbee (2003)	Mary Hayes Holmes (2005)	Janet N. Norton (2005)
N. J. Crawford (2001)	H. G. Jones (2001)	Gail W. O'Brien (2005)
T. Harry Gatton (2003)	B. Perry Morrison Jr. (2005)	Max R. Williams (2001)

© 1999 by the North Carolina Division of Archives and History
All rights reserved

ISBN 0-86526-285-3

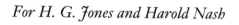

For H. G. Jones and Harold Nash

Contents

Maps and Illustrations

Tables

Foreword

Today few people think of North Carolina as a center of mining activity. Many recognize the state's long agricultural history and its equally important industrial heritage in textiles, furniture making, and tobacco manufacturing. Yet for virtually the entire first half of the nineteenth century, North Carolina was the preeminent state in gold mining.

The 1799 discovery of gold at John Reed's farm in Cabarrus County was the first documented strike in the United States. In its early years, gold mining served as a complement to agricultural activity. Farmers in the central and western parts of the Piedmont never completely abandoned their plows for shovels and pans. For the most part mining techniques remained primitive. Gold seeking merely supplemented agricultural pursuits and never replaced farming.

Even so, gold mining presaged more vigorous industrial activity in North Carolina that would emerge after the Civil War. The most outstanding example of hard-rock mining in the state occurred in the Gold Hill mining district in Rowan County. Gold Hill reached its zenith in the mid-1850s. As in any other mature economic enterprise, Gold Hill reflected essential forms of capital investment, mechanization, labor management, and the extraction of raw materials. As such, Gold Hill represented an anomaly in North Carolina mining.

In *Gold Mining in North Carolina: A Bicentennial History*, Richard F. Knapp and Brent D. Glass present case studies of John Reed and Gold Hill respectively that chart North Carolina's unique role in that industry. Both authors are eminently qualified to tell those stories. Dr. Knapp received his doctoral degree from Duke University. A longtime employee of the Historic Sites Section in the Division of Archives and History, he conducted the original research for the establishment of Reed Gold Mine State Historic Site. Dr. Glass chose the Gold Hill mining district as the topic for his doctoral dissertation at the University of North Carolina at Chapel Hill. Glass, former administrator of the division's historic preservation section, is now director of the Pennsylvania Historical and Museum Commission. Both scholars have published articles in the *North Carolina Historical Review*.

Robert M. Topkins of the division's Historical Publications Section saw the volume through press with the able assistance of Lisa D. Bailey, an editor with that section.

Jeffrey J. Crow, *Director*
Division of Archives and History

July 1999

Acknowledgments

As with so many books, the authors' debts are varied and numerous. Over the years many people have helped each of us with this project and with related previous research. Among all of those individuals, one man stands out—H. G. Jones. For nearly three decades Dr. Jones has played a critical role in the flowering of North Carolina gold-mining history. In the early 1970s, as director of the North Carolina Department (now Division) of Archives and History, he almost singlehandedly orchestrated actions that resulted in acquisition and development by the state of the historic Reed gold mine in Cabarrus County—open since 1977 as a state historic site and visited annually by some sixty thousand people. As director of Archives and History, Dr. Jones hired a young historian to study the history of that mine and aided a young graduate student investigating the story of the mines at Gold Hill. Years later Dr. Jones, a very active honorary chairman of a committee formed to commemorate the bicentennial of the discovery of gold in North Carolina, recommended that the same two researchers (now middle-aged) produce a brief historical survey of gold mining in the state. We are deeply grateful for all of his leadership and help throughout the years, most recently for an extremely thorough reading and critique of earlier versions of the manuscript for this book.

The manuscript has likewise benefited from full or partial readings by professional geologists Henry Brown, Al Carpenter, and Dennis LaPointe, who made numerous helpful suggestions. At Reed Gold Mine, John Dysart and Bob Remsburg patiently answered the authors' queries. Jeffrey C. Reid, chief geologist of the North Carolina Geological Survey, generously agreed to create a map for the volume. Within the Division of Archives and History, Michael T. Southern of the Survey and Planning Branch, State Historic Preservation Office, likewise supplied a map, and Historic Sites Section photographer Rick Jackson and iconographic archivist Stephen E. Massengill both shared their specialized talents in preparing and making available the illustrations for the study. Division administrators Jeffrey J. Crow, James R. McPherson, and Rob Boyette graciously allowed Knapp time to complete his portion of the manuscript.

Since this product could not have been prepared without our past studies of various aspects of the history of gold in North Carolina, we wish to express our gratitude to all who helped us in those endeavors, including people not specifically named here. Former gold miner and educational administrator Harold Nash not only physically saved many of the voluminous records of the defunct Gold Hill mining companies from destruction but also gave countless evenings and weekends to locating research leads, explaining gold mining in the state, finding (often deep in the woods) and preserving large artifacts for Reed Gold Mine, and building public support for that facility. At the University of North Carolina at Chapel Hill, Prof. John Kasson served as dissertation adviser for Glass (who wrote on Gold Hill); Leon Fink, H. G. Jones (again!), and Donald G. Mathews participated in that doctoral committee.

Numerous members of the staff of the Special Collections Department of the Perkins Library at Duke University, the North Carolina State Archives, and the North Carolina and Southern Historical Collections at UNC-Chapel Hill shared their expertise as we examined their historical materials. Researchers Kimberley Hewitt and Mark Schwalm kindly provided significant new information on the Reed mine. George Stinagle and Jeffrey Forret aided Knapp with historical reports on various gold mines. Over the years, particularly before the advent of personal computers, helpful secretaries at Archives and History patiently typed and corrected drafts of various reports.

And, of course, our wives Sharon E. Knapp and Bobbie Glass put up with more gold-mining "business," such as editing and proofreading, than they may henceforth care to recall. We thank them both. To lesser degrees, depending on their ages (none as old as our interest in gold-mining history), our children also shared in the experience of having a writer in the family.

Richard F. Knapp
Brent D. Glass

July 1999

Introduction

The Significance of North Carolina's Gold-Mining Industry

Most historians have depicted mining as a fundamental component of the industrial age, producing vast wealth for a fortunate few and harsh consequences for workers and the environment. In his classic work *Technics and Civilization* (1934), Lewis Mumford wrote that "mining is the prototype of all economic activity," with direct connections to capital formation, mechanization, and labor management. Mumford characterized mining as a "life-destroying" enterprise and mining regions as "the very image of backwardness, isolation, raw animosities, and lethal struggles." More recent studies have echoed Mumford's analysis. Anthony Wallace's *St. Clair* (1987), an in-depth review of a small Pennsylvania town's anthracite-mining region, concludes: "in the interest of saving money, most colliery operators ignored the best engineering practices . . . and tried to work poorly ventilated, inadequately timbered mines, prone to explosions, roof falls, fires, and floods that killed and crippled hundreds of miners annually and eventually bankrupted almost all colliery operators." In *Hard Places* (1991), Richard Francaviglia surveys America's historic mining landscapes and acknowledges that "wherever miners worked and ores were processed, one can see the results of their labor; mining communities huddle amid barren piles of waste rock, and mountains of tailings and slag are left in the wake of historic milling and smelting activity."

With notable exceptions, the history of gold mining in North Carolina does not reflect the grim portrait painted by Mumford and Wallace; nor does the appearance of the state's mining communities reveal the exploitation described by Francaviglia. Although mining was one of the state's leading industries before the Civil War, it never became an all-consuming enterprise. Most mining took place on established farms and provided a complement for agricultural activity in the state's central and western Piedmont region. The story of John Reed's mine in Cabarrus County, which is a major case study in this book, merits special attention not only because it was the place at which the first recorded discovery of gold in the United States occurred but also because Reed's story illustrates a pattern of industrial development that was repeated on dozens of farms throughout the state.

The principal gold region of North Carolina lies in the central Piedmont and extends more or less southwestward from the vicinity of Greensboro to the Charlotte area. Historically the most productive mines in that territory have been found in nine counties—Guilford, Randolph, Davidson, Rowan, Montgomery, Stanly, Cabarrus, Mecklenburg, and Union. Within the region, more than 250 gold mines have been identified (some geologists maintain that there are as many as six hundred mines and prospects), with the large majority being owned and managed by local farmers.

A typical account of one of those mines is found in the recollections of Robert W. Hodson, a Quaker from Guilford County, who began prospecting on his brother's farm in 1825 after gold had been discovered on a nearby farm. Although the Hodsons did not succeed in their first year of gold seeking, they continued their explorations after completing the fall harvest. Eventually they found enough gold to turn a profit for four years. Hodson's account of his enterprise reveals that he knew very little about the techniques and technology of mining and milling. Nonetheless, as he later described his research, "I applied my mind closely to gain a knowledge of Geology, Mineralogy, and Metallurgy from the best books, papers, and men, etc. in my reach—the manner of gathering and working metals in Peru and elsewhere." On the other hand, Hodson conceded that his methods were primitive and wasteful. Although the Hodsons lost much of their product during the milling process, the discoveries at their mine "produced a wonderful excitement. Men came from far and near, and went to work sinking shafts at random and getting no pay."

A corps of self-taught proprietors of small farms, such as John Reed and Robert Hodson, dominated much of the mining industry in North Carolina. Symbolic of the close relationship between agriculture and mining was the establishment of the *Miners' and Farmers' Journal* in Charlotte in 1830. For five years that journal informed the mining community of the intricacies of tracing gold veins, ore milling, fluxing, and other technologies. Advertisements for new equipment and all sorts of gold-saving devices filled its pages. The *Journal* also provided an important connection between the activities of the mine and those of the farm. Invariably the editorial perspective of the *Journal* reinforced the harmony between the two occupations.

While it is true that most gold mining in North Carolina never fully evolved beyond its agricultural base, it is also true that several of the largest mines provided a promise of industrial development that would later materialize in other resource-based industries such as textiles, tobacco, and furniture. In the early nineteenth century, political leaders in the central Piedmont saw the potential of mining as one of several industries that would lift a stagnant economy and serve as a catalyst for progress in education and social reforms. That progressive movement was led first by Archibald D. Murphey of Orange County and later by men such as Charles Fisher, a congressman from Rowan County and himself an investor in mining properties. According to Fisher, "the order and system practiced about the mining establishments will be imitated and introduced into the other pursuits and occupations of life."

Along with the understanding of the larger role that mining could play in economic development came a growing awareness of the role government might play in promoting mining activities. As early as 1823, the North Carolina Board of Agriculture appointed Prof. Denison Olmsted of the University of North Carolina state geologist and commissioned him to conduct the first statewide geological survey in the nation. In 1827 the North Carolina General Assembly began granting charters to mining companies, thus providing legislative recognition and also conferring upon investors a degree of legal protection from potential liability from losses associated with fraud or incompetent management. Government promotion of the mining interests culminated in the December 1837 opening in Charlotte of a branch of the United States mint; that facility coined nearly five million dollars' worth of gold by 1861.

The importance of government actions in support of mining did not overshadow the leadership of private enterprise in exploiting North Carolina's mineral resources. Private interests assembled the essential components for industrialization, including capital, skilled labor, and power technology. From the moment North Carolina's mines evolved from surface to deep-mining operations, mine owners could no longer afford to be part-time farmers but became, of necessity, full-time businessmen heading small companies that attracted investors from throughout the state, major northern cities, and western Europe.

The most exceptional example of a fully developed hard-rock mine in North Carolina was the Gold Hill mining district in Rowan County, the second case study in this book. At its peak of productivity and profitability in the mid-1850s, Gold Hill reflected all the essential conditions of a mature industrial community. Investors traded its stock on a New York exchange. Experienced supervisors and engineers from Cornwall directed three shifts of laborers. Dynamite explosions rocked the underground works, while the rhythmic hissing of steam engines dominated the daily routine above ground. Yet even in the Gold Hill mining district and at the handful of other deep mines in the gold region, industry never replaced farming. Before the Civil War, in fact, mining provided an outlet for slave workers from nearby farms, thus sustaining the farm economy during periods of low prices or poor production. The story of mining in North Carolina offers impressive evidence of industrialization that struck a balance between industry and agriculture, a balance that persisted in other, more successful, industries that fueled the state's economy well into the end of the twentieth century. The result was that North Carolina became an anomaly in modern, industrial America—both a leading manufacturing state and one of the most rural states in the nation. The farmer-miners of nearly two centuries ago would not have been surprised.

1

Antebellum Gold Mining: An Overview

Since the dawn of civilization, gold has been the substance most frequently relied upon to serve as a measure of mankind's accumulated wealth. For countless centuries the metal has attracted the attention and greed of men and nations and played a significant role in history, including that of the ancient empires of Egypt, Greece, and Rome. In the New World—following several centuries of searching and exploitation by Europeans eager for gold and silver—a domestic gold-mining industry in the United States first arose after the accidental discovery of gold in a creek in Cabarrus County, North Carolina, in 1799. In the years following that discovery, workers at several mines in the area sought the metal in creek beds and washed it in pans and rockers. A genuine rush emerged in the decade after 1825 when farmers discovered that gold also occurred in outcroppings of quartz veins on hillsides near creeks that contained the metal. Thousands of individuals, small groups, and companies plunged into the search for treasure by opening surface mines in the weathered outcroppings of gold-bearing quartz veins. This initial bubble finally burst, but in the 1850s larger Carolina mines, with improved and more pervasive technology and new capital, thrived briefly again. Nearly all gold-mining operations ceased during the Civil War.

By the waning years of the nineteenth century, most creek-bed and near-surface deposits of gold had been depleted. As in the 1850s, mining had extended into deeper and harder-to-work ore. Because of these difficulties, and despite technological advances, gold mining became unprofitable. After 1900, except for an interval during the Great Depression, the story was similar. Mines operated sporadically with a downward trend until 1964, when the last operating mill—its site now a residential subdivision—closed its doors.

But gold fever is not easily cured. From time to time, mining companies and geologists still explore for gold in North Carolina. The intensity of such efforts rises and falls with the price of gold, the development of new gold-recovery technologies, and the discovery of new types of gold deposits perhaps previously overlooked. In addition, many amateurs and hobbyists still pan the creeks of the state's old gold-mining regions and peruse geological reports to learn about gold in North Carolina.

Hunters of gold usually encountered it as free gold on or near the earth's surface. Chemical and physical properties of the mineral made identification easy. Gold, with a specific gravity of 19.3, is nineteen times heavier than water, eight times heavier than sand, three times as heavy as iron, and twice as heavy as silver or copper. Insoluble in the strongest acids except aqua regia (a mixture of nitric and hydrochloric acids), gold is the most imperishable, easily worked, and malleable of metals. It can be shaved or flattened with a knife and beaten into extremely thin sheets known as gold leaf. In contrast, pyrite (fool's gold) has a brassy shimmer, and a speck of pyrite tapped with a knife shatters. In sunlight, pyrite may sparkle; between one's teeth it feels distinctly gritty, whereas gold seems softer and is not gritty.

For nearly two centuries, geologists have offered explanations of how gold deposits were formed in North Carolina. The gold-bearing quartz veins and fine-grained disseminated gold deposits in various regions of the state are most commonly associated with ancient volcanic rocks and the effects of hot circulating water. Geologists now believe that some gold deposits, especially the fine-grained disseminated types, were created near the time when those rocks were first formed. Gold-bearing veins of quartz appear to have formed later when those rocks, and possibly nonvolcanic surrounding rocks, were heated, deformed, and fractured during mountain-building. Sulfides of iron and copper (pyritic materials) are common associates of gold in deposits. The easily visible coarse gold derived from quartz veins was the first type of gold mined in North Carolina. Gradual erosion exposed the veins, and their upper, or near-surface, portions decomposed over eons. Weathering not only freed the gold from quartz veins, allowing it to concentrate in soil and creek bottoms, but also weathered some of the associated pyritic materials still in veins and made them easy to remove and separate from the quartz by mechanical means.

Not only quartz veins but also bedrock containing fine-grained dissemi-nated gold weathered into easily excavated and crushed saprolite (rotten, disintegrated rock) near the surface of the earth, especially above the water table. (In most places in North Carolina, the depth of rock weathering extends to some fifty feet and, in some instances, to one hundred feet.) That saprolitic, often gold-rich brown-colored ore, known as gossan, contrasted with still deeper, unweathered gold-bearing material, which frequently was combined with unoxidized pyrites of copper or iron. Deeper, unweathered gold quartz

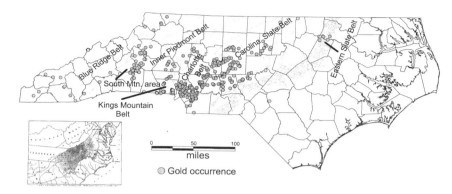

Principal gold regions of North Carolina. Map by North Carolina Geological Survey. Inset: Gold region of the southeastern United States, ca. 1895. Map from Henry B. C. Nitze and H. A. J. Wilkens, *Gold Mining in North Carolina and Adjacent South Appalachian Regions*, North Carolina Geological Survey Bulletin No. 10 (Raleigh: Guy V. Barnes, Public Printer, 1897), 12. (All other illustrations from the files of the Division of Archives and History unless otherwise indicated.)

veins and disseminated deposits were much harder to excavate and crush. In addition, associated copper and iron pyrites made separation of gold more difficult once crushing had been done. Such pyritic gold ore was referred to as refractory ore and, because it still contained sulfur combined with copper and iron, was also called sulfuret ore. Successful recovery of gold from crushed sulfuret ore required sophisticated chemical operations unavailable until the late nineteenth century.

Gold is found in six major regions in North Carolina west of the Coastal Plain. It is difficult to define the precise borders of those areas. They correspond roughly with geologic belts wherein each belt is identified by a specific suite of rocks with a common history. (Some geologists now use the term "terranes" rather than belts.) The eastern gold region in the eastern slate geologic belt comprises at least 300 square miles, the heart of which lies in Warren, Halifax, Nash, and Franklin Counties and features abundant weathered quartz veinlets. To the west is the Carolina slate belt, 10 to 60 miles wide and extending southwestward from Person County to South Carolina. The Carolina slate belt merges on the west into the Charlotte (Carolina igneous) belt, some 15 to 30 miles wide, with gold deposits concentrated in Guilford, Davidson, Rowan, Cabarrus, and Mecklenburg Counties. The Carolina slate belt and the Charlotte belt contained a preponderance of the state's largest and most productive gold mines. Next, to the west, is the Kings Mountain belt, with mines widely scattered in Cleveland, Gaston, Lincoln, and Catawba Counties. The South Mountain gold region, located in the inner Piedmont geologic belt, is ten to eleven miles wide in Burke, McDowell, and Rutherford Counties and extends from a little northeast of Morganton to near Rutherfordton. Lucrative gold deposits there were almost exclusively placers—that is, gold found in creek beds or near the surface in soils. Finally, the metal is found in most counties west of the Blue Ridge mountain front in the Blue Ridge geologic belt, particularly in Ashe, Cherokee, and Henderson. Nearly half of all land in the state is within a gold region.

As previously noted, the first authenticated discovery of gold in North Carolina occurred in 1799; but with the precious metal present in such an extensive portion of the state, it is likely that someone may have encountered it at an earlier date. Did pre-Columbian Indians pan a bit of gold for ornamental use? Certainly the Spaniards' learning of Native Americans' gold and silver in South and Central America stimulated Europeans in North America to seek gold there. Ponce de Leon in 1513 observed an Indian chief in Florida with a store of gold. Spaniards after him wrote of the riches of the southern Appalachians. The English were equally greedy: in 1663 Charles II reserved for himself one-fourth of any gold or silver that might be found in Carolina. In 1774 Gov. Josiah Martin supposedly received a specimen of gold from Guilford County. Thomas Jefferson reported a seventeen-pennyweight nugget found on the Rappahannock River in Virginia. Neither event created much excitement. "Evidence" of pre-Revolutionary mining appeared over the next century. Early Indians probably possessed copper, mica, and gold, but it is unlikely that they systematically *mined* gold. In contrast, mining at John Reed's Cabarrus County farm—scene of the initial discovery of gold—was extensive and led to the nation's first gold rush.

The rush did not begin overnight, however, inasmuch as Reed did not realize that he owned valuable gold until three years after his son in 1799 found a heavy gold-bearing rock in a creek on the family farm. In 1803 Reed formed a partnership with three friends, who supplied equipment and a few slaves to dig in the creek. The following year the United States mint in Philadelphia received eleven thousand dollars' worth of gold from Cabarrus County (perhaps all from Reed). Soon word leaked out. President Thomas Jefferson and readers of the mint's annual report for 1804 learned of the find. A few periodicals carried the news. Congressman Nathaniel Alexander of Charlotte received a beautiful nugget from one of the partners. Moravians around Salem heard of the precious metal when craftsman Jacob Loesch received Cabarrus ore for smelting; soon several people, one using a divining rod, began searching for gold there.

Meanwhile, Reed's miners picked up most of the lumps of gold and began washing sand from the creek in search of finer particles. For such washing, the workers relied heavily and perhaps exclusively upon pans and devices known

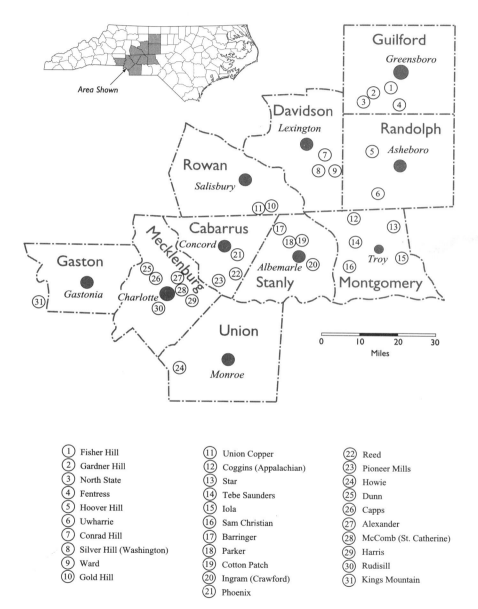

Leading gold mines in Carolina slate belt and Charlotte belt. Map by Michael Southern, Division of Archives and History. Mine locations are approximate.

① Fisher Hill
② Gardner Hill
③ North State
④ Fentress
⑤ Hoover Hill
⑥ Uwharrie
⑦ Conrad Hill
⑧ Silver Hill (Washington)
⑨ Ward
⑩ Gold Hill

⑪ Union Copper
⑫ Coggins (Appalachian)
⑬ Star
⑭ Tebe Saunders
⑮ Iola
⑯ Sam Christian
⑰ Barringer
⑱ Parker
⑲ Cotton Patch
⑳ Ingram (Crawford)
㉑ Phoenix

㉒ Reed
㉓ Pioneer Mills
㉔ Howie
㉕ Dunn
㉖ Capps
㉗ Alexander
㉘ McComb (St. Catherine)
㉙ Harris
㉚ Rudisill
㉛ Kings Mountain

Miner using rocker to recover gold. From Thomas Egleston, *The Metallurgy of Silver, Gold, and Mercury in the United States*, 2 vols. (New York: J. Wiley and Sons, 1887-1890).

as "rockers." An old frying pan could be used to swirl gravel and water and thus separate the heavier gold. The rocker was a box, half-barrel, or half of a hollow tree rocked by hand to wash away lighter material while leaving behind particles of metal. The precise date the first rocker appeared at the Reed is unknown, but the men copied a similar implement employed nearby by a Baltimore man. Soon rockers were in common use.

Perhaps the Baltimore miner was William Thornton—physician, inventor, and designer of the United States Capitol. By the time he arrived, several creek mines were being actively worked. Two of them—the Parker and Harris mines—opened about 1805, possibly preceded by the Dunn in Mecklenburg. Two Marylanders purchased mining land south of Reed and might have employed the rocker-like devices. In 1805 Dr. Stephen Ayres visited the Reed and nearby sites. Panning in all directions, he found gold as far as seventy miles away. Thornton formed a joint-stock company to mine near the Reed. His North Carolina Gold Mine Company apparently purchased 35,000 acres in adjacent Montgomery (now Stanly) County. By 1806 a former governor of Maryland, the treasurer of the United States, and a bank president were directors of the enterprise. A glowing prospectus boasted of easy profits to be had from slaves washing for gold. It is uncertain whether the company did any mining, for shortly it was defunct. Meanwhile Thornton proposed to hire herdsmen to tend sheep and also seek gold, saying he sought "Gold and Fleece, though not the golden fleece."

Gradually surface mining grew as a seasonal, part-time business conducted by amateurs, who still relied upon simple pans and rockers, at times with mercury in them, to catch the gold. By 1810 the Philadelphia mint had assayed 1,300 ounces of Cabarrus gold; even the worst sample exceeded 22 carats fine, the standard for coins. Interest began to rise at various locations in the

Piedmont, but most mining was not very lucrative. For two decades Reed's diggings continued as the principal source of domestic gold in the state and nation. A few other creek mines—the Dunn, Harris, and Parker—were notable. By 1820 gold had been discovered in Anson, Cabarrus, Mecklenburg, Montgomery, and several other counties. One lucky fellow found a nugget that weighed nearly five pounds at the Parker mine in Montgomery (later Stanly) County, and soon more than a hundred men were digging in the creek there. By 1820 methods of extraction throughout the small but growing gold region had scarcely changed since 1803. Local farmers became part-time miners, and haphazard trial and error prevailed over any semblance of science. In 1823 newspaper editors knew of no "person of science" in the gold fields.

Yet about 1824 the small, rising output of gold began to affect the local and national economy. In that year, North Carolina miners sent five thousand dollars' worth of gold to the mint, well above the average of the preceding twenty years. Only North Carolina produced any native gold for the mint. Output had not been constant: a few large nuggets could skew a particular year, and consistent annual shipments to the mint were minor. Perhaps one-third to one-half of North Carolina gold reached the mint; much of the rest was circulated or sold to artisans. A decreasing amount of money in use throughout the nation enhanced the relative value of gold. By 1819 only five dollars circulated for each citizen. North Carolina had merely three principal banks for its 600,000 people. Rhode Island, with 70,000 people, had forty-three banks. Gold served as currency in the growing gold region. Touring the area, geologist Denison Olmsted observed: "Almost every man carries with him a goose quill or two of it [gold], and a small pair of scales in a box like a spectacle case. The value, as in patriarchal times, is ascertained by weight. . . . I saw a pint of whiskey paid for by weighing of 3 1/2 grains of gold." Merchants and farmers offered a variety of supplies and foodstuffs in exchange for miners' gold.

Yale-trained Olmsted was the first of several New Englanders to introduce serious geological study to the state government in North Carolina. In 1823, while a professor of chemistry at the state university in Chapel Hill, he convinced a conservative state legislature to fund four years of fieldwork to assess the state's geological composition. The following summer he began work west of Raleigh in the auriferous Carolina slate belt. In 1825 Olmsted again visited the gold region, hired German miner and mineralogist Charles E. Rothe to conduct a more comprehensive study of that promising area, and then returned to Yale. New Englander Elisha Mitchell, one of Olmsted's classmates at Yale and a colleague at Chapel Hill, completed the final two years of the study. Both Rothe and Mitchell produced reports to the legislature, as well as articles on North Carolina's gold that appeared in the prominent new *American Journal of Science*. Although funding expired after 1827, Rothe and Mitchell's labors represented the nation's first professional (and published) geological

11

work to be conducted at state expense. After Tennessee and New York commenced geological surveys in the 1830s, North Carolina renewed its efforts in the 1850s. Continuing into the 1990s, each new generation of state-employed geologists undertook the periodic study and description of gold-related resources in North Carolina. Many of those scientists, like their predecessors Rothe and Mitchell, continued to recognize the value not only of mineral wealth but also of agriculture to the state's economy.

Nineteenth-century farmers remained interested in seasonal placer mining. While most Carolinians practiced subsistence agriculture without slaves, cotton was expanding in the economy. By 1821 eight states, including North Carolina, individually produced five times as much cotton as had the entire nation in 1790. Farmers in Mecklenburg County, heart of the mining district, grew a considerable amount of cotton, and slaves constituted 38 percent of the county's population as late as 1860. The fluctuating price of cotton created a relationship between farming and mining. When cotton prices declined after 1818, mining attracted some farmers and slave owners. By 1824 cotton production climbed, while prices fell again. The decline continued for decades, but growers' costs did not fall correspondingly. Among options available to growers were emigration from the state or a switch to mining. Numerous citizens tried their luck in the slowly expanding placer fields.

Landowners let others mine their creeks for a percentage of the take. Some owners got one-fourth of the gold; others charged up to one-half. Frequently several lessees worked together, digging gravel and washing it in rockers. As years passed, the system grew varied, with leases specifying as little as one-fifteenth of the gold and terms as long as ten years. Owners ran a great risk: tempted miners and slaves pocketed a goodly share of gold. At some mines, perhaps as much as one-third of the gold was stolen by slaves and trespassers.

By 1824 mines were still worked in a haphazard, inefficient manner with little equipment. Olmsted found "the average product [at Reed] is not more than sixty cents per day" per hand. *Niles' Weekly Register* proclaimed that mining in North Carolina had "all the uncertainty of a lottery." A traveler in Guilford County declared that the miners' scant machinery "looked as though it had been made by children, with a penknife." In a few years some Carolina panners cleared up to five dollars a day; others made only twenty-five cents. As digging for gold slowly evolved into a business with employees rather than self-employed individuals, wages for native whites often were only fifty cents per day. Gold mining was an infant but growing industry and largely a spare-time occupation with irregular results. Each summer a few more farmers became miners; the gold region expanded to several significant placer mines and into portions of half a dozen counties. Knowledgeable visitors such as Olmsted and Rothe began to appear. Their thoughtful suggestions, and some miners' experience, led to limited technological gains and fostered increased, more

Panning was the slowest and simplest way of separating gold from gravel and dirt. Sketch from Egleston, *The Metallurgy of Silver, Gold, and Mercury in the United States.*

dependable production. In 1825 the federal mint received $17,000 worth of Carolina gold, more than three times the total in 1824.

The decade after 1825 was memorable for Carolina mining, which became a socioeconomic factor in the state. Not every mine became large, systematic, and productive; most remained relatively small in scope and erratic in operation. Yet a handful attained an influence that survived sporadically for decades. Characteristic conditions, processes, and aspects of the mining culture blossomed. By the early 1830s, portions of the state experienced a genuine gold rush, and the *Western Carolinian* of Salisbury exulted: "The mining interest of the State is now only second to the farming interest."

The precipitating event, as at John Reed's farm, was unplanned. Early in 1825 Matthias Barringer, a farmer who resided in northwestern Montgomery (now Stanly) County about twenty miles northeast of Reed, was hunting for placer gold. Ascending a stream to a spot beyond which he found no more metal, Barringer noticed a vein of white quartz running from the creek into a hillside. He determined that the quartz contained gold and also identified a quantity of nearly pure gold a few feet from the branch. Soon fifty people were digging on his land, and some men hit large lumps of gold along the vein. For a brief period during the spring of 1825, Barringer's total profits reportedly reached $8,000. The miners followed the 4-inch-wide vein 30 to 40 feet, to a depth up to 18 feet, and extracted gold worth perhaps $13,500. Yet, before long, water hampered continued exploration.

Barringer's discovery verified earlier theories by William Thornton and Stephen Ayres concerning gold in quartz veins. News spread rapidly, and prospectors hunted for veins of quartz throughout the region. Underground deposits eventually proved more extensive and challenging than placers. Mecklenburg shortly became the leading gold county, but most mines, whether of the vein or placer type, continued to be amateurish enterprises. Part-time miners merely moved from creeks to hillsides, sank pits into veins, and continued washing gold in rockers.

The still-declining price of cotton encouraged mining. By 1833 cotton was far beneath values of the 1815-1820 period. Prices remained depressed, particularly in the 1840s and mid-1850s, until the outbreak of the Civil War. Perhaps the seasonal nature of farming spurred mining more than cotton prices. For decades some farmers mined placers when not busy with crops. Into the late 1820s, Reed's placers continued to be the most active in the state, and cumulative production soon passed $200,000.

Alluring new possibilities in vein gold tantalized others. Backward North Carolina was known as the Rip Van Winkle State, and a New York writer called it—despite the gold—"the last state in the world, from which we would expect any thing good to come"; yet the magic metal gained rising prominence. Not only were gold hunters "an order of people that begin already to be accounted a distinct race," but North Carolina soon became known as the "Golden State." In 1826 drivers hauled gold ore daily from the new Rudisill mine through the streets of Charlotte. News spread afar, and on one occasion several hucksters from Connecticut bound for the gold region passed through Washington, D.C., in wagons filled with goods.

Landowners increasingly discovered gold on their property. In a few years, new gold was found in Guilford, Davidson, Randolph, and Rowan Counties. Citizens reported almost daily discoveries, and estimated weekly production in Mecklenburg reached $2,000. In 1827 Prof. Elisha Mitchell toured the district for the state geological survey. The following year he published a map with mines such as the Reed, Alexander, Capps, McComb, Parker, Wilson, Beaver Dam, Barringer, Anson, Cox, and Montgomery. Like the Reed, some new mines were placer mines: Nathaniel Bosworth of Montgomery County reportedly had eighty laborers at his mine. Montgomery's Chisholm (later Beaver Dam) mine daily yielded up to five pennyweights' worth of gold per man. By early 1827, the venture, which had employed more than fifty individuals on shares, used a then-rare steam engine and sought hands to work for wages.

In contrast, Charlotte—as late as 1837 "a quiet little village . . . kept up principally by the mining interest"—and Mecklenburg County claimed most of the handful of vein mines that would remain important for decades. James Capps, a poor man, discovered gold on his few acres in 1827. Within a year his

Caps gold mine as it would appear if the hill was cut down or split where the greates number of pits are dug, and half the hill taken away. Some of the pits are 80 to 100 feet deep.

A sectional view of James Capps's mine, as rendered by William Blanding in 1828. From Special Collections Department, Duke University Library.

mine was the richest in the county. In August 1828 physician and naturalist William Blanding of Camden, South Carolina, described Capps's mine as consisting of about eleven pits, some of them eighty feet deep. Capps and his family plunged into extravagance and excess. He became an alcoholic and died; within months his finely attired widow married a handsome young man. The mine—under new management (which later prohibited alcohol)—continued fruitful. Soon annual output approached fifty thousand dollars' worth of gold, with a labor force of twenty men and eight horses.

Two years earlier, Samuel McComb (the family later spelled its name McCombs) discovered a vein of gold on his Mecklenburg land one-half mile from Charlotte. McComb became a leader in the industry and commissioner of a federal branch mint later built in Charlotte. Workers dug the ore and washed it in rockers. That practice succeeded for a time; on one occasion four men recovered nearly $270 worth of gold in as many days. Before long it was obvious that most of the gold required additional capital and technology for successful exploitation. In 1828 McComb sold part of his mine to J. Humphrey Bissell, a Connecticut native and Yale graduate, for $6,000. Bissell had practiced law in Charleston and studied mining in Europe at Freiburg and Swansea. Contemporaries considered him "a gentleman of unblemished worth, and of high literary attainments," as well as "the most . . . scientific man in the [mining] business." A northern traveler concluded: "Bissell lives the life of a lord and his manners can very well sustain him—though very diminutive, he is not a man to be trifled." Innovative Bissell brought to McComb's mine new technology and men experienced in South American mining operations. He began a tunnel, or drift, and extended it more than four hundred feet in a year. By that time his weekly production exceeded a pound of gold. He also used

15

Gold hunters in North Carolina, probably Burke County, 1833.

carts on a railway inside the mine. On the same vein as the McComb was the promising Rudisill mine. Closed briefly by legal entanglements about 1828, the mine would not be idle for long.

Meanwhile, although the Charlotte area had the best of the new underground vein mines, placers found in 1828 led to a genuine gold rush in mountainous Burke County, which had a major part in the gold story even though it lacked significant vein mines. One day Samuel Martin of Connecticut stopped at the log house of cobbler Bob Anderson for a shoe repair and noticed flecks of gold in the mud from Brindle Creek daubed on Anderson's cabin. The next day Martin and the Andersons panned three dollars' worth of gold and agreed to be partners for six months. Martin made eighteen thousand dollars and departed; the Andersons frittered away their sudden riches. By February 1829 farmers and prospectors had found many placers in Burke. In late spring a rush developed, and "gold fever" became the chief ailment in the county. Soon the State Bank of North Carolina established a branch in the isolated village of Morganton (another branch bank existed in Charlotte). Hundreds of would-be miners appeared with pans and rockers on and near Brindle Creek. The yield of one mine averaged more than two thousand dollars weekly for months. Many hands made five dollars daily, a handsome wage. Several thousand men, including numerous slaves brought in by their owners, worked the creeks. For most of the year, the miners apparently neither searched for nor found veins.

A major factor behind the excitement was increasing publicity. News of gold spread by word of mouth and by letters. For decades periodicals such as the *Medical Repository* and the *American Journal of Science* had reported on Carolina mining. About 1830 several newspapers—especially the *Western Carolinian* of Salisbury and the new *Miners' and Farmers' Journal* in Charlotte—helped convince their readers to take up mining. Other papers copied their articles. Additional stories in periodicals, essays by the aforementioned scientists investigating the geology of the state, and increasing notice by out-of-state papers (the *New York Observer* sent a correspondent) also helped.

Masthead of *Miners' and Farmers' Journal* (Charlotte), 1831.

Carolina newspapers fed gold-related news to the public. Part of the "rush" was the haste of editors to print the latest tales. The *Western Carolinian* warned of a "thousand silly reports which are daily set afloat"—reports such as a story of a nugget too heavy to lift. Faraway newspapers published outlandish stories. A Richmond paper reported that the Capps mine yielded sixteen hundred *pounds* of gold in a week. Editors wrote of a gold vein eighty feet wide. In the gold district, publishers included factual news with exaggerated accounts. The *Miners' and Farmers' Journal* printed countless columns on mining, milling gold, and foreign mines. Papers advertised innumerable mines for sale, as speculation mounted. *Niles' Register* of Baltimore claimed that the price of Mecklenburg land rose whenever a farmer saw quartz. Some investors paid extravagant prices. Land considered sterile and not even worth the taxes rose in value. One Guilford tract, offered at $300, sold for $3,000. Burke parcels once worth under $1 per acre changed hands for $30 an acre. Not all sellers were candid. Some made grandiose claims, and a few salted their "mines." A Carolina paper offered instructions for that practice: "Melt up a silver dollar or a small gold piece. . . . Divide them into small particles by throwing it into a basin of water while hot . . . scatter them about your spring, or in a branch where the road crosses it. . . . Let some of your neighbors discover them by accident." Despite such chicanery, buyers expressed interest.

As capital flowed into the gold region and production jumped, observers saw that corporations with skilled miners might surpass individuals or small groups of miners. Hopes for larger companies blossomed. In the mid-1820s, enterprising citizens, probably from Rowan, sought state approval to form a mining company to operate with expert European miners, but conservative legislators killed the bill. Others suggested that the state subsidize such a venture, as was being done with new railroads, by buying stock. The legislature soon authorized mining corporations. The first concern incorporated, in 1827, was the North Carolina Gold Mining Company. The firm received approval to mine for fifty years if it did not engage in banking or mine state lands. Legislator Charles Fisher of Salisbury helped secure the company's charter and sought funds in Charleston. The founders planned to secure several mines and more than sixty slaves. By March 1829 Fisher committed his own resources, and the company obtained some land. For several years the firm leased tracts in Davidson, Rowan, and Montgomery Counties. Those early efforts probably strengthened interest in corporate mining. Almost no Carolinian alone had the means to develop a deep mine, and the state's wealthiest citizens—planters owning numerous slaves—generally were interested in agriculture rather than industrialism. Of possible new industries for venture capital, textile mills were far cheaper and less risky than deep mines. Only a joint-stock company was likely to succeed in capital-intensive, large-scale underground mining, which required not only costly preparatory work before extracting any ore but also expensive machinery and technology. Despite those risks, corporate mining for a time apparently surpassed the slowly budding textile-manufacturing industry—which later became a dominant force in the state's economy for a century—in attracting northern and foreign capital and in utilizing up-to-date technology symbolized by the steam engine. The number of workers employed by both industries was comparable, but farming continued to dwarf mining and textile enterprises as a means of livelihood.

Within a few years incorporation was irresistible, and the General Assembly in one session approved seven firms. They were the Greensboro, Salisbury, Guilford, Mecklenburg, Cabarrus, Charlotte, and Catawba Gold Mining Companies. Each received a charter for twenty-five years. Authorized capital varied from $100,000 to $300,000, but the largest amount required to commence operations was $100,000. Subsequent legislatures chartered additional companies. Much of the new capital originated in the less agricultural

North. Promoters established a mining company in Baltimore. A New York attorney and a Philadelphian offered to assist mine owners seeking investors. All but one of the Cabarrus Gold Mining Company's initial stockholders were northerners.

Wealthy foreign investors likewise appeared, and in the 1830s a substantial portion of funds from outside North Carolina likely came from Europe. Early in that decade editor Hezekiah Niles estimated a 10 percent return on foreign money in mining. He noted a local benefit too: "Every 100 dollars worth of gold, collected in North Carolina or Georgia, etc. represents, at least, 75 dollars worth of American corn, beef, pork, etc consumed by the various laborers employed, and 10, or perhaps 15 percent more, goes into the general stock of American wealth. . . ."

Most foreign funds and laborers were British, although miners came from numerous nations. European experts arrived by the late 1820s. A French chemist evaluated ore and suggested efficiencies in Guilford. One mine supposedly employed nearly a thousand workmen, who spoke thirteen languages—undoubtedly an exaggeration. With foreign capital came managers from overseas. Foremen in numerous mines were foreign. The chief, and most colorful, of those organizers was Count Vincent de Rivafinoli, flamboyant manager for British interests in Charlotte. The count was an Italian aristocrat, expert mining engineer, former superintendent of large South American mines, and promoter with considerable financial backing and grandiose plans. Rivafinoli's presence awed Charlotte; a man of demeanor and culture, he visited New York to direct a Rossini opera. In 1830 he brought "some of the most learned and practical miners" of England, Germany, Wales, Scotland, Ireland, Switzerland, Italy, and France, as well as eighty other hands, to serve under him. Of Charlotte's 717 residents in 1830, 61 were unnaturalized foreigners. Few of those people settled permanently in or near the town. Nonetheless, nativist resentment of foreigners was important at times, despite disclaimers by such organs as the *Miners' and Farmers' Journal*. There were proposals to exclude foreign capital and workers. On occasion natives refused to work under Europeans. Observers reported riots between domestic and foreign employees. On the whole, however, conflicts over nationality did not greatly hamper mining.

Among Europeans, Cornish miners stood out for decades and boasted an established mining heritage. By 1800 County Cornwall, in western England, was a center of mining technology. By 1830 more than thirty thousand people worked in mines, which by mid-century produced nearly half the world's copper and tin. Men, women, and children labored under conditions "barely tolerable even when times were good." During slack periods, some miners emigrated. John Gluyas, a Cornishman who emigrated to North Carolina, claimed that miners in America earned in a day the same as a week's wages in

Cornwall. A few departures became a flood about 1850, when cheap copper in Michigan and Chile threatened older Cornish mines. Carolina gold attracted skilled Cornish miners, who by 1830 had a reputation in the gold district. Superstitious, clannish, and Methodist, the Cornish miner early rated a verse in the *Western Carolinian*:

> He never was given to swearing or drinking,
> Yet got all his money by damming and sinking;
> He buried himself below all his life,
> And when dead he was buried up here by his wife.

Cornish miner Bill Jenkins, drawn by artist Porte Crayon in 1857.

A common saying in some mining communities was that "wherever there is a hole in the earth, you will find a Cornishman at the bottom of it." By mid-century Cornish miners were known as "Cousin Jacks," since a Cornishman always knew the best prospective employee—his cousin Jack in Cornwall. Cornishmen were recognized experts at financially and physically risky underground mining.

The exact number of Cornishmen in Carolina remains unknown, as does the overall mining population. Native whites, blacks, and perhaps women outnumbered Cornish miners. Precise numbers of miners and related workers—native, foreign, male, female, white, black, adult, or child—varied by time, type, and scale of mine and remain unknown. One company allegedly employed hundreds of workers; most mines operated with a fraction of that number or a few individuals. By the early 1830s, up to thirty thousand people reportedly hunted gold in Carolina. Many were part-time placer miners; far fewer were professionals. The slaveholding elite had a valid concern that a rising white wage-earning class might have no vested interest in slavery. Fortunately for that privileged leadership, many free yeoman farmers were not ready for the regimented schedule and loss of independence required of industrial workers. According to census data, Mecklenburg had only 100 miners in 1840 and 19 in 1850. Of the latter number, 12 were from England, and only 3 had been miners in 1840. A significant percentage of miners and helpers were women, black and white. Many probably worked in family-operated mines, some were expert panners, and others manipulated rockers. Girls labored in Burke and later at Gold Hill. A few ladies in rude mining towns were

African Americans such as this man using a rocker often labored alongside white workers in North Carolina's antebellum gold mines.

surprisingly cultured—one taught a Sunday school class for miners—but they were a decided minority.

Blacks, comprising approximately one-fourth of the one hundred thousand or so people who resided in the rural gold region about 1830, were major participants in mining and related pursuits. While most miners probably were white, hundreds, perhaps thousands, of Negro slaves labored in and near mines and often cut timber and grew food for miners. At the height of the rush in Burke, five thousand slaves reportedly toiled in placer mines. By 1830 ten planters from Granville County together had 293 slaves mining in Burke. Some slaves, like free farmers, mined during slack farming seasons. Various mining companies worked slave labor. The Capps mine employed 33 African Americans (probably all slaves and including 10 women) for a time, and partners J. Humphrey Bissell and Samuel Barker hired 59 slaves in 1830. Rental of slaves was popular at mines such as Gold Hill. About 1850, a year's rented work cost between $150 and $175. Slaves' tasks varied with individual owners' attitudes concerning the reliability and capabilities of blacks. Occasional observers felt that African Americans were unfit to be miners, and managers commonly used slaves for unskilled physical labor. While blacks proved effective at Gold Hill and elsewhere, the industry produced no long-term shifts of locations or occupations under slavery, and only 5 percent of southern slaves worked in *any* industry. Owners had some concern that industrial mining, with its opportunity for time off and extra wages, weakened their authority over bondsmen. Gold led to freedom for various slaves, but free Negroes seemed disinterested in mining. By 1826 slaves reportedly hunted for gold on their own, and some acquired money to buy liberty. Yet in 1860 only fourteen of four thousand free blacks in the state were miners, and none were in Mecklenburg or Cabarrus.

By 1830 social conditions in Mecklenburg mirrored the life of the miners, which was often hard and given to excess. Observers reported "deplorably bad" morals around mining towns and larger mines early in the great rush. Writers cited as causes an unregulated society and the "usual effects" of easy gold upon the minds of the poor and ignorant. One northerner could "hardly conceive of a more immoral community. . . . Drunkenness, gambling, fighting, lewdness, and every other vice exist here to an awful extent. Many of the men, by working three days in the week, make several dollars, and then devote the remaining four [days] to every species of vice." Elisha Mitchell found "shocking fellows . . . drinking and fighting" at the Capps mine before liquor was proscribed there.

Many miners abused alcohol. Loafing near major mines were worthless hedonists who worked only enough to buy bread and whiskey from convenient liquor carts. Liquor flourished in Charlotte, where drunks routinely abused peaceable citizens, and stores boasted "the best foreign spirits and wines." Tippling was not confined to one race. One writer complained that "At every camp whiskey shanties were plentiful, and most of the Negroes thought more of what those shanties contained than of their freedom, and the moment they found gold they would quit work and invest it in drink." Vices did not overcome all miners or only gold seekers, a portion of whom were gentlemen and social reformers. Some mine managers strictly forbade liquor; others, including several Cornishmen, arranged for the preaching of the Gospel to miners. A gold hunter in Montgomery County admitted that "any dissipation, however vivid as it might be, would fail to come up to the reality," yet spent his idle hours reading and playing the violin. In Burke County the upper classes used liquor freely, but morals there among miners and the general public were quite similar. For many miners, liquor was an escape from an uncomfortable existence. Mining life could be harsh; disease and untimely death were frequent visitors. At placer mines, a fortune hunter might live outdoors without any cover. He carried provisions and "a few necessary tools, such as a mattock, a shovel, a bucket, or water dipper, and a rocker." Burke miners, even if wealthy, lived in small cabins. Mining "towns" were often bare frontier villages of a few huts and no amenities.

Yet mining life was not without some merriment and social activity. Christmas and the Fourth of July might be celebrated with a mining flavor. On Christmas in 1825 immigrant German miner and geologist Charles Rothe amused Charlotte in his "miner's uniform" of "a round coat with three rows of buttons having a hammer and pick stamped on them." The coat was of leather and scarlet cloth; a cape and cocked hat completed the outfit, in which Rothe spent the morning visiting and drinking eggnog. On one Fourth of July, Burke miners enjoyed a barbecue and many toasts: "May the farmers around us be encouraged by the Miners of Burke." "May the gold miners meet with shallow pitting and rich grit for their reward." "Health of body, peace of mind, and four pennyweights to the hand." Not all social life centered on holidays. Mining expert Capt. John E. Penman, a "large, red-faced, typical Englishman . . . used to being waited upon," who was a fixture in Mecklenburg mining for two decades, and his sixty miners once marched into Charlotte escorted by fifes and drums for a banquet at his expense.

Miners' wages varied according to skill and luck. Few miners grew rich. As time passed, they increasingly became wage laborers toiling for others. A miner working for himself or on shares at a small mine in the 1830s received from twenty-five cents to five dollars daily. The average was a dollar or less. Poorly paid as a group, miners could always dream of finding a big nugget. Whatever a miner's income, he had costs beyond subsistence. A dollar bought a pound of quicksilver or a shovel. A "machine," perhaps a rocker, cost fifteen dollars, and a hand pump two dollars. Larger operations required more capital. In 1829, equipping a sizable gold-washing operation with spades and rockers took $500. Horse-driven "pounding and grinding mills" cost as much as $2,500. Waterpower required $500 to $1,000 more. A complete steam-powered arrangement ran up to $4,500. More complex devices had to be imported, as did certain staple provisions. Burke miners are reported to have purchased up to $20,000 worth of goods each week, including local corn, Kentucky pork, and Philadelphia shovels. Many miners avoided expenses of sophisticated machinery by continuing the haphazard use of minimal equipment. Unfamiliar with technology and unwilling to risk loss, placer owners preferred immediate gain from men using pans and rockers on shares to the cost and uncertainty of machinery. Even important vein mines were backward; at Barringer's in Montgomery (later Stanly) County, men wastefully sank random pits far from the major lode.

Nevertheless, technology crept into the gold fields after the mid-1820s. Charles E. Rothe, who had come to aid Denison Olmsted with the state geological survey, remained for several years. Knowledgeable about European mining, Rothe promoted machinery and leased a mine in South Carolina. By 1830 other foreign experts appeared. The *Miners' and Farmers' Journal* printed technical articles. Although some were copied from European periodicals, others described leading Mecklenburg mines. By late 1830 that paper characterized rockers as "the old mode" of obtaining gold.

Water-powered German stamp mill, 1557.

One new machine that employed old technology was the stamp mill, which dated to sixteenth-century Germany and broke quartz into fine pieces so that gold could be more easily separated from it. In 1829 J. Humphrey Bissell installed at the Capps the first stamp mill used in the United States. Stamp mills pounded ore (already broken, first by gunpowder and then by hand, to fragments measuring several inches across) into fine gravel. The machine, made of wood, was covered in key places with iron and resembled a mortar and pestle. Ore flowed through a trough, or mortar, and received countless blows by stamps rising and falling via a camshaft arrangement.

Yet stamps did not reduce ore enough for efficient gold recovery. Miners used other machines for further crushing and amalgamating the golden particles with mercury. One such device, the Chilean mill, usually featured two stone wheels perhaps five or six feet in diameter that rotated around a shaft set into a circular stone base containing ore, water, and mercury. The heavy wheels broke ore into fine particles. The mill—with no antecedents in Chile—became common in North Carolina. A variation was the arrastra, which substituted heavy drag stones for the wheels and a circular pavement of flat rocks for the stone base. Arrastras, simpler and cheaper to build, were more dependable and efficient. Both were extremely slow compared to stamps. By the early 1830s, advanced mines—most near Charlotte—had such machines, coupled with pumps if necessary and driven by horse, water, or steam power. Other mines, including the Reed and rich Burke placers, continued operations with pans and rockers.

One exceptional mine was the Capps, leased for several years by the heirs of the unfortunate James Capps. From several dozen to a hundred blacks and

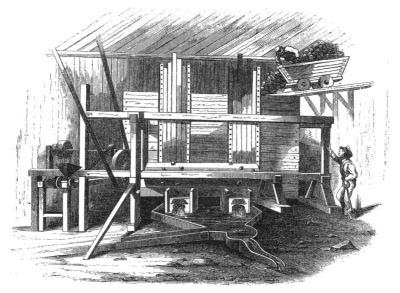

Wooden stamp mill, early 1850s. Engraving from Robert E. Clarke, "Notes from the Copper Region," pt. 2, *Harper's New Monthly Magazine* 6 (April 1853), 579.

 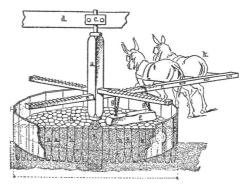

LEFT: Chilean mill for crushing ore beneath rolling wheels. RIGHT: Mule-powered arrastra with a single drag stone. Drawing at right from Thomas A. Rickard, *Journeys of Observation* (San Francisco: Dewey Publishing Company, 1907).

whites labored there. A steam engine pumped water from a one hundred-foot shaft; horses raised ore to the surface. Miners used gunpowder to loosen ore underground but only human muscles to break ore on the surface before feeding it to crushing mills. The Capps relied upon stamp and Chilean mills, both of which briefly produced profits handsomely.

Within a few years, the Capps was run by the Mecklenburg Gold Mining Company, a corporation that purportedly employed six hundred persons. Its managing incorporator was Vincent de Rivafinoli. Associating himself with entrepreneur Bissell, he promptly leased the leading Capps, Rudisill, and McComb (renamed St. Catherine) mines. With dozens of skilled European miners, he installed three steam engines used primarily for pumping. Spending large sums, Rivafinoli deepened the Rudisill's engine shaft and added timbered, horizontal galleries roofed with boards and ventilated by machine-driven bellows.

At the opposite end of the same mass of ore, and one-half mile northeast of the Rudisill, was the St. Catherine mine on Sugar Creek. When Rivafinoli arrived, attorneys Bissell and Barker were erecting gold mills there. Nearby the two had bought an old water-powered flour mill (renamed the St. Catherine mill) for use in processing ore from several mines. A 110-acre pond supplied water to the mill via a 150-yard-long, 45-foot-wide canal. Bissell and Barker had converted a water-powered cotton gin to a Chilean mill and were replacing flour-mill machinery with ore mills. At Rivafinoli's suggestion, the partners began changing the Chilean mills into arrastras and added a steam engine. They built a new brick enginehouse and two frame buildings, each to house six large arrastras. The sum of water and steam-powered arrastras was eighteen machines, together capable of processing four hundred bushels of ore daily. The St. Catherine mill also featured twelve water-powered stamps, described in the *Miners' and Farmers' Journal* as follows:

The stamp heads are of wrought iron, weighing each 75 pounds, and the upright shafts to which they are severally attached, measure 11 feet in length and 6 inches square. They are divided into sets of three and three. . . . Extending under the stamp heads, and solidly based, is a stick of oak, upon the top of which are secured blocks of wrought or cast iron . . . upon which the heads strike. . . . [T]he pounded material roils upon a succession of scives [sieves], coarse and fine, while the part which the scives reject as not enough reduced, is thrown back to receive another blow of the stamps. The upper scives are of sole leather, perforated with holes of any required size, or of strong iron wire, of extraordinary fineness, insomuch that the powder passing through them, if it is not of the sulphurets . . . is fitted for immediate amalgamation. . . . Eight workers for 24 hours [are] necessary to keep twelve stamps in full operation. . . .

Such machinery represented only the handful of advanced mines in the state.

More typical in operation, although not in location, were gold fields in northeastern North Carolina, discovered in the early 1830s. Eastern mining centered where Franklin, Nash, Warren, and Halifax Counties joined. Although never comparable in overall scale to Piedmont mining, operations in that locale were conducted intermittently for a century. The most noted mine belonged to a Mr. Portis, a cobbler who reportedly continued his shoemaking until he made a pair of right and left shoes on the same mold and resolved to quit. Portis leased his mine to a group employing thirty-six hands with several rockers. One laborer unearthed a fabulous twelve-pound nugget. Gold was recovered at twenty nearby sites.

In the early 1830s the state counted numerous active mines besides those in the eastern counties or in the Piedmont. The Dunn and Alexander mine, eight miles west of Charlotte, with surface and vein gold and a solitary, horse-powered Chilean mill, continued in operation. The Harris mine produced remarkable concentrations of gold. In Cabarrus, work continued at the Reed, and the new Cabarrus Gold Mining Company planned a mining venture at Pioneer Mills. The Barringer mine in Montgomery (Stanly) County, noted for veins and nests of gold, appeared exhausted to some analysts. Rowan, later a major gold county, had some profitable placer mines. Placers continued preeminent in Burke County, where daily production reached twenty-four hundred dollars from the richest creeks in the state. In one six-month period more new post offices were established in Burke than in any other county in North Carolina. In what became Cleveland County, prospectors discovered a gold vein (later to be a major mine) near Kings Mountain. Another mine of rising importance was the Haile, near Charlotte but just inside South Carolina. In Davidson County a corporation leased five thousand acres near the Conrad Hill mine, using water-powered stamps and Chilean mills. British experts were more impressed with Conrad Hill, where workers dug to seventy feet and ran a mill four miles away on an undependable stream. The Englishmen proposed to establish steam power, a stamp mill, and other machinery.

By the early 1830s the industry increasingly affected parts of the state, with benefits exaggerated by local editors and promoters. A Salisbury paper claimed that the $1,000 to $1,500 weekly production of Mecklenburg gold "infuses life and activity into all branches of business." Counties within the mining region enjoyed greater prosperity than their counterparts elsewhere. Future governor William A. Graham exclaimed: "Those who have been esteemed prudent and cautious embark in speculation with the greatest enthusiasm—bankrupts have been restored to affluence, and paupers turned to nabobs." While few made fortunes, the industry expanded regional economies. A Charlotte weekly listed various advantages: a rise in business, employment for mechanics and artisans, an influx of visitors and residents, more circulation of money, and rising property values. Mining created interconnected gains. Gold provided income for individuals. New northern and foreign capital led to more jobs and had a multiplier effect locally when miners sought goods and services. Trade prospered with gold as currency in a state plagued by discounted paper notes. Gold reduced national dependency on foreign bullion and supposedly bolstered social values. Editors declared that gold prompted "many lazy, lounging fellows, who once hung as a weight upon society, into active and manly exertion." The industry fostered technology, orderly society, and education, declared miner Charles Fisher. Citizens considered their region with enhanced pride. Finally, emigration from stagnant North Carolina—considerable by the 1820s—was in part slowed, with some internal migration to the gold region.

Mining also had negative effects. Observers cited alcoholism, moral degeneracy from easy money, neglect of agriculture, and decaying work ethic and thrift. Speculation made some rich and others poor: the *Charleston Courier* luridly described the "corrupting treasure." The human cost was men maimed or killed in accidents from blasting, tunnel cave-ins, falling rocks, and other mishaps. Editors often glossed over such news. A few observers noted a negative environmental impact. One writer predicted that the Burke placers would fail and leave land ruined for farming, a situation repeated in varying degrees in all gold counties. Other effects, such as water pollution, often went unrecorded.

Despite such consequences, gold production rose in those years. Inasmuch as one-third or more of the total output was delivered to the United States mint at Philadelphia, that facility's reports are a starting point for estimating total production. The state supplied most domestic gold received at the mint, and all such gold ($110,000) prior to 1828. In 1827 the mint received $21,000, 11 percent of receipts, worth of North Carolina gold. The following year deposits from the Old North State reached $46,000. In 1829 Virginia sent $2,500 worth and South Carolina $3,500 worth, while the North Carolina sum jumped to $134,000. Georgia and North Carolina each shipped just over $200,000 worth in 1830. North Carolina regained the lead with $294,000 in 1831, $458,000 in 1832, and $475,000 in 1833 (a record lasting more than a decade). That increase provided native gold for 80 percent of the mint's gold coinage by 1830. In 1834 the mint coined more gold than the total of the preceding nine years.

Nevertheless, the mint's usage supposedly accounted for only one-third to one-half of all production of gold in North Carolina, and the state's total output of the metal cannot be determined. The short lives of many companies and attempts to avoid taxation hindered accurate record keeping. Perhaps individuals never reported much gold and pocketed choice nuggets before they reached the owners. A considerable amount of the metal went to domestic and European artisans, manufacturers, and other users. Many leading mines, such as those of Vincent de Rivafinoli, sent output directly to Europe, where large

VICTOR G. BLANDIN,
MANUFACTURER OF JEWELRY, &C.
ONE DOOR ABOVE THE SHERIFF'S OFFICE,

BEGS leave to inform his friends and the public, that he has lately commenced the manufacture of JEWELRY, from North-Carolina Gold, in the French fashions, at the most moderate prices.

NEW FURNACE.

He has also erected a new FURNACE, for melting Gold, by which no particle of metal can be lost, even if a crucible happens to break.

The patronage of the public is respectfully solicited.

Charlotte, March 2, 1831.

Advertisement for goldsmith Victor G. Blandin of Charlotte, 1831.

American nuggets were popular. Jewelers in New York and elsewhere preferred Carolina gold and paid a premium for it. Some Charlotte jewelers, such as Victor Blandin and Thomas Trotter, specialized in local gold. The metal went from country merchants to market towns such as Fayetteville and thence to users in Charleston, New York, and Europe. Perhaps one-fifth of North Carolina's gold production in 1832 went into the arts. Finally, some Carolina gold reached the mint labeled as "Georgia gold."

Southerners began promoting the creation of branch mints in 1830. The trip to Philadelphia was long and dangerous. The gold region lacked a uniform circulating medium, with much gold of uncertain purity in circulation. United States representative Samuel P. Carson from Burke called for a congressional inquiry and asked miners about output, new technology, and future prospects. Charles Fisher, J. Humphrey Bissell, and others responded thoughtfully. The state legislature endorsed a regional mint, but the matter bogged down in Congress for years. Local desire for a mint remained high, and William Davidson of Charlotte proposed the following toast: "to turn our gold into money, and the money into the pockets of the people."

Private initiative met the need. In 1831 German immigrant Christopher Bechtler began minting gold coins in Rutherford County. A year earlier, watchmaker Templeton Reid had coined Georgia gold, but Bechtler was more successful. The middle-aged goldsmith, who also made guns and clocks, landed in New York in late 1829 and reached Rutherfordton early in 1830. He produced coins with homemade, hand-operated equipment. Besides $2.50 and $5.00 coins, he produced in 1832 the first gold dollar minted in the nation. Each coin bore a value and its maker's name. Bechtler's integrity assured success. In four years he coined $109,000 worth of gold (a figure that grew

29

Christopher Bechtler of Ruther-fordton customarily marked his coins, such as this gold dollar, with his name and the amount of gold they contained.

twentyfold by 1840) and fluxed nearly 400,000 additional pennyweights' worth. The mint lasted until 1857, although Christopher Bechtler died in 1842. His trusted coins circulated in western North Carolina and neighboring areas for many years.

Meanwhile the village of Charlotte got its mint, after sectional conflict snarled the issue in the U.S. Senate, with the South and West favoring the facility and the North and East opposed. A proposal to establish at New Orleans a mint to coin gold and silver and branch mints at Charlotte and Dahlonega, Georgia, to coin only gold was voted into law in March 1835. Samuel McComb supervised local preparations for erecting the Charlotte facility, which was designed by noted Philadelphia architect William Strickland. The two-story brick building was 125 feet wide and cost $29,700. Construction required fourteen months. The new mint marked a decade of mining progress. In 1825 the Philadelphia mint had received only $20,000 worth of native gold, all from North Carolina. By 1834 production had increased immensely and spread to neighboring states. That year, North Carolina deposits at the mint reached $380,000, but Georgia sent $415,000. By the mid-1830s, significant and enduring aspects of the mining culture had appeared. Nonetheless—despite foreign capital and expertise; slaves, stamp mills, and steam engines; and continuing output—mining moved toward events that tested its stability.

In the late 1830s mining quickly but temporarily lost much of its vigor. Various factors, some long-lasting, weakened the industry. Deposits at the main government mint fell sharply. From $475,000 in 1833, the value of shipments of North Carolina gold to Philadelphia dropped by 1837 to $116,900. By spring 1836 Burke County's placer gold rush was over, and the diminished enterprise was left to poor whites, free blacks, and perhaps some slaves.

Alternative uses drew labor and capital from picked-over creeks. Vein mining in other counties or in Georgia provided one option. Agriculture and railroad construction utilized slaves who had previously served as miners. With Carolina placers largely exhausted, vein mines also faced challenges. After the disastrous panic of 1837, most large firms were short of funds, bankrupt, or dormant. Fertile Alabama cotton fields drew off slave labor. Remaining "miners" were primarily farmers. The federal census enumerated only 589 miners in 1840, one hundred of them in Mecklenburg County.

Mining was accompanied by its own peculiar problems. Vein mining was always risky, requiring major outlays of capital in advance of actual production. Errors in management, lack of planning, and poor technology plagued mines. Even Rivafinoli received censure—from the head of his company, Prof. James Renwick of Columbia College in New York—and criticism for hiring too many salaried administrators and losing one-half of his gold during milling. As early as 1830, some mines closed as a result of ineffective direction. Over time miners removed most upper vein material, generally decomposed rock, and went deeper. Mining below the water level, generally encountered fifty to sixty feet underground, led to complications such as the need to pump water out of the mine. Deeper ore often was combined with pyrites of copper, iron, or sulfur; refractory sulfuret ore beneath the water table was not decomposed and difficult to work. Without good pumps and a means to deal with such ore, most mining ceased where pumping began. Initial, simple efforts to deal with pyritic ore failed: sulfurets required a chemical or metallurgical process. A common response was "roasting" ore to drive off the sulfur, but inadequate knowledge of chemistry prevented that process, whether in open air or special furnaces, from working successfully for many years. Efforts to smelt ore at the Smart mine in Mecklenburg also failed. In addition, many deep mines yielded a low grade of unprofitable ore. Some commentators derided as indolent those natives who lacked the fortitude to develop mines in a skillful, scientific manner.

In any case, the late 1830s were difficult times for mining. The Cabarrus Gold Mining Company, despite northern money, a promising mine at Pioneer Mills, and a steam engine, battled bankruptcy. Rivafinoli's company in Mecklenburg began an extravagant program that outstripped returns, and he disappeared from the historical record. In late 1837 the county sheriff sold at auction all of his leased mines, as was the case with many lesser mines. John Penman bought the Rudisill, once highly advanced and productive. He cleaned out old workings and tried to dewater the engine shaft, but Rivafinoli's worn-out pumps failed, and Penman abandoned the mine. Penman also worked the St. Catherine for several years. Similar failures occurred at other mines.

Nevertheless, the Charlotte mint opened in December 1837—in a town of fewer than one thousand souls and a county that in 1840 counted fifteen mines and an equal number of distilleries in operation—with Democratic legislator John H. Wheeler as superintendent. Some $25,000 worth of gold arrived that month. The staff gave depositors certificates for gold coins or made their gold into bars for a fee. Wheeler's assistants included a coiner, an assayer, a chief clerk, and laborers. Soon the mint was receiving some $130,000 worth of bullion annually. In slightly more than two decades, the mint coined about five million dollars in half-eagles ($5.00, its most common product), quarter-eagles ($2.50), and gold dollars. Congressional Whigs, opposed to ostensibly wasteful and patronage-serving branch mints, sparred with Democrats for years, but North Carolina's Whigs prudently defended the mint. Deposits rose to $272,000 in 1843. In 1844 fire destroyed much of the facility, and political squabbling delayed repairs; the mint was out of operation for more than two years.

If coins symbolized the persistence of mining in hard times, new corporations evoked the eternal lure of gold. The unprecedented record of ten charters granted in 1835 lasted more than a decade, but soon the legislature approved companies with broader activities beyond mining. In 1836 legislators chartered the General Mining and Manufacturing Association, with authorized capital up to $1,500,000, ten times the previous average. That firm's leaders included William J. Alexander and J. Humphrey Bissell of Charlotte, two men from Burke County, and a

One-dollar gold coin made at Charlotte mint, 1855.

New Yorker. In 1839 the state chartered the Washington (silver) Mining Company. Gold remained a major interest, and in the 1840s firms received rights to engage in related activities such as copper mining, landholding, and manufacturing. New companies included the North Carolina Mining, Manufacturing, and Land Association and the Philadelphia and North Carolina Mining and Smelting Company. Lawmakers greatly broadened the franchise of the Guilford Gold Mining Company (formed in 1831) to include "operation of mills, factories, and machinery, to manufacture grain, lumber, iron, copper, and other metals, also cotton, wool or either by water, steam, or otherwise."

By the mid-1840s mining had largely recovered. Annual North Carolina deposits at federal mints in the decade after 1837 averaged some $289,000. Deposits at Charlotte approached $400,000 by the late 1840s. Various mines were increasingly active. Guilford's Deep River mine produced gold and copper for direct shipment to England. New leaders tried to reorganize the battered Mecklenburg Gold Mining Company, lessee of the Rudisill, Capps, and

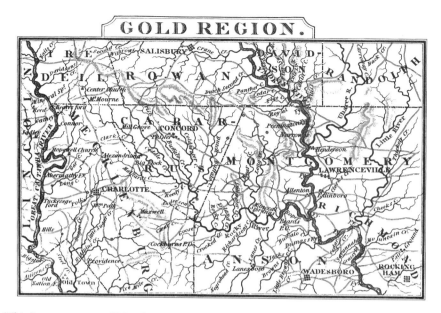

This inset to a map of North Carolina published in 1839 defines the state's gold region as encompassing portions of several Piedmont counties.

St. Catherine mines. Thomas Forney proposed to move machinery to Rutherford County and hire John Gluyas, a Cornish mining engineer for the old firm, as superintendent. Soon John Wheeler declared that the Rudisill was "yielding handsomely." In 1844 a British traveler found men extracting ore from the 160-foot level of the Capps. In 1848, however, Capt. Charles Wilkes of the U.S. Navy—whose family for decades would own in Charlotte a number of mines, as well as a factory that manufactured mining machinery—acquired both the Capps and the St. Catherine through foreclosure. Miners found a vein of gold at the Parker, an early placer mine. "Gold fever" reappeared in Randolph County, and a new mining corporation began work in Rutherford County. At the Lewis mine in Union County, men planned expansion with new capital. In 1843 imaginative J. Gibson mined the Catawba River. His men used shovels to lift sediment and gravel onto flatboats and washed it on shore in rockers, but the scheme failed.

By 1845 owners of the Washington (Silver Hill) silver mine in Davidson County had acquired 446 acres of land at a reputed price of $479,500 and established a mining village. The project included sixty buildings with houses, a laboratory, offices, workshops, millhouses, smelting and washing structures, a school, and a store inside a board fence. The mine was more than 160 feet

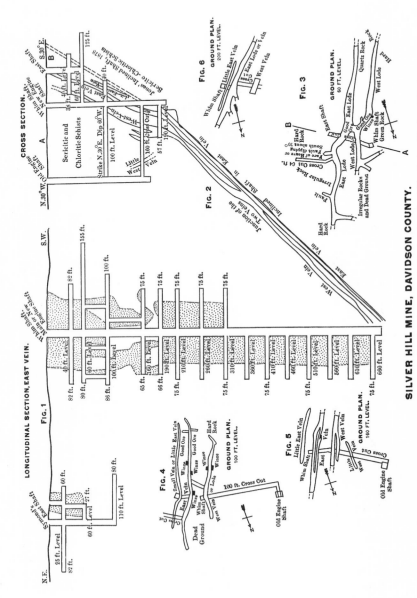

SILVER HILL MINE, DAVIDSON COUNTY.

Stippled spaces and the ground plans showing the area worked out up to May, 1854.   Scale : 1 Inch = 150 feet.

deep. In 1844 workers recovered about $24,000 worth of silver and $7,253 worth of gold.

In 1842 mining operations commenced at Gold Hill in Rowan County on land that a few years earlier had been offered for sale for fifty bushels of corn. By 1843 workers began mining veins there, and soon there were three principal mines. The minuteness of the gold caused great losses in crude refining, but its immense quantity made Gold Hill the state's leading mining district (see chapters 3 and 4). The initial vein eventually produced $400,000 worth of gold. At first, companies mined on short-term leases, with horses supplying the only power. By 1850 ten groups, three with steam power, mined or processed ore; employed 169 men and 2 females, perhaps girls; and reported production valued at $76,083. Gold Hill, major supplier to the Charlotte mint, became a small village. A few miles southwest, activity resumed at the Reed, closed for a decade by legal problems. Mining was much as in the 1830s, with about twenty men and a few horses.

The census of 1850 surprisingly lists no active mines in Mecklenburg, Randolph, or Stanly Counties but includes 50 mining concerns, with 6 in Burke, 6 in Cabarrus, 1 in Davidson, 3 in Gaston, 3 in Guilford, 5 in Montgomery, 10 (at Gold Hill) in Rowan, 8 in Rutherford, and 8 in Union. The fifty companies each produced more than five hundred dollars worth of gold and were the most significant in the state that year, but operations varied greatly. Total capitalization amounted to $755,880, with Silver Hill claiming 70 percent of that figure. The mines had various power sources individually and in combination, including steam power at 5 places, water at 20, horses at 13, and human muscle at 11. Only 48 females worked at the mines, which employed 742 men. The average monthly pay for males was $13.18; for females, $7.58. The total monthly expense for labor by some 800 miners was about $10,148. The fifty firms produced precious metal valued at $308,553. The total annual value of North Carolina gold registered at the federal mints reached $473,543 in 1848 (previously surpassed only in 1833) and in 1849 hit a record $485,793. That year Charlotte receipts climbed to $391,000. In 1850 totals declined to $335,523 for all federal mints and $320,000 for Charlotte.

The zenith of North Carolina mining (likely in 1832, 1833, 1848, or 1849) passed, just as California production after 1848 dwarfed southern mining. Annual California output burgeoned from $245,000 in 1848 to $41 million in 1850, when fifty thousand miners hunted gold there. Placers predominated initially, but by 1853 much of the surface gold was gone. Production peaked at $81 million annually in 1852 and slid to $45 million by 1857. The California placer gold bonanza did not, however, cause a major decline in North Carolina, where production compared favorably with that of the early 1830s. The initial discoveries of gold and other precious metals in the West siphoned off some

Table 1
Selected Mining Data from the Census of 1850

County	Name of Mine	Capitalization	No. of Workers	Annual Production
Burke	McKesson	$37,000	45	$8,000
	Erwin	$250	11	$2,150
Cabarrus	Phoenix	unknown	30	$3,000
	Reed	$20,000	20	$7,500
Davidson	Washington	$500,000	25	unknown
Gaston	B. F. Briggs	unknown	106	$82,800
	High Shoal	unknown	62	$10,136
Guilford	Frederic Fonbus	unknown	unknown	
	Coffin, Shelly, and Co.	unknown	unknown	
	Nathan Coffin and Sons	unknown	unknown	
Montgomery	five firms	unknown	85	unknown
Rowan	Gold Hill (ten companies)	$87,110	171	$76,083
Rutherford		unknown	80	unknown
Union	Jones, Howie, & Co.	unknown	3	$1,000
	Houston, Armfield, & Co.	unknown	35	$12,000

investment capital and skilled laborers from the southern mines. Californians greatly desired the services of skilled Georgians, North Carolinians, and Cornishmen. Indeed, veterans of the southern gold districts introduced many of the machines and techniques to the first surface mines in California.

Although one journalist lamented during the 1850s that several gold mines east of Charlotte were "but little worked, partly on account of the more inviting field for miners in California," in reality the lure of treasure in the West did not attract great numbers of North Carolinians. Out-migration, a critical problem in the state in the 1820s, had subsided by 1850. One principal California mining district counted only fifty North Carolinians among several thousand people. Cabarrus County reported half a dozen departures. Some émigrés worked at California's North Carolina Copper and Gold Mining Company. Two Burke County men took with them several slaves to exploit California placers; one owner returned to Burke, while a trusted slave miner (whose wife was in Burke) remitted funds to his owner and his spouse. The total number of North Carolinians in California rose from 1,027 in 1850 to 1,582 a decade later. Indeed, California events fostered renewed mining in the Old North State, with its resources far closer to eastern investors.

North Carolina enjoyed relative prosperity in the early 1850s, helping lure outside investment. Low wages and improved transportation were added incentives. Land values doubled, and there were gains in agriculture, manufacturing, and commerce. Such factors stimulated corporate mining. In 1851 the legislature aided four companies, including the existing Washington Mining Company. Promoters of mining began selling stock in various firms such as the Lewis Gold Mining Company. The lawmakers also incorporated the North Carolina Manufacturing, Mining and Land Company, capitalizing it at up to one million dollars. An 1852 law deliberately promoted mining and manufacturing, allowing easy incorporation. Shares had to cost at least one dollar, companies could not declare dividends if in debt, and financial disclosure was optional. Within a few years the law encouraged the creation of numerous new concerns authorized to mine gold and other metals, although some of the companies did little or possibly no mining. Incorporators often were promoters and northern investors, but a few initiators owned bona fide mines.

Table 2
Selected Mining Companies Authorized by
the North Carolina General Assembly in the 1850s

Alamance Mining and Manufacturing Company
American Exchange Mining and Smelting Company
Baltimore and Montgomery Mining Company
Beaver Dam Gold Mountain Vein Mining and Plank Sluicing Company
Boss Gold and Silver Mining Company
Cambridge Copper Company
Capps Hill Gold Mining Company
Central Gold and Copper Mining Company
Charlotte Copper and Gold Mining Company
Christian Gold Mining Company
Conrad Hill Gold and Copper Mine
Conrad Hill Gold Mining Company
Consolidated Mining Company of North Carolina
Cowee Mining and Manufacturing Company
Excelsior Gold Mining Company
Fisher Hill Mining Company
Gardner Hill Mining Company
Gillis Copper Mining Company

Gold Hill Mining Company
Greensboro Mining and Manufacturing Company
Guilford Copper and Gold Mining Company
Guilford County Mining Company
Guilford Gold and Copper Mining Company
Halsey Mining and Smelting Company
Hodgin Hill Mining Company
Lewis Gold Mining Company
Lizarddale Copper Company
McCullock Gold Mining Company
Manteo Mining Company
Montgomery Mining Company
Nantahala Gold and Copper Mining Company
North Carolina Central Gold and Copper Mining Company
North Carolina Copper Company
North Carolina Mining Company
North State Copper and Gold Mining Company
Perseverance Mining Company
Phoenix Gold Mining Company
Phoenix Mining Company
Portis Gold Mining Company
Potosi Mining and Manufacturing Company
Silver Hill Mining Company
Southern Mining and Manufacturing Company
Stewart Gold Mining Company
Stokes Iron Mining Company
Tuckasege Mining Company
Union Gold Mining Company
Ward Gold Mine Company
Way-Yehutta Mining and Manufacturing Company

In incorporating such mining companies as those shown above, the state legislature generally declined to limit those firms to particular minerals (for example, gold, silver, copper, or any combination thereof) or geographic locations within the state. The legislature authorized the creation of additional companies as late as 1863.

Numerous gold mines also contained copper ore, and most major copper mines had been worked for gold. Copper was found in Ashe County as early as 1827 and perhaps mined in Chatham in 1828. In 1838 the Deep River Gold Mine in Guilford shipped one hundred tons of copper to Liverpool. As miners dug deeper over the years, they increasingly found yellow copper pyrites below the water level. Following major discoveries in 1850 in eastern Tennessee, North

Carolina was ready for copper mining. Mines with significant deposits of copper ore included the Gardner Hill and McCullock in Guilford, Gold Hill in Rowan, and the Conrad Hill in Davidson. Particularly in Randolph and Guilford Counties, miners began removing copper. The state's chief copper-mining enterprise in 1853 was Guilford's old Fentress gold mine, renamed the North Carolina. The mine—which sold ore in Boston and New York—employed about a hundred workers, who began constructing smelting works and reached a depth of more than three hundred feet before activity ended in 1856.

The company was among many selling stock in northern cities. Stock mania and disreputable companies affected some Carolina mines as much as physical mining. After the California rush, investor interest in mining spread around the world. By 1853 British companies mining worldwide numbered more than five hundred. Brokers established the New York Mining Board, and the stock of the Conrad Hill, Gold Hill, Lindsay, McCullock, North Carolina, and Phoenix mines was publicly traded in that city. New York papers bulged with "golden statistics." Inevitably, speculation arose. Quick profits on Wall Street fueled new companies, and early investors made money at the expense of later stockholders. Entrepreneurs might form a business with nominal capital of $500,000 and subscribe 40 percent of it ($200,000) to buy a mine. The original partners then sold half the stock for $250,000, making $50,000. Such firms "mined" only enough to make their stock active. By 1855 nearly a hundred mining firms had issued $50 million in stock, exceeding banking capital in New York. Directors, "men of good wind, and plenty of it," dealt in inflated reports on mines. Rewards were lucrative on "the Great Wall Street Vein." Dependence upon New York funding was dangerous. Contractions of the money supply decimated shaky mines. In late 1853 the money market tightened; a year later most mining shares were worthless or nearly so. Many mining properties lacked real value, and at others managers had no funds for production. State geologist Ebenezer Emmons lamented the North Carolina mines' "unfortunate notoriety in Wall Street." Only a few companies, such as Gold Hill, survived such times. Mining stocks had not revived when the crippling panic of 1857 dealt a serious, if not fatal, blow to mining in the Old North State.

North Carolina in the 1850s had a number of significant mines. By 1853 the mine at Gold Hill (see chapter 3) was 340 feet deep and equipped with four steam engines, Cornish pumps 350 feet long, and Chilean mills. Shipments to the Charlotte mint quadrupled in four years. Estimated production since 1842 exceeded two million dollars. The American Mining Company developed the Cabarrus mine. Fifty men constructed buildings, installed steam machinery, and explored underground, but by 1855 the mine was deeply in debt. Owners of the Beaver Dam mine in nearby Montgomery County enjoyed profits. Various parties worked the Rudisill successfully for short periods. One firm reactivated the mine, showcase of earlier decades: workmen restarted the steam engine, refurbished the mine, put stamps to work, and raised much ore, but quit after a year. James W. Osborne—mining investor, politician, and former superintendent of the Charlotte mint—operated the mine for a time. The Capps achieved good returns in late 1854. John Penman remained actively involved with mines such as the Capps and the Howie (in Union County) until his death in 1855. The Mecklenburg Gold and Copper Company acquired machinery for the Catha mine and expanded the Rhea, where previously the only machinery had been an arrastra. Like the Rhea, Conrad Hill also had potential for both copper and gold; miners expanded old workings, excavating to one hundred feet by 1856 before running into financial problems. By 1856 the new Fisher Hill Mining Company had installed a 70-horsepower steam engine and eight Chilean mills. At Hoover Hill, groups worked the mine on leases.

A corporation led by Commodore Richard F. Stockton of New Jersey purchased the Howie mine, which by 1854 had produced $250,000 worth of gold, and operated it with slave labor. The firm installed tons of machinery worth $30,000 or more and began development. Stockton also began mechanizing the Kings Mountain mine west of Charlotte and perhaps worked the Lawson mine in Union. The Manteo Mining Company installed a steam engine, forty light stamps, bowls for washing ore, and a shaking table at the Jones mine in Davidson County, but half the gold was lost in processing. A three-hundred-foot railroad linked the mine and millhouse. In Guilford in 1852 the McCullock, profitable on a small scale for nearly thirty years with copper and gold, returned $31,000 worth of ore at a cost of $6,000. Then a northern company acquired the property, sent in Cornish miners, and erected ten Chilean mills, a massive 100-horsepower steam engine, and twenty-five stamps. The mine ran at a loss for nine months before suspending operations.

The Phoenix mine in Cabarrus County also experienced incorporation, brief operation, and failure. In 1853 profits from one Chilean mill covered expenses, so the company erected four more mills, a steam engine, stamps, a residence, and a millhouse. By 1854 manager William H. Orchard was profitably grinding 120 bushels of ore daily. Near the 140-foot level, the quality of the ore plummeted. In 1857 the sheriff sold forty acres of Phoenix land for unpaid taxes. Curiously, Orchard purchased the tract. Adjoining the Phoenix was the Vanderburg, which, along with Pioneer Mills, was one of few noteworthy Cabarrus mines in the 1850s. Pioneer Mills yielded gold above the water level and copper beneath it. At the Vanderburg, much gold escaped during processing, and the company (later the Excelsior concern) faced numerous lawsuits. Miners dug only one hundred feet deep, with underground workings 176 feet long.

Notable mines were active in other parts of the state. The Portis in Franklin County continued to show profits. The old Parker in Stanly County yielded perhaps $200,000 by 1856. At the Russell in Montgomery County, the Perseverance Mining Company in 1853 added an eighty-horsepower steam engine, forty stamps, Chilean mills, shaking tables, stirring bowls, and a 158-foot-long building. Men removed ore from pits sixty feet deep and broke it by hand for feeding to the stamps. Previously, workers carried ore two miles to a mill. Mining continued sporadically at the state's largest silver mine, the Washington (or Silver Hill), which for a time was said to be the only one in the nation. Workers dug silver at other mines in Davidson County—the Conrad Hill, Peters, Cross, Emmons, and Ward—and at the McMachin, near Gold Hill. Nonetheless, silver was a major product only at the Washington, which also yielded lead.

About 1856 Stephen Leeds of the *Mining Magazine* experimented at a mine in Rutherford County, hoping to end the speculative reputation of eastern mining and exchange technical data. He hoisted four hundred tons of ore for processing in various machines powered by steam. Leeds placed pulverized ore in settling tanks for sprinkling with mercury and amalgamated the sand in arrastras. After months, he concluded that ore must be crushed to the finest size and the resultant slime of water and ore amalgamated in the slowest manner. Others likewise sought panaceas for southern mines. While crushing, washing, and amalgamating devices had existed for decades, a new host of inventions for handling ore arose after discovery of gold in California and Australia. The South became a testing ground for "almost all the patent gold-saving processes invented," most of which were failures. The *Mining Magazine* deplored the "huge bombshells that make the mineral regions of the South resemble some Titanic battlefield." The endless roster of machines, many worthless, included Silliman bowls, Sullivan bowls, Hungarian bowls, and Tyrolean bowls. Yet experience proved that new machinery (as at the McCullock) did not necessarily enhance mines. Miners continued struggling with pyrites and attempted to improve roasting. Commodore Stockton presumably succeeded about 1857 in concentrating pyritic ore. A Massachusetts man, H. Holland, roasted sulfurets and nitrate of soda near Charlotte. Near Rutherfordton C. Ringel attempted another roasting technique. Metallurgy progressed, and a transition from practical miner to college-trained mining engineer began. Thoughtful scientists began trying to dissolve gold with chemicals such as cyanide or potassium.

In 1857 mining engineer Dr. Marinus Van Dyke successfully introduced hydraulic mining—washing away a hillside with a high-pressure hose—in McDowell County placers after observing the process in California. He moved water four miles by flume, canal, and a trestle one hundred feet high, and lifted it to a nozzle aimed at a hillside. Sluices filtered the material washed away. The procedure economically reworked old placers in McDowell and Burke; a yard of gravel reputedly cost 250 times less than if washed by a rocker. The process yielded profits of up to ten dollars daily for a pipe tended by two men.

Gold mining in North Carolina declined as the decade ended. The Charlotte mint received only $156,000 in deposits from within the state in 1859. Receipts from Gold Hill fell drastically, but the mine was—along with the Howie and Rudisill—among the state's most successful. Many mines were closed or in serious trouble. One bright spot was a new mine opened in 1858 on Sam Christian's land in Montgomery: miners there reportedly dug up twenty-five pounds of gold in ten days. The census of 1860 confirmed the decline and recorded no working mines in Burke, Cleveland, Cabarrus, Franklin, Guilford, Halifax, Iredell, Mecklenburg, Rutherford, or Stanly Counties. Production for all listed mines in the state was a mere $80,000, with a labor force of 303 people, mainly men. Most mines utilized steam power. Two other mines were very active: Silver Hill in Davidson, which turned out a yield worth $16,750, almost all in silver, and employed one hundred people, and Gardner Hill in Guilford County, at which 190 men and 10 women processed 1,920 tons of copper ore worth $100,000. North Carolina's total reported production of $80,000 worth of gold was less than the $95,000 in Carolina gold received at the Charlotte mint. One expert declared that the state's actual output in 1860 was $156,000, still lower than any year since the panics of 1837 and 1857. The Charlotte mint received only $32,000 in deposits in 1861 before North Carolina seceded from the Union in May. Nearly all remaining mining ceased during the war.

Table 3
Selected Mining Data from the Census of 1860

County	Name of Mine	No. of Workers	Annual Production
Catawba	J. J. Shuford	7	$3,200
Gaston	B. F. Briggs	20	$12,000
Montgomery	Thomas J. Forney	10	$2,580
	Baltimore and Montgomery	35	$500
Randolph	Hugh McCain	9	$1,230
	Daniel and Company	15	$1,339
Rowan	Gold Hill	132	$35,400
Union	Howie	75	$24,000

Secession was but one factor in the decline of mining, for most mines had closed before the war. No single theory explains the industry's fate. While California placers lured some Carolinians westward, California also spurred new technology and enthusiasm that benefited North Carolina. Economic factors detrimental to mining included panics in 1837 and 1857, speculation in mining stocks, and attractive alternative uses for labor and capital. There were problems related to inadequate technology and inherent riskiness in deep mining. In an industry that demanded careful accounting and large initial outlays of capital, ineptness and mismanagement, as well as inefficiency in general, were important hindrances. As in all gold fields, miners simply exhausted easily recoverable gold, and separating the precious metal from remaining refractory ore and pyrites was costly and difficult if not impossible. Some critics faulted slavery, southern laziness, or agrarians' lack of adaptability to industrialism. Specific failures often resulted from combinations of those factors.

Nonetheless, antebellum mines produced a significant amount of gold, a livelihood for miners, a foretaste of the coming industrial society, and markets for food and supplies in a rural, relatively backward state. Until 1860, North Carolina gold valued at the following amounts went to three major mints: $9,100,591.37 to Philadelphia, $4,663,273.35 to Charlotte, and $3,746,930.46 to Bechtler (before 1840), for a total of $17,510,795.18. The mines produced far more gold than that, but the total output can never be known. No one can calculate precisely how much gold was lost, stolen, sold for jewelry and arts, or shipped overseas. One estimate was that coinage was half of total output, which then would have been $35 million. Historian Fletcher Green posited at least $60 million for the period 1799-1860, while a geologist offered $24,638,108 as a reasonable estimate for the years from 1799 to 1962.

Table 4
Reported Gold Production in North Carolina, 1804-1963

Year	No. of Troy Ounces	Value	Year	No. of Troy Ounces	Value
1804-1823	2,274	$47,000	1831	14,224	294,000
1824	242	5,000	1832	22,158	458,000
1825	822	17,000	1833	22,980	475,000
1826	968	20,000	1834	18,384	380,000
1827	1,016	21,000	1835	12,724	263,000
1828	2,225	46,000	1836	7,165	148,000
1829	6,483	134,000	1837	5,656	116,900
1830	9,869	204,000			

43

1838			1880	4,596	95,000
1839			1881	5,564	115,000
1840			1882	9,192	190,000
1841			1883	8,079	167,000
1842	140,232	2,898,505	1884	7,596	157,000
1843			1885	7,354	152,000
1844			1886	8,466	175,000
1845			1887	10,885	225,000
1846			1888	6,580	136,000
1847			1889	7,102	146,795
1848	22,910	473,543	1890	5,733	118,500
1849	23,502	485,793	1891	4,596	95,000
1850	17,200	355,523	1892	3,801	78,560
1851	15,814	326,883	1893	2,593	53,600
1852	19,512	403,295	1894	2,330	48,167
1853	13,334	275,622	1895	2,622	54,200
1854	10,018	207,073	1896	2,143	44,300
1855	10,954	226,416	1897	1,674	34,600
1856	8,276	171,070	1898	4,064	84,000
1857	4,058	83,870	1899	1,669	34,500
1858	9,325	192,742	1900	1,379	28,500
1859	10,381	214,574	1901	2,685	55,500
1860	7,556	156,182	1902	4,388	90,700
1861	536	11,088	1903	3,411	70,500
1862	112	2,313	1904	5,994	123,900
1863	63	1,309	1905	6,081	125,685
1864	295	6,094	1906	3,973	82,131
1865	614	12,693	1907	3,976	82,193
1866	6,818	140,937	1908	4,716	97,480
1867	3,208	66,306	1909	1,946	40,230
1868	4,350	89,906	1910	3,292	68,045
1869	5,645	116,672	1911	3,400	70,282
1870	4,892	101,111	1912	8,032	166,014
1871	4,633	95,766	1913	6,117	126,448
1872	5,557	114,863	1914	6,344	131,141
1873	5,822	120,332	1915	8,321	172,001
1874	5,180	107,070	1916	1,269	26,237
1875	5,255	108,628	1917	590	12,187
1876	4,411	91,181	1918	79	1,631
1877	3,872	80,026	1919	5	101
1878	3,634	75,123	1920	72	1,479
1879	3,971	82,076	1921	156	3,229

1922	95	1,971	1943	137	4,795
1923	68	1,415	1944	21	735
1924	220	4,540	1945		
1925	897	18,540	1946		
1926	79	1,631	1947		
1927	49	1,015	1948		
1928	114	2,366	1949	13	455
1929	245	5,054	1950		
1930	705	14,582	1951		
1931	368	7,598	1952		
1932	367	7,591	1953		
1933	725	18,522	1954	214	7,500
1934	509	17,779	1955	190	6,650
1935	2,176	76,145	1956	882	30,870
1936	1,940	67,900	1957	1,373	48,000
1937	949	33,203	1958	876	31,000
1938	1,878	65,730	1959	965	34,000
1939	495	17,325	1960	1,826	64,000
1940	1,943	68,005	1961	2,094	73,000
1941	3,313	115,900	1962	460	16,000
1942	4,396	153,860	1963	33	1,000

Officially recorded production of gold in North Carolina ceased in 1963, although a tungsten mine yielded a very small amount of gold as a by-product in 1971. The amounts cited above are undoubtedly incomplete but are the only substantive government figures available. Readers should note that, despite the best efforts of state and federal geologists and others, no totally reliable records of total production of gold exist. Information from promoters and enthusiastic newspaper writers is especially suspect, as are some estimates relating to earlier years. This volume relies both upon state and federal records, which are not always in agreement. Source: P. Albert Carpenter III, *Gold in North Carolina* (Raleigh: North Carolina Department of Environment, Health, and Natural Resources [N.C. Geological Survey, Information Circular 29], 1993 [reprinted 1995, 1999]). Carpenter obtained his information from J. T. Pardee and C. F. Park Jr., *Gold Deposits of the Southern Piedmont* (Washington, D.C.: Government Printing Office [U.S. Geological Survey Professional Paper 213], 1948), as well as the U.S. Bureau of Mines. Data from the earlier decades originated as returns by the United States Mint.

As with total production, many observers have questioned the overall profitability of the prewar mines. Surviving data on the amount of capital expended and profits earned are fragmentary and suspect. Fletcher Green felt that $100 million was invested in return for more than $50 million in gold. Yet much capital found its way into "paper" companies active only on Wall Street, and experts have estimated that western mining firms—with far more ore— scarcely broke even overall. Perhaps that also was true in the South, but in 1860 a dwindling mining industry mattered far less to people than possible secession.

During the Civil War years, gold mining virtually ended in the state, which seceded on May 20, 1861. For four years North Carolina supported the South with manpower and supplies. On the day after secession, the state militia occupied the Charlotte mint, which operated for a few weeks as a state mint, producing about a thousand five-dollar gold coins for the Confederacy. Some mine owners, such as Commodore Stockton of the Howie, returned north when war came. The sheriff seized and auctioned his property. Remaining active mines closed one by one. "Millions to buy guns but not a dollar to buy a pick or shovel," complained one mine promoter, who acknowledged the "discouraging" prospects of mining "in the face of a draft which is depleting our population rapidly and leaving scarce enough hands to work the farms." The only significant gold mine that operated during the war was the Rudisill. The Confederate army recovered sulfur and saltpeter from the ore extracted there. Slave miners worked eight-hour shifts at the facility, which also supplied acids and sulfates for the army's medical needs. While vein mining ceased at Gold Hill in 1861, surface ore provided stone and chemicals for the Confederacy. But despite the war, some intrepid miners still searched for placer gold, just as John Reed had done sixty years earlier.

2

Reed Gold Mine: From Discovery to Historic Site

The story of North Carolina's Reed Gold Mine reflects the remarkable accidents, drama, and ironies of history that, with variations, occurred in connection with gold rushes around the world. It is the story of an illiterate Hessian citizen-soldier—an illegal immigrant from Germany—who deserted from the British army in Savannah and made his way to backwoods North Carolina, where he settled, married, and reared a family. It is the saga of a twelve-year-old boy who went fishing one Sunday and found a seventeen-pound rock that served as a doorstop for three years before being sold to a merchant for a mere $3.50, although it was gold worth a thousand times that modest sum. It is the account of an impoverished slave who found a twenty-eight-pound nugget of gold in a creek. It is the report of a rich mine that was closed for a decade while its owners argued over a chunk of gold in legal battles that reached the state supreme court. It is the topsy-turvy tale of a mine whose last original family owner went broke and sold the property at auction, only to see it resold ten months later for an 800 percent jump in price. It is the narrative of a mining company that, despite tens of thousands of dollars and the latest technology, equipment, and management, failed within a year. It is the legend of a woman murdered by a family member and shoved down a mine shaft. It is the tale of a mine only twenty miles from Charlotte abandoned and kept for a private hunting retreat for seventy years, eventually to be preserved as a state historic site.

The Reed Gold Mine in Cabarrus County held out the initial golden promise to the people of the Piedmont and the nation. Unhappily, because there are no known Reed manuscripts, many questions about John Reed and his mine remain unanswered. The very spelling of the apparently illiterate man's name may be questioned. Born in Germany, John Reed must have Anglicized his original name, which probably was Ried, Riedt, or Rieth. Many German surnames in Piedmont North Carolina received American equivalents by transferring the sound or meaning of the word to English. Inasmuch as "Reed" meets both of these criteria when compared with Ried, and several of his sons signed their names in that manner, the spelling seems logical. Equally imprecise until recently has been the date of John Reed's birth. Various sources place his birth between 1757 and 1759 in the province of Hesse-Cassel.

John Reed's Hessian military records in the Staatsarchiv at Marburg, Germany, list him as Johannes Rieth with a town of origin of Appenfeld, presently a small village perhaps twenty miles southwest of Kassel near the main highway to Frankfurt. The Rieth and Ried families originated in nearby villages, Raboldshausen (founded before A.D. 800) and Salzberg. Reed's mother, Anna Elisabeth Ried, was born in 1728 in or near Raboldshausen.

For centuries in Germany, births and other important life events were recorded in parish records of local churches. The Lutheran church book at Salzberg lists under baptisms for 1759: "Mother—Anna Elisabeth Ried, her illegitimate son Johannes was born 14th April at 10 o'clock in the morning. Father is Johann Jakob Helmerich son of the Herrschaftlichen Pächter [rental agent and general manager] of the lands belonging to the lords of [the castle at nearby] Neuenstein." Both parents did penance for their adultery, and Anna took young Johannes with her when she married Adam Hahn, a widower, in 1764. The Hahns lived near Raboldshausen until at least 1773, when Johannes was confirmed in the local Lutheran church. Perhaps Johannes served an apprenticeship in nearby Appenfeld and lived with his uncle Johann Heinrich Ried. That village was poor and had neither a school nor its own church; most villagers were tenant farmers. One branch of the Ried family had moved there and changed its name to Rieth.

In any case, Johannes Ried, or Rieth, joined the Hessian militia from the district of Appenfeld. He probably enlisted rather than being drafted and stood five feet four inches tall, the minimum acceptable height for recruits. Young Ried served in the Garrison Regiment von Wissenbach, which, not unlike present-day military reserve forces, was made up mainly of citizen-soldiers who trained several weeks each summer. In 1776 Frederick II of Hesse-Cassel mobilized the regiment to aid the British in the developing American Revolution. The troops disembarked at New York that October.

Ried, however, was probably a replacement who reached America in 1778, arriving at Long Island to join the regiment for its transfer south to capture Savannah in late December. American forces failed to retake the city after a siege and a final bloody attack in October 1779. As the long months passed, the Hessians suffered from the food and climate and complained bitterly of both. During the occupation, the British dispatched daily patrols to the outlying areas to protect foraging troops and carry out military reconnaissance. The patrols went at least as far out as the German-speaking settlement at Ebenezer, twenty-five miles up the Savannah River. Undoubtedly Ried participated in his share of such patrols.

At least 10 to 15 percent of the Hessians in America deserted, and Ried did so on June 21, 1782, from a post "outside of Savannah," taking with him his arms and equipment. By that time rumors probably were in the air that the British were about to evacuate the city and sail for the West Indies. In October 1781 British general Cornwallis had surrendered to George Washington in Virginia, ending English hopes for victory in North America. Three weeks after Ried absconded, the British left Savannah for Charleston (their last stronghold in the Carolinas and Georgia), which they abandoned in December. Meanwhile, on the same day Ried deserted, two other men in his unit—both from near Appenfeld—deserted from Savannah. One of them, Phillip Jordan, later owned land on Meadow Creek near John Reed.

To desert from Savannah was dangerous because many German colonists in the area were Loyalists. The senior Hessian officer in Savannah offered rewards for the return of live deserters—or scalps and uniforms—brought back by search parties of tories, Native Americans, and African Americans. A deserter had to beware of German-speaking civilians. His best chance was to find a change of clothes, get behind the American lines, travel with sympathetic patriots, and take the road northwest toward present-day Columbia, where it turned north to Rock Hill and Charlotte.

John Reed and several Hessians made their way either singly or in groups to the rural Germanic area around Dutch Buffalo Creek in eastern Mecklenburg—now Cabarrus—County. Reed may have gone to Mecklenburg with Philip Jordan or others. In that isolated, ethnic farm community built around St. John's Lutheran Church lived numerous German farmers. They tended to reside in crude log houses, continued to speak German, and rarely saw the outside world except on marketing trips each spring and fall.

In that setting, although a few miles away near Meadow Creek, Reed spent his life and raised a family. Perhaps he first found work as a hired hand on a farm owned by Peter Kiser. Within a few months, probably in the fall of 1782, young Reed fell in love and married Sarah Kiser (or Kizer), daughter of Peter (who farmed and operated a gristmill) and Fanny Kiser. The union produced nine children—four sons and five daughters. Reed, helped by his brother-in-law, Frederick Kiser, began acquiring land to farm. After buying an initial thirty acres from Kiser, Reed obtained land from the new state of North Carolina. At the time (and as late as 1959), the state allowed citizens to enter claims on tracts that appeared to be unowned. By 1800 Reed, who already had seven children, had acquired 330 acres in that way.

Although Reed would later have more children—as well as sixty-eight grandchildren—and possess much more land and wealth, little is known of his personal life and qualities. Public records reveal as much about him as any other available source. Unlike many Hessians, he likely was illiterate, for he signed deeds, his will, and his application for citizenship with an X. And, contrary to the habits of most of his peers, he apparently did not join any Germanic churches, for no records have survived of any births or baptisms of his children in Lutheran or Reformed parishes in his area. Reed and his family might have attended a nearby Baptist church, inasmuch as one of his neighbors was Rev. James Love, a Baptist preacher. Love became Reed's partner in gold mining, and in 1805 Love's daughter married Reed's first son.

When John Reed died decades later, an obituary credited him as being a Christian and a friend of the poor. Local historians characterized Reed as "honest but unlearned," "a rather primitive character, but a good liver in his way and a respected citizen." Reed performed his share of civic duties and was a successful farmer and businessman. By 1799 this ordinary, middle-aged yeoman farmer was at least forty years old and owned several hundred acres of land in a backwoods county twenty miles east of the village of Charlotte. Given the life expectancy of his day, one might have imagined that this immigrant with his curious background would die in obscurity within a decade or so, but such was not to be the case.

In 1799 Reed's life and the history of his adopted homeland were changed by the accidental discovery of gold on his property. One Sunday—supposedly in the spring—twelve-year-old Conrad Reed, son of John and Sarah, went fishing with several siblings in Little Meadow Creek on the family farm rather than attend church with his parents. At the creek he saw "a yellow substance shining in the water." Wading in to retrieve the object, he discovered it to be some kind of metal. The wedge-shaped rock was about the size of a small smoothing iron, or flatiron. Its weight was later said to be about seventeen pounds. Conrad showed the yellow stone to his father, but John Reed, unable to identify it, set it aside as a doorstop and continued life as usual. Only once during the next three years did Reed pay any particular attention to the object. At some point he took the stone to William Atkinson, a silversmith in Concord, North Carolina, for identification. The latter, however, could not identify the rock.

In 1802 Reed encountered a person who instantly recognized the composition of the rock. A jeweler in Fayetteville whom Reed visited on an annual marketing trip told Reed the metal was gold and asked that the nugget be left for fluxing. Later the artisan showed Reed a bar of gold six to eight inches long. It appears that Reed had no concept of gold as precious; when the craftsman offered to buy the nugget, Reed asked what he felt to be a "big price"—$3.50. The merchant gladly paid him and received roughly $3,600 worth of gold.

Conrad Reed finding the first gold nugget, as depicted by artist Porte Crayon in *Harper's New Monthly Magazine* 15 (August 1857), 289.

Tradition has it that Reed then bought gifts for his family, including cloth and coffee beans for his wife. (Sarah, however, reportedly was unfamiliar with coffee and became frustrated when the beans failed to cook well in a stew.)

It was not long before Reed (possibly aided by James Love) supposedly recovered about a thousand dollars from the jeweler. The Reeds soon began searching at random for other valuable rocks up and down Little Meadow Creek. The chief hunts occurred in the summer, when farming did not require much labor and the creek was dry. Reed shortly turned a profit and in 1803 took three men of relative substance—his brother-in-law Frederick Kiser, James Love, and wealthy landowner Martin Phifer Jr.—into partnership. In late summer, after the crops were in the ground and the stream had nearly dried up, each of the three others supplied equipment and two slaves to dig for gold in the creek bed. The four planned an equal division of returns. They were not disappointed. Before the end of the season, Peter, a black man owned by Love, unearthed from merely six inches below the creek bottom (near a deep spot called the "lake") a twenty-eight-pound nugget worth more than sixty-six hundred dollars. One story was that Love offered Peter a walnut-sized knob off the nugget before it was fluxed, but Peter—fearing a jest at his expense—refused to risk damage to his dinner fork by trying to pry off the piece.

The gold later enabled intelligent but uneducated Reed to become a man of significant wealth. He invested in land and slaves but otherwise lived modestly. Reed eventually bought some two thousand acres of land and retained nearly half of it until his death. He also engaged in the unfortunate southern habit of slaveholding, purchasing three African Americans—Dinah, Charity, and Sam—in 1804. Reed ultimately may have owned more than a dozen additional blacks. Thirteen unmarked stones, which may mark slave graves, have survived in the family cemetery. Each of Reed's three partners held more than a dozen enslaved Americans. At that time only about a fourth of white families in the state owned any slaves at all.

With slaves, partners, and family members engaged in part-time mining and a need to market the gold, it was inevitable that by late 1803 or early 1804 the outside world would learn of the fabulous creek. Apparently the partners shipped Peter's nugget to the United States mint in Philadelphia. In 1804 Reed's workers at Little Meadow Creek found five nuggets weighing from one to nine pounds each, as well as gold in dust and fine particles. One observer reported that the four partners garnered more than fourteen thousand dollars in a mere six weeks. That same year eleven thousand dollars' worth of Cabarrus gold, probably most or all from Reed's creek site, reached the federal mint. Congressman Nathaniel Alexander of Charlotte received a beautiful yellow nugget from one of the partners. A few periodicals mentioned the mine, and word of the gold circulated through Washington, Philadelphia, and New York.

In 1806 William Thornton of Baltimore, who planned to conduct elaborate mining operations in the area, examined the Reed. Some laborers still merely turned the gravel in the creek bottom with spades and picked out any visible gold. Thornton apparently found one improvement: the use of mercury, known since ancient times for its ability to bond chemically with grains of gold. Reed's men gleaned gravel for visible gold and probably panned the remaining sand, with mercury in the pans, to obtain finer gold by "amalgamating" it (i.e., combining it chemically) with mercury. Heating the amalgam of gold and mercury in a sealed iron retort vaporized the mercury, leaving gold behind. In that way the men obtained six or seven ounces of gold several times a week. Thornton learned that the estimated cumulative production of the mine extended as high as $40,000 and that the proprietors still valued the site at $100,000. Like Stephen Ayres before him, Thornton believed that the hills around the creek must contain gold; but the owners were either ignorant of or uninterested in that observation. Reed continued his farming and dealing in land. The tracts reflected little or no rise in price as a result of gold.

For about twenty years placer operations at the Reed mine and nearby continued on a technologically crude, part-time basis, perhaps because mining was an unfamiliar pursuit with unpredictable, sporadic rewards for the simple agrarians. Similar activities soon began as neighboring farmers found gold in their creeks. Reed's diggings became known as the "bull of the gold mines." Before long, workers at the site had dug up and gathered the obvious larger nuggets and had begun to pan for smaller, infinitely more numerous, particles of gold. Rockers soon superseded pans and became the usual machines in which to wash gravel at the Reed and other North Carolina placer mines. Like the pan, the rocker depended upon the high specific gravity of gold (more than nineteen times as heavy as water) to separate the valuable metal from sand and gravel. A typical rocker was a box, a half-barrel, or half of a hollow log. After adding auriferous gravel and water to the device, the miner rocked it by hand or used foot action to wash away the lighter material and leave behind heavier bits of gold. In 1805 a visitor to Reed's creek saw workers using a machine, somewhat like a rocker, that consisted of sliding boxes with tin bottoms full of holes, through which hand-powered pumps washed water and gravel. Reed had copied the device from that of a neighboring miner (perhaps William Thornton), who had ordered it built in Baltimore.

By 1824 haphazard digging at Reed's property had yielded an estimated one hundred thousand dollars' worth of gold, and seasonal placer mining was common in Cabarrus and nearby counties. Yet farming predominated, and little if any technological progress had been made in two decades. Like other mines, the Reed was inefficient, and tolerable wages could be made by working gravel already washed several times. There was, however, always the hope of additional large nuggets, for which the Reed, above other North Carolina mines, was famous.

After James Love died in 1821, Reed and his two remaining partners apparently joined with three Virginia investors to expand operations. The reinvigorated enterprise prompted the new state geologist, Denison Olmsted, to make a visit. He found the mine to be the level portion, some fifty to one hundred yards wide, of a floodplain created by Little Meadow Creek between two hillocks. The space was "nearly all dug over" and contained "numerous small pits, surrounded by piles of rubbish, for the distance of a quarter of a mile up and down the stream." Workers dug down three or four feet to reach a layer of gold-bearing gravel and "tenacious blue earth," which was processed by hand with rockers and pans. Yet the creek did not appear as productive to Olmsted as in earlier years. He believed that its output might be enhanced by new capital, the introduction of currents of running water on inclined planes, and diversion of the creek for more systematic mining of its bed.

The Reed mine remained, however, essentially a low-budget, family-run operation and embraced neither the most advanced technology nor perhaps the decade's frenzied search for gold, although one Cornish entrepreneur named Matthew Thomas attempted to lease the mine for ninety-nine years. John Reed apparently preferred to continue his profitable placer operation rather than risk his capital in the uncertainty of a shift to extensive, potentially costly, vein mining. Furthermore, he forbade mining on lands he cultivated. Large nuggets occasionally turned up, and before 1826 the total quantity of gold found at the Reed mine in pieces exceeding one pound each amounted to eighty-four pounds. That productivity eventually reached one hundred fifty pounds. Despite stories of an eighty-pound hunk of gold, Peter's twenty-eight-pound nugget remained the largest authenticated find. Within a few years the estimated value of the total yield from the famous creek reached two hundred thousand dollars. By that time the mine had been worked more than nearly any

Little Meadow Creek, for decades North Carolina's principal source of native gold.

other placer deposit in the state. While several other mine owners employed steam power and hundreds of skilled miners at increasingly extensive underground operations, Reed avoided such a scale or mode of operation. The aging German continued the close-knit family operation at his mine and farm rather than import outside workers, values, technology, and perhaps capital. He had attained a comfortable existence and saw no point in changing a successful policy or disrupting his life-style.

During the early 1830s work at the Reed finally progressed from placer mining to hard-rock underground efforts. In 1831 Isaac Craton, a Reed in-law, dug the first pit on Upper Hill above the stream and found a vein yielding ore worth five dollars per bushel. With little expertise, the miners made considerable progress in excavation within the next few years while continuing some of their creek mining. Various miners, perhaps nearly all sons or relatives of Reed, deepened pits into shafts. It is likely, given the expanded activity, that the family utilized local men, black and white, as laborers. There were at least four or five shafts with depths of up to ninety feet on Upper Hill and probably another set of shafts on Lower Hill, which at one point supposedly produced four or more pounds of gold a day.

Exactly how the miners dealt with the increased output of ore remains unknown. They apparently erected horse-powered whims near the chief shafts to raise the ore and put up an arrastra, or drag-stone mill, near the creek to crush the ore. The whim was a large vertical drum around which a rope could be wound or unwound to raise or lower the ore bucket. A horse or mule harnessed to the ends of a fixed horizontal sweep extending out from the drum walked in a circle to turn the drum and raise the ore bucket out of the shaft. The workers might have processed the ore in rockers after crushing it. By then European miners operating a handful of large mines at Charlotte used steam engines for power. One August, probably in 1832, the largest concern (the Mecklenburg Gold Mining Company) milled 756 bushels of ore from the Reed mine for a fee of $226.80. The extent of dealings between the company and the family is uncertain. Perhaps the Reeds relied upon the Charlotte-based mills only until they arranged for additional ore-crushing at their mine. Transporting hundreds of one-hundred-pound bushels of ore some twenty miles to Charlotte by wagon on poor roads was not a desirable way to process ore.

Tales, some dating to the early underground mining, soon circulated about conflicts and fabulous wealth at the Reed. Isaac Craton reportedly was so successful in his original efforts to engage in pit mining that Timothy Reed (a grandson of John Reed) forced him out of the shaft and then quickly recovered up to twenty thousand dollars' worth of gold there. Timothy Reed worked intermittently at the mine for decades. Robert Motley, another in-law, claimed to have recovered fourteen pounds of gold one day before breakfast. A Captain Biggers said he worked his weight in gold at the mine. Miners dug gold "like potatoes" from one trench on Upper Hill. The family partners reportedly paid their employees with pieces of gold pounded in a common hand mortar. Slaves at the mines were said to remove gold and spend it at nearby groceries and liquor shops, paying for a single drink with a hunk of gold and quartz as large as a hen's egg.

In early 1834 Conrad Reed, who had found the initial nugget in 1799, died. On November 15 his son and seven remaining children of John Reed or their representatives entered into an oral agreement to govern work at the mine. Old John Reed was to receive a royalty, and the rest of the gold was to be split among partners working on the day of the discovery. George Barnhardt (husband of Reed's youngest child, Martha) was named manager. Several parties understood that no substitute miners were permissible.

John Reed authorized mining to resume on the following Monday. Three of his grandsons guarded the property Sunday night, but he postponed work because of heavy rains and flooding. Soon Robert Motley found a chunk of gold that weighed nearly ten pounds when fluxed and precipitated a lengthy legal struggle within the family. Motley argued that George Reed, absent at home with a sick wife, did not merit a share of the gold. Within a few days, the family unearthed additional large nuggets, in all perhaps more than thirty pounds of gold, and friction continued. Consequently on November 25 the eight male family members and old John produced a written agreement, which in large part probably reiterated the oral covenant. The paper specified penalties for idleness, neglect, stealing gold, or sickness and clearly stipulated that no substitutes or slaves were allowable. The manager was to be obeyed, and each partner was to provide a horse for hauling. Yet despite Reed's attempts to maintain family unity, even to the point of an offer to reimburse some relatives personally, selfishness caused the deal to fail. George Reed demanded a share of the earlier nugget. When most of the family disagreed, he brought suit and secured an injunction that closed the mine. As a result, formal work there ceased for about a decade.

The case eventually reached the state supreme court. The dispute focused on which of Reed's sons and sons-in-law, who had been working the mine under the oral agreement, owned the nugget. George Reed had sent his sixteen-year-old son Arthur to work as his substitute on the day of the find. Some of the elder Reed's associates maintained that young Arthur was not doing a man's share of work. Chief Justice Thomas Ruffin upheld a lower court's decision in favor of George Reed on the ground that his son, the substitute, had been at work for the group. Ruffin argued that the defendants had accepted Arthur as a co-worker, since one of them had ordered him to perform certain tasks and he had complied. Although legal expenses reportedly consumed much of the value of the nugget, George Reed presumably received $535 for his share of the gold, plus interest accrued during the long years of litigation.

Shortly after the settlement, and before any substantial renewed mining, John Reed died on May 28, 1845, at the age of about eighty-seven. The family buried the patriarch beside the creek with his wife, and their graves remain there to this day. In 1842, three years before his death, Reed had gone to the Cabarrus County Courthouse to apply for and receive citizenship in his adopted land. Sarah Reed had died in 1843 after a marriage of sixty years. Thus ended the story of John Reed, except for two curious footnotes that reunite him with his German birthplace. Cabarrus County court records tell of a young man named Conrad Reed from Hesse-Cassel who arrived in America about 1844, sought citizenship in Cabarrus, and died there in a few months. Yet there is no indication of any connection to John Reed. Just as inexplicable is an entry in the old church book in Salzberg, Germany, that records the birth and baptism of Johannes, son of Anna Elisabeth Ried. Next to the entry is a cross, the German symbol for death in such books, and the date "6/3 45," perhaps meaning June 3, 1845, and possibly the burial date of John Reed. If this is so, did some of his children (he was apparently illiterate) arrange correspondence with relatives back in Germany? Or did Reed have Hessian friends who wrote home?

Reed had appointed his son John Jr. and son-in-law George Barnhardt as executors, directing them to sell his property. In August 1845 they adver-

A VALUABLE

GOLD-MINE

For Sale.

THE undersigned having qualified as the Executors of the last Will and Testament of John Reid, senr. dec'd., will sell upon the premises, in Cabarrus county, in the State of North Carolina, on Thursday the 5th day of February next, the valuable **Gold-Mine**, so well known amongst Miners in this region of Country as,

"THE REID MINE."

This Gold-Mine has the reputation of being one of the richest mines ever opened in this section of the country, and this character is as old as the history of Mining in North Carolina ; it being among the first Mines opened in this State.

Although this is one of the oldest mines in the Country, it has as yet been but partially explored, the late proprietor never would permit any persons out of his own family to work the Mine, and they never were permitted to enter the lands he cultivated. There are about seven hundred and fifty acres in the tract, and but a small part of the tract has as yet been tested ; but the part worked has yielded more Gold to the labor than any mine ever opened in this Country.

Some of the rarest specimens of pure gold have been found at this Mine that have ever been found in the United States ; and with one or two exceptions, the largest mass of pure gold was found here that we have any history of : it weighed twenty-eight pounds, avoirdupois weight : a number of other large pieces have been found, weighing sixteen, thirteen, eleven, and eight pounds, and so on, to the smallest particles.

These large pieces were found in an alluvial deposite near the surface. This deposit has been found very rich as far as it has been tested, but the largest portion of it has been in cultivation by the late proprietor, and has never been worked ; but it is believed to be equally as rich as the part that has been worked.

There are a number of VEINS runing through this tract of land which have been but partially tried, but as far as they have been tested are equal, if not superior, in value to any veins that have ever been opened in this Country.

This valuable property has been thrown into the public market by the testator in order that an equal distribution might be made among his children.

Payments will be divided into three equal instalments, and one, two and three years' time will be given, interest at the rate of six per cent. per annum will be charged upon the whole after the first year, the purchaser entering into bonds with approved securities ; or a discount of six per cent. will be made for cash payments. The notes of, or checks on, any specie paying Banks in North Carolina, Philadelphia, New York, or Charleston, will be received.

Further particulars will be made known on the day of sale.

This Mine is situated fifteen miles south-east of Concord, in the State of North Carolina.

GEORGE BARNHARDT, } Ex'rs
JOHN REED,

August 7th. 1845—18:3t

*** The Raleigh Register is requested to give the above *three* insertions, and forward account to Gold-Hill, Rowan county.

Newspaper advertisement for sale of Reed mine, 1845.

tised the mine for sale by auction in February 1846. Reed's estate was valued a few years later at some $40,000 and apparently included $18,070 in notes from the sale of his land. The next round of mining, however, ultimately failed, and the estate probably grossed only about $25,000 (about $540,000 in 1999 dollars).

Reed's son-in-law Andrew Hartsell and grandson Timothy Reed purchased the tract entirely on credit with three years to complete payment. For a few years, they worked the mine with some success in more or less the fashion pursued in the 1830s. How much development they added to the underground workings remains unclear; perhaps they dug three new shafts on Upper Hill. Although exploratory digging may have occurred in the 1830s on Lower Hill (south of Upper Hill), Reed and Hartsell also dug shafts and drilled tunnels there. Timothy Reed and his men pushed one tunnel 140 feet through solid rock beneath Lower Hill to intersect a vein that on the first day reportedly yielded enough gold to cover the entire expense of the tunnel. By that time, Reed's miners apparently employed gunpowder for blasting, because Timothy Reed was wounded in an explosion. Compared to other leading North Carolina mines, however, the Reed was a small operation using obsolete equipment and a few horses. The partners deposited about $4,500 in gold at the Charlotte mint between April 1848 and November 1850. Timothy Reed reported to the federal census that he produced ore worth $7,500 with twenty hands at a labor cost of $400 monthly. Some of the laborers probably were slaves owned or rented by the partners. The partnership was not as profitable as some other mines. Within another year, deposits at the mint for the previous three years reached more than $6,000. While the ore at the mine reportedly was very rich, the owners were having problems putting into operation a suitable mill to grind it. By 1852 Reed was unable to pay debts to his relatives, and a mortgage in the amount of $18,070 plus interest had remained unpaid for three years.

The venture obviously was not going well, and the last significant involvement by the Reed family was at hand. Thomas J. Shinn, a neighbor and grantee in a deed of trust from Reed and Hartsell, foreclosed and advertised the mine for sale at auction. In October George Barnhardt and Caleb White, a Cabarrus man of some wealth, bought the property for only $3,005. They leased the mine to Conrad Hardwick for one-eighth of the gold found in pieces below "twenty penny weight" and one-fourth of the larger nuggets, but the owners soon found a better opportunity. In July 1853 Barnhardt and White sold the mine for $10,000—a very handsome profit of 200 percent in nine months apparently not shared with the heirs of John Reed—to James W. Osborne, a Charlotte lawyer and political appointee as superintendent of the mint, and Emmer Graham, coiner at the mint. Osborne and Graham resold the mine the same day, obviously by design, to Philip W. Groot of Albany, New York.

The property changed hands again and became, at a price that in ten months had risen 800 percent, the possession of the Reed Gold and Copper Mining Company of New York. In July 1853 Groot sold the entire tract—measured at 745 acres—for twenty-five thousand dollars to trustees for the company, which hired professional miners and installed new equipment. The Reed mine was under the direction of Dr. Louis Posselt, formerly professor of chemistry at the famous German university at Heidelberg and mill superintendent at the renowned and up-to-date Jesus Maria silver mine in Mexico. Although the Reed was not the largest of the major Carolina mining endeavors, it was certainly typical of them and had more expertise and up-to-date mining equipment than at any other time in its history.

Within a year the company spent considerable money repairing and developing the Reed mine underground and erecting new machinery and buildings on Upper Hill and nearby, although the surrounding area was under cultivation. On the hill the corporation used native stone (for foundations, a boiler pit, and a chimney twenty-nine feet tall) and timber to build a small village with a substantial enginehouse and millhouse under one roof, a large whim house and whim to raise ore, an office, a powder house, stables, a blacksmith shop, and eleven cabins for miners. By mid-1854 the major

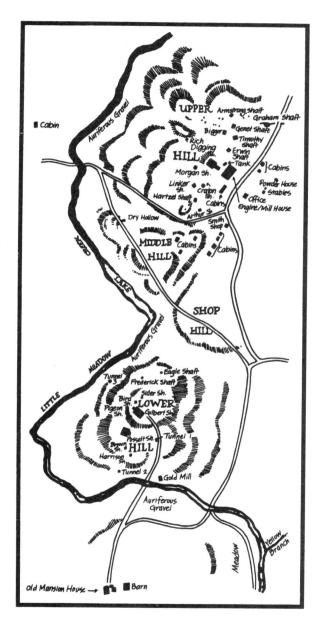

Reed mine in 1854, based on a map by August Partz that appeared in *Mining Magazine* 3 (August 1854).

underground portion of the Reed at Upper Hill comprised no fewer than fifteen separate shafts, many connected by a series of tunnels more than five hundred feet long. Candles provided lighting underground. The firm delayed the start of new work at Lower Hill, which had nine shafts, a number of tunnels and underground chambers, and two whim houses remaining from earlier mining.

Posselt undoubtedly instructed his employees in centuries-old European techniques of mining. If a shaft intersected a vein of ore, the miners cut tunnels, or drifts, following the ore at different levels. Working either up or down from different drifts on the same vein, the laborers eventually chiseled out fair-sized rooms, or stopes, in their efforts to remove the vein material. After discarding waste rock, miners probably loaded the loose ore into low wheelbarrows for the trip back through the tunnel to the shaft. Underground mining was dangerous, backbreaking work, and sensible miners moved as little heavy rock as possible.

As in Europe, major Carolina mines frequently utilized iron buckets, or kibbles, to hoist both ore and miners to the surface. At the Reed this lifting took place chiefly in the 110-foot-deep engine shaft on top of Upper Hill. Atop the shaft on a timber headframe was a sheave, or pulley, connecting a rope or chain from the kibble to a hoisting device, called a whim, similar to an outsized windlass. A single horse moving in a circle might have powered this machine. The engine shaft also had a pumping function and contained a new steam-powered submersible Worthington pump capable of raising water for the millhouse and draining portions of the mine below the fifty-five-foot water level. Then or later miners also installed a much different Cornish-style pump there. The reliable Cornish pump, standard for underground mines around the world for centuries, was much more cumbersome and included heavy wooden pump rods (not unlike telephone poles hooked together) that ran the entire depth of the shaft.

A fifty-horsepower horizontal steam engine in the approximately twenty-four-hundred-square-foot millhouse across the shaft opening from the whim operated the pump(s) and machinery for crushing the ore and isolating the golden particles. The engine was coupled to a large boiler fired with wood cut on the property. Oral tradition is that the boiler was purchased in England and shipped via Charleston to Charlotte, then hauled overland by teams of mules. The equipment run by the engine included a stamp mill for crushing the ore by a series of pounding blows. Supplementing the stamp mill were three large Chilean mills that crushed the ore to a finer size. Still other machines, among them an arrastra, or drag-stone mill, aided in crushing and separating the gold. Shaking tables shook in a reciprocating motion to separate the gold particles from lighter sand and quartz. The mill workers used all of these steam-powered machines, as well as water and quicksilver, for catching bits of precious metal in the devices before purifying it in retorts to recover gold from the ore. At the

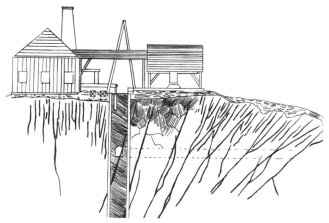

This ca. 1880 drawing by an unknown artist depicts the millhouse and chimney, engine shaft, and whim house at Upper Hill, all of which remained little changed since the mid-1850s.

Reed, Posselt probably placed mercury in the bed of the arrastra. Like miners in the state before and after him, he also might have employed mercury elsewhere—common places included pans, rockers, sluices, Chilean mills, and stamp mills.

Despite an impressive array of machinery, the Reed Gold and Copper Company was defunct before the end of 1854. The Reed company, whether primarily a speculative venture or not, might have suffered in a general collapse of mining shares that year. On the other hand, decisions at the mine itself could have hastened its failure. Perhaps Posselt should have spent more of his limited capital exploring underground ore reserves rather than erecting costly machinery. Within a year or so, the state geologist of South Carolina, Oscar Lieber, reported that the gold at Reed, while remarkably coarse, was nearly depleted. His counterpart in North Carolina, Ebenezer Emmons, wrote that a vein at the famous mine yielded only $1.15 per bushel, a mediocre return in those days.

In 1855, following a confluence of such problems and local unpaid bills, the sheriff of Cabarrus County auctioned the property to satisfy creditors. By January of that year the Cabarrus County court had resolved at least three lawsuits against the Reed Gold and Copper Mining Company. When claims against the bankrupt enterprise exceeded $6,050, the sheriff sold the mine. Some of the buyers were already extensively involved with the Reed. For $6,700—about one-fourth the amount the corporation had paid for the mine— Emmer Graham, Charles J. Gilbert, Samuel T. Armstrong of New York, and

Charles Winslow of Massachusetts acquired the 745 acres in June 1855. By then, recorded gold production in North Carolina had fallen more than 50 percent from its high point in 1849, and the group conducted little if any organized mining. Local people continued panning and digging in the creek, and in 1856 and 1857 unidentified miners unearthed two nuggets of about four pounds each at the Reed. Nevertheless, census takers in 1860 found operations suspended at the mine of "S. T. Armstrong and Company" and did not record a single mine in operation in Cabarrus. The mine remained closed during the Civil War, along with virtually all Carolina gold mines except the Rudisill.

Over the next three or more decades the Reed mine, despite its ups and downs not unlike other mines in the region, lured fortune seekers, some more serious than others, to southeastern Cabarrus. One person closely connected with the mine during most of that time was Robert Gadd (b. 1832), an articulate Englishman who had deposited $830 in gold from the Reed at the Charlotte mint in 1859 and served about a year in the Confederate army. Just a few months after the Civil War ended, Gadd was a principal in the partnership of Gadd and Parker, which leased the mine. The firm dewatered and perhaps deepened the engine shaft. The following year a representative of the new *American Journal of Mining* observed that the mine was in operation and that the engine shaft was 120 feet deep; however, the efforts by Gadd and Parker may have amounted to little more than pumping out and shoring up old underground workings.

Late in 1866 William L. Hirst (ca. 1802-1876), a Philadelphia lawyer and investor, paid about $25,000 to purchase the tract from the four parties, or their heirs, who had obtained the mine a decade earlier at the sheriff's sale. The sellers accepted short-term mortgages from Hirst in the amount of $11,350. Within a few months Hirst sold half the mine for $15,000, subject to half the mortgages, to James P. Bruner, a Philadelphia manufacturer. Several years later one of the mortgage holders, Emmer Graham, foreclosed on Hirst and forced another auction of one-fourth of the mine. Hirst refused to lose his mine and had a Philadelphia attorney buy the property back for him—at a one-third reduction of the mortgage debt—during a sheriff's sale in late 1870. After some ten years Bruner's unpaid debts connected with the Reed amounted to $1,135, and the Cabarrus sheriff in 1881 seized Bruner's half of the mine and held another auction. This time the purchaser, apparently for a mere fifty-nine dollars, was attorney A. A. Hirst, the son of deceased William Hirst, and the family regained complete control of the mine.

The Hirsts never resumed activities at the site on a sustained, substantial scale but did allow others to work at least portions of the mine. Two local men in particular had a fascination with the mine: Robert Gadd and Dr. James Parks McCombs. Gadd's relationship with the mine over forty years did not end until 1899. He was intelligent, hardworking, driven, almost always optimistic about future prospects for the mine, and a knowledgeable if not always practical miner. Gadd also became involved in controversy: with his brother William he cluttered the Cabarrus court docket with more than forty appearances in three decades on issues ranging from adultery to shooting and charges of murder. Physician J. P. McCombs (b. 1836) was from a prominent Mecklenburg family, attended Davidson College, and graduated from the New York Medical College. After three years as a surgeon in the Confederate army, he returned home to practice medicine. Deeply interested in gold mining in Mecklenburg and Cabarrus, he dealt with partners and prospective investors in New York, Philadelphia, and Britain. During three decades he had a part in operation of seven or more mines; most did not return his expenses.

Although little activity took place at the Reed in the 1870s and William Hirst died in 1876, McCombs considered leasing or buying the facility at the time of Hirst's death. The heirs, however, seemed uncertain what to do with the mine, and nothing immediate resulted. Five years later the Hirsts arranged for Philadelphia investors to operate it. A Mr. Nesbit spent several months there directing workers who tested the creek for gold and prepared the long-silent steam engine erected in 1854 for service. In three months Nesbit spent more than eight hundred dollars for equipment and spare parts in Charlotte. The following year the mine reopened to process low-grade ore found not far underground, but lack of water prevented much milling of the material.

About that time the Hirsts hired S. C. Johnston, a man of lengthy experience with mining around Charlotte and presumably a mining expert or geologist, to evaluate the site. He reported that the hundreds of acres contained enough timber—extensively used as a fuel for steam boilers and for shoring up underground workings—to support large-scale mining for many years. A Cornish pump, likely added after mid-1854, rested in the engine shaft, which needed some new timbers and about two hundred dollars' worth of repairs. Much exploratory work, including nine shafts and a tunnel, had been undertaken at Lower Hill. Johnston believed that a remarkable potential existed at the Reed for hydraulic mining—exposing gold by washing away hillsides and creek bottoms with high-pressure water—as done in California, where large profits were made despite operating expenses twice those of Cabarrus. Johnston recommended pumping water from Rocky River a mile away and using hydraulic techniques at Little Meadow Creek. He concluded that "great value may be attached to the property."

With such a reference, the Hirsts and their associates undertook restricted operations sporadically in the 1880s and early 1890s, but profits, if any, did not justify full-scale development. During that time McCombs and Gadd had their chance at the mine. The two men, along with Charles McDonald of Concord, leased it for a period including at least the years between 1885 and 1889. McCombs slowly funneled more than four thousand dollars into the mine, with

McDonald and Gadd contributing unknown amounts. Gadd lived at the mine apart from his family for three years as manager, obtained a modest remuneration—averaging less than twenty dollars a month, the wages of a common laborer—for his work, and contacted McCombs several times monthly. Gadd constantly seemed to beg McCombs for more money and a personal visit to the mine.

Often with shortages of rations or supplies, Gadd struggled along but remained optimistic that the mine someday would yield great rewards. In the summer of 1885 he dewatered the engine shaft on Upper Hill. By December he had that shaft retimbered and cleaned out to the fifty-five-foot level, less than halfway to its bottom. Soon men were below the water level with a new find of quartz at the seventy-foot level; the ore was so promising that Gadd began planning to run the thirty-year-old Chilean mills. Then he discovered a rotten pump rod and had to remove the heavy Cornish pump for repair. Meanwhile miners continued underground blasting and digging. The following summer Gadd and his crew were busy raising ore and had the mills for grinding the ore—a steam-powered arrastra and Chilean mills installed in 1854—working eighteen hours a day. The mills operated for several months, and a large amount of ore remained below in the mine, ready for raising and milling. Gadd also set up a sawmill. The miners might have used the mill both to cut wood for the boiler that powered the old steam engine and to produce rough-cut lumber for constructing a second millhouse on Upper Hill to replace the decaying millhouse built in 1854. Workers erected a second, much smaller, house perpendicular to and over a portion of the original building. The second structure—not as well built as the first and also of wood—sheltered little more than the arrastra.

Gadd's crew of workers ranged from more than a dozen men in the early months to only a man or two as time passed. Some of the men bore names still familiar in southeastern Cabarrus—Barbee, Barnhardt, Bost, Cox, Hagler, Linker, and Ridenhour. Other miners—"Eury and his men"—were African Americans. Daily pay was average for Tar Heel mine workers at the time: 75 cents to $1.25 for miners; $1.50 for a man who probably supervised with Gadd; $1.00 to $2.00 for haulers, who probably moved wood and perhaps ore and at times provided their own horses; 75 cents for a fireman to keep the steam engine running; and 30 cents for the one woman on the payroll—Mary Barbee, possibly a cook. The mine had its own small store, where the miners bought supplies and personal items. Goods available there included bacon, cornmeal, flour, sugar, coffee, plug tobacco, salt, and soap. Gadd bought such items in Charlotte and Cabarrus, along with shoes and clothing for the men and mining supplies such as candles, machine oil, iron, nails, gunpowder, and blasting fuses. Some of those items, as well as pay, were often in short supply, making for

This ca. 1930 photograph shows the chimney and boiler (foreground) at Reed, used intermittently for decades since 1854, and a smaller, later, millhouse.

unhappy laborers. At times Gadd had to pay the men with gold recovered only days earlier, and he incurred troublesome debts to area merchants.

By January 1887 problems old and new began to overwhelm Gadd's efforts. He suspected that some of his men were stealing gold, and the crew was becoming recalcitrant. Extremely cold weather froze the crucial Cornish pump, as well as the arrastra and Chilean mills, breaking the granite base of one Chilean mill. Operations halted for a time. Shortages of rations and supplies recurred, and one local merchant announced that he would sell to the mine only for gold and not on credit. Gadd considered that statement an insult. The episode, along with comments by his brother and others, revealed that Gadd had a violent streak and at times had difficulty getting along with people. As time passed, he and his partner McDonald each accused the other of missteps with money. Lacking operating capital, Gadd was often behind on his payroll and debts. As a result, he had smaller crews, at times only two or three hands, and seemed to accomplish little except keeping the mine from refilling with water. He managed to install a hoist atop the engine shaft but by November had only one man cutting wood for the steam engine. If the woodcutter stopped, the mine would have to shut down for lack of pumping capability. Gadd warned McCombs: "We must either sell out, go to work and fix it up, or surrender the lease."

Selling or leasing increasingly preoccupied the partners, but none of their efforts led to success. Gadd and his crew tried to keep the water down and make the mine attractive for potential buyers. As early as January 1886, when things still seemed promising, McCombs had drafted a contract for A. F. Lucas of Charlotte to sell the property. Throughout 1887 an English investor was interested but wanted the unwilling partners to advance one thousand dollars, refundable upon a sale, for an examination of the mine by an English engineer. In 1888 McCombs apparently gave an option to a northern investor named S. E. Greeley. Greeley visited the mine several times, raised almost enough money in Boston to buy it, and reputedly was going to offer ten thousand dollars to the Hirsts. By mid-1889 an English group, perhaps a second consortium, desired the mine. Again Gadd prepared for a visit, leaving piles of ore—with gold easily visible—where guests would see them. When the Englishmen failed to raise adequate funds, the Hirsts refused to take anything less than twenty-two thousand dollars.

For several years after 1890 little happened at the old mine, although Gadd continued to haunt the property. Local residents must have panned surreptitiously in the famous creek during winter months. Technology at the Reed had not advanced since 1854 except for possible installation of the Cornish pump, and innovation was no longer present. For instance, the chlorination process for extracting gold (a chemical procedure conducted nearby that employed chlorine to free the precious metal) was not used at the Reed. By 1894 the 120-foot-deep engine shaft was inaccessible, despite efforts by a Mr. Church, who fired the old boiler and started one of the pumps.

That year the lure of the century-old mine attracted seventy-year-old Oliver S. Kelly of Springfield, Ohio. Kelly had gone to California for that state's gold rush in 1852, prospered as a contractor rather than a miner, and returned to Ohio in four years to become a successful businessman. One of his sons would make the Kelly company a vast tire manufacturer. Kelly arranged for a Springfield associate, physician Justin D. Lisle, to inspect the Reed mine in September 1894 with Prof. C. A. Mezger, a mining engineer from Charlotte. With Mezger's favorable report, Kelly, Lisle, and Kelly's son O. Warren Kelly purchased the mine and more than eight hundred surrounding acres of land from the Hirsts for fifteen thousand dollars. The buyers gave a mortgage— repaid on schedule in 1900—on the property to a Philadelphia insurance company.

Mezger spent a week at the Reed with Lisle and a crew of ten men. Gadd provided almost the only specific verbal data on the mine, which Mezger found "very contradictory and little trustworthy." On Lower Hill, for instance, the team sank two test shafts, which Gadd had "recommended urgently," but neither produced the promised result. Mezger did, however, suggest good prospects for ore from below the water table at the hill. He did not have time to pump out and examine the underground workings at Upper Hill. Mezger believed that, while the quickest returns would come from systematic surface mining along the creek below the two hills, careful deep mining of both hills might yield one thousand dollars a month in profits. He declared that eighteen months and fifty thousand dollars in cash would be needed to reach this sustained profitability, less any returns from the mine.

With Mezger's report in hand, Lisle arrived with his wife in early 1895 to manage the mine. He soon had local men placer mining the floodplain of Little Meadow Creek between Upper and Lower Hills, as well as the lower slopes of the two hills. In October the men, working under Gadd, opened and re-timbered an old shaft on Lower Hill. About that time someone supposedly found a woman's watch chain, a fob, a possible piece of a gold tooth, and some hair, which re-ignited local gossip and the sporadic feud between brothers Robert and William Gadd. Rumors and legend arose that a miner, perhaps Robert Gadd, had murdered a woman years before and thrown her down a shaft. Lisle discounted the matter, and work continued with disappointing results underground despite extensive prospecting work.

Like others before him, Lisle became disheartened in that search, and he turned his attention toward placer mining along Little Meadow Creek. The owners, in return for half of any gold found, leased surface mining rights to four local men—Jacob Shinn, Jesse Cox and his son A. M. Cox, and Dr. J. R. Jerome. On April 9, 1896—almost a century after Conrad Reed's accidental discovery—the miners' efforts produced the last great nugget found at Reed: a spectacular piece of nearly 23 pounds, only 3 1/2 feet underground. Shinn carried the heavy but ordinary-looking rock to the creek to wash it off, realized what he had, and screamed, "Boys, I've got it!" The eleven-inch-long nugget was a total surprise; on the previous day, discouraged Jesse Cox had offered to sell out for five dollars. Lisle took the jubilant men to nearby Georgeville in his wagon to weigh the rock, and the entire countryside was aroused. As the men passed the Georgeville Academy, principal William Brooks exclaimed that they were either all drunk or had found a nugget. Lisle, who received telegrams from Milwaukee, Philadelphia, and New York offering to buy the golden stone, had it taken to the Charlotte assay office at the former mint. Employees there made casts of the nugget for the state museum and the Smithsonian Institution before crushing it for the gold, which at the time was valued at some forty-eight hundred dollars.

The find and the profits from it rekindled the owners' enthusiasm. In 1897 the mine was producing gold, perhaps largely from placer mining, and Lisle tested the underground ore again. Still active, Gadd convinced Lisle to let him begin work again at Lower Hill, which had been generally inactive since Timothy Reed's efforts. Gadd and his men brought up about five barrels of very rich ore; each yielded one hundred dollars' worth of gold. The men also

A 22-POUND GOLD NUGGET.

FOUND AT THE REED MINE IN NO. 9 LAST THURSDAY.

Mr. J. L. Shinn the Lucky Finder---Description of the Find, and Other History of This Famous Mine.

On last Thursday morning about 11 o'clock a nugget of gold weighing 22⅜ pounds Troy was found at the already famous Reed mine in No. 9 township, this county. Messrs. Jacob L. Shinn, D. M. Cox, Jesse Cox and Adam Canup were working the mine at the time. They were digging about three and a half feet under the surface. Mr. Shinn unearthed the precious nugget, and came near casting it aside. He took a second look at it, however, and its appearance made him examine it more closely. He alone (the others not knowing about his find) took it to the branch and washed it. He at once saw what he had found, and cried out: "Boys, I've got it!" The other men went to where he was, and when they saw the treasure they could hardly contain themselves.

Dr. Lisle, one of the owners of the mine, who lives near, was at once informed, and they say the doctor was almost as much excited as uncle Jesse Cox, whose excitement and joy found expression in continued shouts. One of the other men told him if he didn't hush he would alarm the neighborhood, but Dr. Lisle told him to shout on, as he had something to shout for.

The men worked on until 4 o'clock in the afternoon, when Dr. Lisle had his conveyance hitched up and carried them and their find over to Georgeville. As they entered the village Mr. Cox heralded the fact as he went, and soon the whole neighborhood was all excitement. Hundreds of people went to

In its issue of April 16, 1896, the *Concord Times* credited Jacob L. Shinn (pictured at right) with finding the last great nugget at Reed in 1896.

dewatered and retimbered the engine shaft and cleaned out part of the Upper Hill workings. With the aid of one of the old Chilean mills, Lisle sampled that ore, but the results were unsatisfactory. Consequently, in October 1898 he sold his quarter-interest in the mine to O. Warren Kelly for sixty-five hundred dollars.

With the mine completely in his family's hands, Warren Kelly, convinced that a new, faster stamp mill and amalgamation would extract more gold than did the old Chilean mills, again attempted underground mining. Within two months Kelly ordered a heavy ten-stamp mill from the Mecklenburg Iron Works of Charlotte, a principal postwar manufacturer of gold-mining equipment for the South. The change made the Reed again somewhat typical of leading southern mines of its day. All the key working parts of the sturdy mill, as in dozens of similar southern mills, were made of cast iron rather than a combination of wood and iron. Additional changes included a larger mortar, as well as round stamps that rotated to equalize wear each time they descended to crush ore. Those technological advances had originated in California, where earlier miners had improved on the old wooden European stamp mill inherited

California-style ten-stamp mill erected by Warren Kelly near Little Meadow Creek.

from the South about 1850. Kelly had the mill set up between Upper and Lower Hills beside Little Meadow Creek, a convenient source of water. He, or perhaps Lisle previously, hastily constructed a new, even smaller, house atop Upper Hill for some of the machinery remaining there.

In March 1899 Warren Kelly's son Armin, who knew nothing about mining but was a fast learner, arrived to manage the mine. Gadd, who had promised Warren Kelly gold worth a thousand dollars a ton, and his men were deepening a shaft on Upper Hill. When delays and other problems developed, and Gadd's new shaft simply cut through into a previously accessible subterranean location, Armin fired Gadd and some of the men, essentially ending Gadd's half-century-long role at the mine. Young Kelly found Gadd difficult to work with and of surprisingly modest circumstances despite his supposed extensive knowledge of ore. Kelly talked with other old-timers, including some of the Coxes, and used the new stamp mill to test surface ore from Upper Hill. Results were dismal. He had ore raised from the ninety-foot level and then analyzed all the veins in the hill. Some samples yielded a pitiful sixty cents in gold per ton of ore. Reasoning that earlier miners had taken the best ore, Kelly moved to Lower Hill, where he retimbered the ninety-foot pump shaft and drained the mine. He found much mediocre ore and evidence that there, too, past

Curiosity seekers on 1854 flywheel at Upper Hill, ca. 1940s.

miners had taken out the best rock. In November 1900, before Armin Kelly finished at Lower Hill, a telegram called him to the family business in Ohio, and operations at the mine were suspended again.

As with most—but not all—other Tar Heel mines during the twentieth century, there was little significant mining at the Reed. Various people (not always with the owners' authorization) tested parts of the old mine, but the results each time were negative. Yet a stream of amateur panners washed gravel in Little Meadow Creek. About 1912 local miners did some placer work and sifted through the old ore dumps. That year Warren Kelly supervised limited underground excavation at Upper Hill at the 120-foot level and deepened the engine shaft to about 140 or 150 feet. That was twice as deep as any subsequent effort and the last new underground work until state ownership in the 1970s.

In 1934 and 1935 Armin Kelly had Frank Cox, a local man, strip several surface veins on Upper Hill, but results were not worthwhile. During the Great Depression, lean men again attempted to extract any gold still hidden at the Reed. Some, such as A. L. Nash of Rowan County, openly asked the Kellys for permission to work the gravel. The owners did not mind local folks panning for small amounts of gold and asked for a share of any nuggets discovered. In 1934 a few miners washed placer material in barrel rockers of the type used a century earlier and also opened up an old tunnel on Upper Hill. As the national

70

economy recovered, however, that rudimentary mining ceased, and the Reed once again became a secluded spot where hobbyists panned and dreamed while tenant farmers worked their fields. Various Kellys visited their rural retreat for country living and horseback riding. During World War II most of the old machinery was carted off to scrap-iron dealers. In 1962 the last of the resident caretakers, Charlie Barbee, left the property, and the famous old mine lay abandoned until the North Carolina Division of Archives and History opened it as a state historic site in the 1970s.

For nearly two centuries John Reed's gold mine has retained an important, albeit sometimes forgotten, place in North Carolina history. The mine, initially the result of historical accident, produced nuggets of remarkable size and purity. That reputation led pioneer miners to discover and perhaps develop countless other gold prospects and mines—as well as related enterprises—in the South. Some of them, such as Gold Hill, surpassed the Reed in certain respects. Presently, however, this earliest known operating gold mine in the nation is the single major mine in North Carolina to survive unspoiled down through the years and be restored and preserved as a state historic site. Astonishingly, its hundreds of acres have remained almost intact since John Reed's death more than 150 years ago.

3

The Gold Hill Mining District, 1842–1865

The Gold Hill mining district developed after a period of general decline that nearly ended the mining industry in North Carolina in the 1830s. After 1835 many ambitious North Carolinians moved to the rich farmlands of the Mississippi River valley to take advantage of rising cotton prices. The major deep mines around Charlotte apparently had played out, and many mine workers headed to Georgia and South Carolina, where intensive development continued. The panic of 1837 further eroded the potential for investment. Squabbles over questions of ownership plagued other mining properties, such as the Reed mine in Cabarrus County.

The establishment of the branch mint in Charlotte late in 1837 created a somewhat more favorable climate for the revival of gold mining over the next several years. The mint offered a stable marketplace for gold bullion and encouraged new explorations along the western section of the Carolina slate region. Among those new properties was the district at Gold Hill.

The Gold Hill district extended through southeastern Rowan County, northeastern Cabarrus County, and into a narrow strip along part of Montgomery (now Stanly) County. The Yadkin River formed its northeastern boundary for eight miles, from which the district ran in a southwesterly direction for eighteen miles to the village of Mount Pleasant. In the center of that district grew the village of Gold Hill, located about fourteen miles southeast of Salisbury along a two-mile ridge or narrow plateau that ran from the Yadkin River southwest through the village itself. The ridge formed a watershed with streams to the northwest flowing to the Yadkin River and those to the southeast flowing into Rocky River. To the southwest were the Beaver

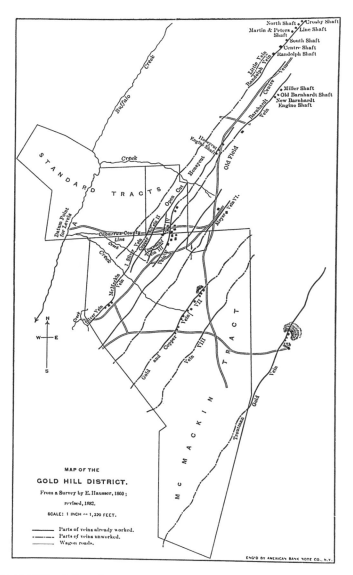

Map of Gold Hill mining district, 1882. From Henry B. C. Nitze and George B. Hanna, *Gold Deposits of North Carolina*, North Carolina Geological Survey Bulletin No. 3 (Winston: M. I. and J. C. Stewart, public printers, 1896), facing p. 87.

Hills, the only other prominent topographical feature in the otherwise flat valley.

The most important geological feature in the area was the Gold Hill fault, which ran north to south along the west central section of the district. This fault divided the igneous rocks on the west from the sedimentary rocks on the east. The sedimentary series of rocks, mostly slates and schists, contained the district's important mineral deposits. The character of the ore bodies at Gold Hill resembled that of other mineral regions in the Carolina slate belt. Gold-bearing ores occurred in auriferous pyrites as isolated crystals or as small masses within narrow quartz stringers. These deposits formed at least ten distinct veins, which generally pitched in a northern direction. Two types of veins were found in Gold Hill: one marked by silicification, containing gold; the other with a minimum of silicification, in which copper ores dominated. Those copper-bearing schists were chalcopyrites rather than pyrites. Each type of vein also included quantities of silver and lead. All ores found in the district contained some amounts of those minerals, although ores with a higher percentage of gold usually held a minimum of copper and vice versa. Most geologists believe that the gold and copper veins formed at different geological times during periods of minor faulting that occurred after the formation of the Gold Hill fault.

Before 1840 the area that became known as Gold Hill was better known for its diversified agriculture and mineral waters than for its mineral resources. Several families—Heilig, Earnhardt, Troutman, Isenhour—settled there as part of a large migration of German Americans from Pennsylvania to North Carolina following the Revolutionary War. By the mid-nineteenth century, about a dozen small farms ranging in size from one hundred to eight hundred acres produced corn, oats, and potatoes. For labor, farmers relied on their large families; a small number of black slaves, no more than three to five per farm, supplemented that source.

Geological surveys in the 1820s had identified mineral resources in the Gold Hill region—indeed, the celebrated Barringer mine, site of the first gold vein discovered in the Carolina slate belt (1825), was located along the eastern border of the Gold Hill district. Nevertheless, serious exploitation of the Gold Hill district did not occur until about fifteen or twenty years after the gold rush began in other parts of the state. There were two reasons for the delay in mining activity in the district. First, the mining population had focused its attention on the Burke County placers and on the mines in the western slate belt around Charlotte. Those mines remained productive through the mid-1830s. Therefore, there was little demand to explore the gold fields that lay to the east in Rowan, Montgomery, Randolph, Davidson, and Guilford Counties.

The second reason for the delay in mining had to do with agricultural practices. The farms around Gold Hill were established later and continued to be productive longer than the farms closer to Charlotte. The first wave of German-American immigrants from Pennsylvania had occupied the better farmland of the Carolina Piedmont in the early 1750s. However, much of that land had declined in value within two or three generations as a result of erosive land use, inferior tools, poor management, and soil exhaustion, all practices common to European agriculture. In southern Rowan County, those problems did not become acute until the late 1830s, when lower prices for crops and labor shortages resulting from out-migration reflected a weakening economy. Soon the farmers there were negotiating leases with the "gold hunters," much as their predecessors had done in the central Piedmont in earlier decades.

The first discovery of gold at Gold Hill occurred in September 1842 when two farmers—Archibald Honeycutt and Daniel Culp—began "Washing the surface on the head of a drain" on the land of another farmer, Andrew Troutman. The men soon struck a rich vein of ore and sank a shaft that would eventually reach two hundred feet below the surface. Gold hunters identified at least five additional vein deposits on neighboring farms over the next year. "We were utterly surprised," wrote a visitor in 1844,

to find almost the whole surface of a ridge, some one and a half or two miles in extent, torn up by the pick and shovel of the miner. Here was a deep deserted pit with gaping mouth, inviting as it were, man and beast to sudden destruction by a misstep. There was a long trench running through the woods for many yards, which had been made in "searching for the veins." Here again were a company of operators in and about a shaft or pit of some 60 to 75 feet in depth pursuing a vein into the bowels of the earth, and from thence drawing the rich ores. A little way off and there is another company similarly engaged. A little beyond and there is still another, and another, and another, and so the woods are filled.

Many of those miners were veterans of the gold boom of the 1820s and 1830s in the Charlotte region. Some were quite familiar with the basic techniques of excavation and extraction. They understood simple pumping procedures and had used gunpowder in deep mining. Hoisting equipment, railroad tracks to move ore from underground, and quicksilver for milling gold were all utilized in other mines and reintroduced at Gold Hill.

Nevertheless, poverty and backwardness rather than technological progress characterized the settlers in this new mining frontier. The settlers' "shafts" were nothing more than open pits. They knew little about timbering or ventilation in the shafts. Although they employed blasting, they usually cleared the underground works with "sheer muscle power." Pumping techniques were so crude and irregular that most extraction rarely proceeded below the water table. Hoisting and milling machinery ran chiefly by horsepower or waterpower and an abundance of hand power. Despite the earlier use of steam power at mines in Mecklenburg County (less than forty miles away), the native miners at Gold Hill initially had little or no familiarity with steam engines or steam-driven machinery. One of the earliest historical accounts of Gold Hill recorded thirty or forty horse-powered mills, including "circular runners and drag mills." Another observer noted that scattered among the "diggings" and makeshift mills were the "log cabins" of the miners, most of these being "of a real primitive order." A longtime resident later recalled the first miners at Gold Hill as "poor men with rude machinery."

Throughout the 1840s local farmers leased mining tracts to the gold hunters, usually charging between one-sixth and one-tenth of the profits as a rent or land toll. These leases were short term and rarely exceeded ten years. The miners formed partnerships among themselves as well and worked their leaseholds in small "companies" of from ten to thirty men. Some of these companies owned slaves or, more likely, rented slave workers from nearby farms. Between 1842 and 1853 at least twenty of these partnerships worked the mines in the Gold Hill district, and as many as eight operated at the same time. By 1850 only four mining companies and two milling companies, along with several small independent operations, had survived.

The story of two of the most successful companies that operated during the first decade of mining at Gold Hill is critical for understanding the development of the entire district. Both companies relied on the experience of men who had worked at other sites in North Carolina, and both companies eventually imported the expertise of foreign-born miners to utilize the techniques and technology of deep mining. Each company operated on the two most productive veins in the district, and these shafts—the Barnhardt and Earnhardt—became the core properties in building the reputation of Gold Hill as the South's most successful gold-mining district.

The first firm, Barnhardt, Heilig and Company, was established by Col. George Barnhardt, a prominent mining pioneer in the state. Barnhardt was a descendant of German immigrants who had settled first in Pennsylvania and then migrated to North Carolina after the American Revolution. He was born on a farm in Cabarrus County not far from the Reed gold mine, worked at the mine in the 1830s, and made his mark as a civic and political leader. Unfortunately, he became embroiled in the legal squabbles that suspended mining at Reed. In 1843 Barnhardt moved to the gold fields in southern Rowan County. There he entered into a partnership with five other miners "for the Purpose of Diggin[g] and searching for gold and other precious metals" on a section of a farm owned by George Heilig. For the privilege of working this land, the Barnhardt company paid Heilig one dollar a year as rent and one-seventh of all the gold found at the mine. The Barnhardt-Heilig vein quickly became a leading producer in the area. By July 1843, after only a few months

Mining pioneer George Barnhardt married Martha Reed, John Reed's daughter, and became a leader of gold-mining operations both at Reed and at Gold Hill.

of operations, the company recorded deposits of more than twenty-five hundred dollars' worth of gold bullion at the branch mint in Charlotte. Colonel Barnhardt also became the acknowledged leader of the small mining community, and, according to local legend, he selected "Gold Hill" as its name.

Other veterans of mining in North Carolina moved to Gold Hill as its reputation spread. Ephriam Mauney (pronounced "Mooney" in Rowan County) joined the Barnhardt partnership sometime after 1845. His Pennsylvania German family also had migrated to the state in the eighteenth century but settled in Lincoln County. During the 1840s, Eph Mauney and his brother, Valentine, moved to the Carter gold mine in Montgomery County, where they gained some experience in deep mining and milling ores from vein deposits. A few years later the brothers moved to the Cabarrus County side of Gold Hill and set up a profitable water-powered gold-milling business. One of their principal customers was Barnhardt, Heilig and Company. The Mauneys soon joined this company and eventually became two of Gold Hill's most prominent citizens, the owners of mercantile outlets and real estate, and principals in the promotion and management of the Gold Hill mining district for the next thirty-five years.

The second major property developed during these formative years was owned by the family of Phillip Earnhardt. During the initial years following the discovery of gold, that mine was not considered very profitable. However, the arrival of Moses Holmes and his brother, Reuben, brought an infusion of capital and mining experience that resulted in a dramatic change for the better. The Holmes brothers were sons of a wealthy Davidson County planter. They worked briefly for a merchant in Lexington and moved to Gold Hill in 1846. The brothers borrowed five hundred dollars from local merchants and also entered into a lease to operate the Phillip Earnhardt mine, agreeing to pay Earnhardt a land toll of one-seventh of all profits and an additional one-half of the remaining profits to other members of the Earnhardt family. Despite these rather unfavorable terms, the brothers slowly accumulated a cash reserve, enough to purchase steam-driven pumps and to employ thirty workers, including six slaves. By 1850 their basic investment of twenty-five thousand dollars was producing seventeen thousand dollars' worth of gold a year.

The Holmes operations expanded dramatically in 1852 through a partnership with two Cornishmen—David Martin and John Peters—who had also arrived in Gold Hill in 1846. Initially Martin and Peters contracted with George Barnhardt to mine a second shaft on the Heilig property "in a mining like manner" and to bring their ore to Barnhardt's mill. Their company was poorly financed and operated only with horse-powered equipment. By 1850 they employed eighteen workers and started to show a small profit. When they combined with the Holmes brothers in 1852, they were able to install new pumps, powered by steam engines, to remove water from the Earnhardt shaft. In its first year of operations, the new company of Holmes, Martin, and Peters grossed more than sixty-four thousand dollars; the firm earned a profit of more than fifty-six hundred dollars a month the following year. Those earnings were seven times greater than the 1850 profits of both companies combined.

A third partnership of importance in the formative years at Gold Hill was Coffin, Worth and Company. The company organized in February 1844 when five gold hunters leased an eight-acre tract of land from Dr. Hugh Kelly on what was called the "tavern lot" of Gold Hill. There the men established a mill and ground ore from various mines in the district. The principals in this partnership were members of two enterprising Piedmont families. John Milton Worth lived in Montgomery County, where he farmed and also invested in gold mines. Worth's brothers—Joseph Addison and Thomas Clarkson—joined this company, as did a Salisbury businessman, John M. Coffin. Throughout the 1840s and early 1850s, Coffin, Worth and Company was a leading producer in the Gold Hill district. With a modest investment in steam-powered Chilean mills and in raw materials—mercury and wood—and a labor force of thirty-seven, including two women, the company produced twelve thousand dollars' worth of gold annually.

The few records that have survived indicate that most of these partnerships and small companies were quite profitable. Beginning in 1843 and continuing through the early 1850s, the branch mint at Charlotte recorded large deposits

Slaves, women, and children labored at Gold Hill. This Porte Crayon drawing (1857) shows young workers operating log rockers there.

of gold bullion from George Barnhardt and other miners from Gold Hill. The superintendent of the mint estimated that one-third of the gold coined in Charlotte came from Gold Hill. In 1851 Barnhardt reported that eleven companies and several smaller partnerships at Gold Hill had recovered more than eight hundred thousand dollars' worth of gold up to that time.

As for the profitability of those companies, *DeBow's Review* in 1848 described eight mining interests at Gold Hill as "averaging fifty percent on their capital on the yield of gold." The census of 1850 reported three large mining companies and one milling company in operation, and those enterprises continued to earn handsome returns—ranging from 22 to 48 percent on their original investment. It is not surprising, then, that observers agreed that "Gold Hill mine has been operated with more perseverance, skill, and success than any other in the State; or perhaps in the South."

The success of the dozen or so large companies that operated in the district during the first decade did not chase the independent operators and entrepreneurs from the field. Regrinding and rewashing the "wastes" and "sands" from the mills of the larger concerns could be a very lucrative business. Grinding required only a horse-powered or water-powered mill and a small labor force. Sand washing often involved no more than fifty or one hundred dollars to purchase mercury, which lined the bases of Chilean mills and log rockers. The cost of labor for this process was quite low because operators relied upon slaves, women, and children to tend the milling equipment, haul ore in wheelbarrows, or rock the machinery with their hands and feet.

The independent operators at Gold Hill rented what was known as "wasted" ore from the larger companies and paid a percentage of their profits to the supplier of that material. For example, George Moose and two laborers washed the "waste" of the Barnhardt Company and could produce nearly $1,500 in gold annually with an investment of only $110. One miner, using the help of two boys, was able to make $181 a month rewashing wasted ore of the Holmes, Martin, and Peters company. Another made one dollar per bushel from his regrinding enterprise. Still another earned $6,000 in one year regrinding sand wastes "(excepting) the labor of two men and five or six small girls."

Of all the independent operators, the Reverend James Morphis enjoyed the greatest success. Morphis began rewashing sand wastes by hand in the late 1840s. By 1850 he barely broke even on his initial investment. Within a year, however, he had constructed two water-powered Chilean mills about four miles from Gold Hill and had worked out an agreement with Moses Holmes to regrind his company's wasted ore for one-sixth of his gross revenues. Using the labor of two hired men and three slaves, Morphis produced more than thirteen thousand dollars' worth of gold in 1852.

Although independent miners would always play an important part in the mining industry in the Gold Hill district, by 1850 most workers were wage earners employed by the major mining and milling companies in twenty- to thirty-man crews. The 1850 census reported approximately 171 workers in and about the Gold Hill mines. Slightly less than half the workers called themselves "miners," and the others described themselves as "laborers"—the difference being that miners worked in skilled jobs underground, while laborers worked at various jobs on the surface.

Half of the "miners" were Cornishmen recruited because of their knowledge of deep mining techniques and their expertise with the pumping equipment and milling machinery needed in a large-scale mining operation. Some of these men—an example was John Gluyas (see chapter 1)—had worked in several southern mines in the 1820s and 1830s. Others, such as David Martin and John Peters, were part of a more recent migration that began in the 1840s—the "Hungry Forties"—a migration caused as much by the potato blight in Europe as by opportunities in the New World. Political and economic conditions in Cornwall hastened that exodus. "Wages are low, poverty is intense, and taxes exorbitant," wrote one migrant in 1843, "operative resistances, political commotions, and gubernatorial coercion reign with insecant [incessant] fury in the country of 'crown heads.'" Although the number of Cornishmen was never large in any gold-mining community in North Carolina, the influence of those men was considerable.

About one-third of the "laborers"—above-ground workers or assistants to miners below ground— were black slaves. The remainder of the work force was native white North Carolinians. Underground miners could earn from $25 to $35 a month; common laborers, including slaves, earned $13 a month during this period. Children below the age of fifteen received three to ten dollars a month. Occasionally a company might list one or two women as

Among a number of Cornish miners at Gold Hill were Matthew Moyle (*left*) and Nicholas Trevethan, shown at work in 1857 by artist Porte Crayon.

Young female workers at Gold Hill often washed gravel in log rockers. Porte Crayon rendered this sketch of Sarah Jackson, probably one such worker at the mine.

employees, probably as sand washers, earning $4.50 a month.

In the two decades prior to the Civil War, mining provided a foundation for a stable industrial and commercial community of 700 people, including about 60 slaves. It is likely that the population of the district fluctuated. The several small companies operating at Gold Hill hired and dismissed workers as their level of operations and their finances required, and the population rose and fell accordingly. Lawsuits, mud slides, equipment breakdowns, and disease could suspend operations for a period of time. It seems likely that the number of people living at Gold Hill never exceeded 800 or fell below 500 during the antebellum period. If the population ever approached 1,000, it would have been during the peak years of activity in the mid-1850s.

The mining population, as might be expected, was dominated by young, white males. In the 1850 census, men outnumbered women by 26 percent and confirmed the observation of one female visitor that "there are so many young men . . . but few ladies in the place." Most of the white workers—about three fourths—were under thirty-five years of age. Almost 90 percent of the slaves were likewise under thirty-five. Sixty percent of the white workers were married, although among the skilled underground miners more than half were single. The families of the married workers were surprisingly small by the standards that prevailed in most mining communities. The average Gold Hill household included two or three children. In all, four hundred to five hundred people—men, women, children, and slaves—depended directly upon the mines for their living.

The other residents in the community were either farmers or members of a small mercantile and professional class. Gold Hill represented a growing marketplace in the rural economy of the Piedmont. The task of providing food, clothing, and shelter for the mining population attracted investments from some of the state's leading businessmen, including a former governor, John M. Morehead, and a future governor, Jonathan Worth. Local merchants advertised "the largest and cheapest stock in Rowan County . . . selected with the greatest care in Northern cities for cash."

A wide range of artisans and professionals provided essential services. A report in 1849 noted no fewer than five physicians and an attorney living in Gold Hill. The community also included five stores, a hotel, a tavern, and six blacksmith shops. A carriage maker, a boot- and shoemaker, a saddler, carpenters, and brick- and stonemasons found ready employment in the small industrial district. Many of these men were native North Carolinians, but several had migrated from the North or from Great Britain.

Gold Hill's location along the main route between Salisbury and Cheraw, South Carolina, also contributed to its growth as a center of trade and industry. Farmers from five counties—Rowan, Cabarrus, Montgomery, Stanly, and Davidson—found an easy outlet for home-grown produce. "There are neighborhoods in all these counties," observed the Salisbury *Carolina Watchman*, "much farther off from the County seat of each respectively than from Gold Hill where, on account of its conveniences, citizens from these counties frequently go to sell their produce and deal in the stores."

The mining district boasted a cultural and political vitality, as well as the basic foundations of commercial and industrial activity. The German background of the local farmers ensured a prominent place for the Lutheran Church. Visitors to the district took note of the German-language services that were still conducted as late as 1850. The Reverend Joseph A. Linn became the first Lutheran pastor in Gold Hill in 1844. He extended his involvement in the community beyond spiritual affairs, investing in gold mines, a gristmill, a tannery, and several local businesses. The establishment of the Methodist Church reflected the influence of the Cornish miners. Cornwall had been a hotbed of Wesleyan reform efforts, and the miners carried strong, conservative beliefs with them to their new country. In May 1848 one of the mine operators, David McMakin, donated three acres of land on the Rowan-Cabarrus county line "for the purpose of building a Church for the use of the members of the Methodist Episcopal Church in the United States of America." The first burials on the Gold Hill Methodist Church property occurred in the early 1850s.

Attending church or an occasional political debate was the chief diversion from the business and industry of the mining community. Temperance was an important local issue, influenced by the Cornish. The company store offered its customers Bibles and other books, including "a History" for one dollar. No libraries or newspapers existed in Gold Hill during this period. Two schools served about forty or fifty pupils, most likely the sons and perhaps the daughters of the merchants, professionals, artisans, and high-paid mining "captains" who formed Gold Hill's political and social elite. These men were among the few who owned property of any kind—houses, carriages, watches, and furnishings.

The material prosperity of this small elite class suggested that at least some of the "poor men with rude machinery" had indeed found their pockets "well-lined with gold." By the late 1840s Gold Hill was emerging slowly from its rough pioneer stage into a town of some economic and social consequence. In 1848, for example, a newspaper editor from Asheboro wrote to a friend of "a great Ball to come off at Gold Hill . . . to which all the young people in this place have tickets. Ladies and gentlemen are invited from Salisbury, Wadesborough, Concord, Mocksville and other places and a grand affair is expected." The young editor was so awed at the imposing guest list, however, that he regretfully added: "I shall not attend as I am too poor to shine honorably in a company so fair and fashionable."

Just as Gold Hill was becoming the South's leading mine, the California gold rush captured the imaginations and ambitions of tens of thousands of migrants worldwide. California gold inspired renewed enthusiasm for mining in North Carolina—and brighter prospects than at any time since the early 1830s. Newspapers discerned new investment throughout the region, especially in Rowan, Davidson, Guilford, and Randolph Counties. Promoters hailed the renewed activity as "only the beginning of what is to prove [North Carolina's] inexhaustible wealth." Northern entrepreneurs visiting the state shared the contagious mining fever. "It is only a matter of time," wrote one visitor, before "the wealth that for countless ages has lain buried in the earth is . . . brought to the light of day. . . ."

In that optimistic atmosphere, the mines at Gold Hill attracted the attention of serious investors from New York. In the spring of 1853 Prof. Charles U. Shepard of the College of Charleston (South Carolina) visited Gold Hill to assess its accomplishment and potential. It is not clear who employed Shepard to undertake this field survey, but his report reads more like an investment strategy than a technical evaluation. Shepard was immediately impressed by the geological features of Gold Hill. He counted at least nine gold-bearing veins in a square-mile area. The veins were "well-defined, of large size, and are judged to be of unending depth as they are entirely in their positions." Shepard also noted the handsome profits of some of the companies in the district; however, he concluded that the industry could not grow with so many companies competing for scarce capital for investment and for skilled labor required in deep mining. Short-term leases and high land tolls were particularly debilitating, in Shepard's opinion, because they discouraged investment in steam-driven machinery and pumps.

Shepard was more enthusiastic about the potential at Gold Hill than about its past performance. To resolve some of the managerial problems caused by the number of small companies in the district, Shepard recommended the consolidation of the mines under a single owner. For a relatively small investment, he projected an annual return of one hundred thousand dollars and hoped that his report on Gold Hill would "attract a large attention, and . . . convince the most cautious capitalist that an investment in these mines . . . must secure large and regular returns." Despite the underdeveloped state of the mining industry as Shepard found it in 1853, Gold Hill indeed had a very bright future. "I have seen no mines in our own country, or even in Great Britain, which have left so strong an impression of their intrinsic value as has been produced by the inspection of the mines of Gold Hill in North Carolina," Shepard wrote.

Shepard's report apparently reached the audience for which it was intended. Not long after its publication, the Holmes brothers (Moses and Reuben) and the Mauneys (Ephriam and Valentine) undertook the ambitious task of bringing the mines of Gold Hill under single ownership and management. These men were in a fortuitous position to take advantage of the situation that existed in 1853. Unlike some of the pioneer miners, such as George Barnhardt, who had retired to his farm in Cabarrus County, they were young men, under forty. All had experience with the problems and possibilities of deep mining. They knew the Gold Hill region well. They knew the miners, the farmers, and the merchants of the region. They also had access to financiers in the North through their own businesses and through other merchants in North Carolina. Probably through this network, they were able to bring Gold Hill to the attention of a large New York mercantile firm, Sackett, Belcher and Company.

In the spring of 1853, as many of the original leases expired, Moses Holmes began taking bonds—or options—on most of the mining properties in Gold Hill. Those bonds indicated that Holmes would receive title to the properties provided he sold them before a given time and for no less than a minimum price. By August he had gained a commitment from his northern contacts to purchase three of the major properties in the district—the Old Field, Heilig, and Earnhardt mines—for $315,000, a substantial increase over the terms of the bonds. He also obtained a ten-year lease on the Honeycutt mine and purchased the engine lot from Coffin and Worth, along with their "engine and Gold Mills, cabins and work shops," for twelve hundred dollars. The buyers—six New Yorkers and two Bostonians—organized as the Gold Hill Mining Company and appointed Moses Holmes their local representative. In August 1853 the company issued two hundred thousand shares of stock at five dollars per share. For the first time, a single owner controlled the major gold-mining properties in the district.

Gold Hill experienced its greatest productivity and prosperity between 1853 and 1858, a period during which the district attracted recognition as "the prince of mines" in the Atlantic states and the richest mining property east of the Mississippi. The new Gold Hill Mining Company made this success possible through an aggressive investment program that began late in 1854 after the miners struck a new rich deposit of gold ore just a few hundred yards southwest of the Earnhardt mine. That deposit, later known as the Randolph mine, eventually reached a depth of 800 feet and became the single most valuable gold-bearing mine in the South. Geologists, miners, and investors agreed that the Randolph mine "has contributed most to the celebrity of the Gold Hill district and is in reality 'the Gold Hill mine.'"

The discovery of the Randolph vein touched off a new wave of development at Gold Hill, more extensive by far than any mining activity that had taken place in the previous decade. Within a few months the company erected new buildings, enlarged existing structures, and extended its underground operations. By 1856 the company had completed an ambitious building campaign that included eleven dwelling houses; numerous structures for shafts, milling, and supplies; a reservoir; and more than two thousand feet of elevated trestles to transport water throughout the mining and milling operations. It installed at the Randolph and Center shafts an eighty-horsepower steam engine purchased at a New York auction for $4,400. The estimated cost of this above-ground work was in excess of thirty-three thousand dollars.

Equally impressive was the investment in developing the various underground shafts at Gold Hill, especially at the Randolph shaft, where the new engine pumped water from a depth of 360 feet and, through a series of flat connecting rods, pumped a shaft nearby to a depth of 390 feet. Opening those

This Porte Crayon drawing of Gold Hill shows several millhouses, trestles for transporting water, and a large stock of logs for use at the mine.

shafts cost from $15 to $20 per foot—a total of $13,000—and took more than a year to complete, without, according to company president Isaac Smith, "one cent return to the Company. It was, however, obliged to be done for the purpose of opening the mine." In addition to the buildings, equipment, and underground work, the company maintained a large inventory, valued at more than sixteen thousand dollars, that included expendable and durable goods, food, tools, quicksilver, animals, and building materials.

Operations at Gold Hill's deep mines began with what was called "dead work"—clearing shafts and removing water. The miners penetrated the underground works in two ways: manual labor and blasting. Blasting with gunpowder began in British and German mines in the mid-seventeenth century. The nature of Gold Hill's geology encouraged the early use of gunpowder to excavate subsurface areas. "[Miners] cannot advance a step without blasting, as the slate commences eight inches from the surface and increases in hardness as it descends," wrote one observer in 1851.

The first step in blasting was drilling, which required bars of cast steel about 1 1/2 inches in diameter and about 3 or 4 feet long. One end was flat for striking, and the other end was shaped like a chisel with the edge flared. The drill was driven at a 45-degree angle into the wall of the shaft to a depth of from 18 inches to 3 feet. After each strike, the miner rotated the drill, creating a hole of about one inch in diameter. Miners could work alone with a drill and

BORING.

Porte Crayon depicted two African American workers drilling holes for underground blasting at Gold Hill.

hammer, but they often worked in pairs. Cornishmen (nicknamed "Cousin Jacks") perfected that team approach, and drilling operations came to be called "double-jacking." Before setting a charge, the "nipper," or powderman, scraped the hole, dried it with sand or clay, and then poured gunpowder into the dry hole along with filler material placed on top to close the opening. Then he inserted through the filler a fuse in contact with the gunpowder, struck a match, and warned the workers to clear the area before the explosion.

After blasting, shafts provided access to strictly vertical deposits such as those at Gold Hill, and adits served as nearly horizontal passageways to bodies of ore located in a hill. Crosscuts—horizontal tunnels perpendicular to the general direction of a vein of ore—ran to different locations or to new discoveries. Those passageways were narrow in width to save on construction expenses. To facilitate extraction and movement of ore, the miners also constructed drifts (tunnels following the course of a vein) or sank winzes (shafts running from one level to another).

The miners carved out sizable rooms called "stopes" at points along the shafts and other excavations where ore was to be extracted. In mines such as Gold Hill, where veins were vertical and large, miners cut levels at or near the lower part of the vein (or lode) and again at regular intervals (fifty to one hundred feet) above the original level. Stopes were either overhand (worked upward from a level) or underhand (dug downward from a level). In the shafts,

87

the miners of Gold Hill occasionally employed a method of wall support known as timbering, although in many hard-rock mines in North Carolina the native rock generally held together as well as a natural wall. Only when a shaft had to bear considerable extra weight, such as a ladder or pump, was timbering needed.

Because any new underground development work or exploration required blasting, that operation became a part of daily life at Gold Hill and received dramatic coverage in contemporary newspaper accounts. A visitor to the mines in 1851 wrote: "When within a hundred feet of the bottom we halted at a signal just below us. It was a warning that a blast was to be fired. We waited a few seconds in suspense—the match had failed—but another instant brought a convulsive shock, and a loud report as of rolling thunders. The noise, though almost deafening below, cannot be heard above ground."

David Hunter Strother, a writer and illustrator for *Harper's New Monthly Magazine* under the name "Porte Crayon," compared the blasting at Gold Hill to battlefield conditions: "[We] heard a stunning crash as if they had been fired out of a Paixhan gun, then came another and another in quick succession. They soon enveloped in an atmosphere of sulphurous smoke, and as the explosion continued [we imagined ourselves] in the trenches of Sebastopol."

The president of the Gold Hill Mining Company, Isaac Smith, reported in 1856 that the company needed four kegs of powder each day to sink 970 feet of shafts, clear 894 feet of levels, and add 30 feet to any existing shaft. "The mere cost of gunpowder, some $8 per day," Smith observed, "is but a trifle when compared to the men required to drill the holes and remove the worthless slate." The total cost of underground preparation was more than $48,000, and this was simply to put the mine in good working order.

Following blasting and the completion of shafts, clearing the mines of seeping water and keeping them dry was the next important preparatory step for underground work. Many shafts at Gold Hill initially were abandoned once work reached the water table at 60 to 100 feet below the surface. In the late 1840s the two largest Gold Hill companies, headed by Moses Holmes and George Barnhardt respectively, installed Cornish pumps driven by steam-powered engines with capacities of 40 horsepower. A visitor to the district in 1851 noted that "the first sound that salutes your ears is the monotonous cough of the [Cornish] 'pump engine' which unceasingly forces up the water from the bottom of the mines." The engine "works continually night and day (Sundays excepted) to draw off the water which is constantly rising in the mines." The European immigrants of the mid-1840s or before introduced these widely used pumps and the piping needed to move them as deep mining intensified.

Clearing the mines of water and removing worthless rock underground set the stage for hard-rock mining. The gold-bearing rock at Gold Hill appeared in veins lying on both sides of a stratum of slate or between two strata. Along

Operators of the mines at Gold Hill frequently employed whims—large vertical drums around which rope was wound and unwound—to raise and lower buckets of ore. Shown at right is a typical horse-powered whim. Engraving at left from sketch by Porte Crayon; drawing at right from J. W. Foster and J. D. Whitney, *Report on the Geology and Topography of a Portion of the Lake Superior Land District*, Pt. 1: *Copper Lands* (Washington, D.C.: House of Representatives, 1850), 127.

one vein, for instance, there occurred at least four bodies of good to rich ore interlaced with equally large portions of poor ore. By the mid-1850s, the miners at Gold Hill had driven six shafts along that vein, including the celebrated Randolph and Center shafts, a ladder shaft, and an auxiliary pump shaft. Two long crosscuts connected the ladder shaft with the rich ore bodies of those shafts at the 270- and 330-foot levels.

After removing and breaking down a large quantity of ore from a vein, laborers loaded the material into a bucket raised by a horse-powered whim. At Gold Hill at least four horse-powered whims operated at various shafts in the 1850s, and the whim at the Randolph mine powered a double operation, with one bucket descending as another rose to the surface. The bucket, or kibble, was a copper vessel "about the size of a whiskey barrel," weighing between 100 and 400 pounds and capable of holding from 200 to 1,500 pounds of ore. When the ore reached the surface, the whim attendant loaded it onto wheelbarrows, and "top ground" laborers hauled it to the mill house at the Barnhardt shaft. There "cobbers" further broke down the ore manually, chipping waste rock from lumps of ore, and then as many as five types of milling machinery crushed, dragged, stirred, shook, and rocked the ore in an effort to extract the fine flakes of gold. As in most deep mines in North Carolina, the gold at Gold Hill was in such thin deposits that only extensive milling could effectively extract and save the precious metal.

Machinery of every description marked the rhythm of daily life in the Gold Hill community. By the mid-1850s, steam power typically drove pumps, Chilean mills, and log rockers, although smaller companies continued to use horse-powered and water-powered milling machinery. Only a Sunday holiday or a "cleanup" provided a break from the daily "music" of the steam engine. Writer Porte Crayon observed that "the measured strokes of the mighty pumps thumped like the awful pulsations of some earth-born giant." Another visitor wrote: "The steam mills seem to partake of the general feeling of confidence and puff, puff as deliberately and grand as if they knew every breath was worth a dollar. Hundreds of long, wide rockers with quicksilver gliding in their bottoms roll lazily from side to side and seem to say, 'We'll save it, no use in fretting.' The creeking [sic] joints of connecting rods, the spatter of small jets of water, the rattle of cogs and the deep base harp of monster crushers unite in a sort of chorus of which 'O take your time Miss Lucy' is the prominent idea." Of all the machinery, concluded this visitor, "the piston is the only part that seems to care whether anything is done. It is leaping out and in like the tongue of the excited viper; and small steam leaks, here and there, persistently, but vainly hiss it, every motion, for its indecent haste."

The mining, milling, and extraction methods used at Gold Hill dictated a well-defined division of labor. In addition to back-breaking work, specific skills were necessary. Each procedure required supervision, teamwork, and skill. The miner below ground, for instance, needed an understanding of the veins in which he worked and the ability to follow rich deposits deep into the earth. Above ground, the skills of the engineer, blacksmith, carpenter, and wheel-wright were needed to construct and maintain the milling machinery. Each of these specialists relied on the support of common laborers. To the mine manager or agent of the company fell the responsibility of accounting, payroll, and supply. In short, deep mining in the nineteenth century involved the coordination and management of a large group of workers with various skills and occupations.

As long as mining in the Gold Hill district remained a simple operation confined chiefly to surface deposits, management and labor were virtually one and the same. When deep mining commenced in earnest, however, the organization of the work force became more complex. The first indication of this change came with the development of work shifts in the late 1840s. An early reference to that practice can be found in the correspondence of a female visitor to the district in January 1850: "I was frightened the first night after I came," she wrote, "being waked . . . by a bell ringing. I thought that there was a fire somewhere but . . . I soon found that it was for another set of hands. . . ." A newspaper correspondent who traveled to the district in 1851 observed that "two relays of hands are employed numbering in all between forty and fifty. . . . One half the miners commence their labor at 6 in the morning and come out at dark, the other half work all night." In 1851 another reporter wrote that "labourers underground work eight hours per day; those above[,] twelve." In

1856 state geologist Ebenezer Emmons visited Gold Hill and noted three shifts of eight hours each for underground work.

Management divided each work shift into an "underground force" and a "top ground force." Each "force" included both miners and laborers, which is the way the 1850 census and the Gold Hill Mining Company categorized the workers. Miners performed the skilled jobs—drilling, timbering, and blasting underground or, above ground, mechanical operations related to the power and milling technology. Laborers performed manual chores such as ore cobbing or carrying ore underground and at the mill. In many cases laborers assisted miners in drilling or milling activities. Most laborers were either native-born whites or slaves. Thus, in the hierarchy of labor in the gold-mining district, foreign-born workers held positions of prestige with support from native whites and slaves. Wages at the mine further reflected this difference in status, for the miner could earn twice as much in monthly salary as the laborer.

Each day the workers donned flannel shirts, coarse trousers or overalls of white duck, and jack boots. An underground miner also wore a thick heavy wide-brimmed hat lined with felt. For light in the mine, he attached a candle with a soft mud candlestick to this makeshift helmet. Into the shaft he carried his mallet, drills, and other hand tools common to hard-rock mining. At Gold Hill in the 1850s a miner descended into a shaft through an opening "partly occupied by an enormous pump. . . ." He made his way down into "the black throat of the shaft" by means of "a narrow ladder that was nearly perpendicular. . . . The ladders were about twenty inches wide, with one side set against the timber lining of the shaft, so that the climber had to manage his elbows to keep from throwing the weight of the body on the other side. Every twenty feet or thereabout the ladders terminated on platforms of the same width, and barely long enough to enable one to turn about to set foot on the next ladder. In addition, the rounds and platforms were slippery with mud and water." Sixty or seventy men took this route to work every day to a depth of 300 to 750 feet.

When *Harper's* sent Porte Crayon to Gold Hill in 1857, the reporter/illustrator sensed danger the moment he entered the shaft. As he descended, he found his footing hampered by mud and water on the platforms and rounds. As he reached the bottom of the third or fourth ladder, Crayon made a misstep that threw him slightly off-balance, and he felt the iron grasp of the foreman on his arm:

"Steady, man, steady!"

"Thank you, Sir. But, my friend, how much of this road have we to travel?"

"Four hundred and twenty-five feet, Sir, to the bottom of the shaft."

"And those faint blue specks that I see below, so deep down that they look like stars reflected in the bosom of a calm lake, what are they?"

"Lights in the miners' hats, who are working below, Sir."

Porte Crayon sketched miners at Gold Hill descending by ladder three hundred or more feet underground to conduct their daily duties.

Porte Crayon felt a numbness seize upon his limbs.

"And are we, then, crawling like flies down the sides of this open shaft, with no foothold but these narrow slippery ladders, and nothing between us and the bottom but four hundred feet of unsubstantial darkness?"

"This is the road we miners travel daily" replied the foreman. . . .

Following this exchange, Crayon decided to "remove his slippery buckskin gloves and grip the muddy rounds with naked hands for better security. . . ." He proceeded down the shaft "as if he were walking on eggs, and when ever and anon some cheery jest broke out, who knows but it was uttered to scare off an awful consciousness that, returning again and again, would creep numbingly over the senses during the intervals of silence?"

Once he reached his destination, a miner entered a surrealist world described by contemporaries with a mixture of terror, wonder, and confusion. The darkness was particularly disorienting. "Some fifty feet down, both our candles were extinguished by the dropping moisture from the dark and jagged slate rock which on all sides surrounded us," a visitor related in 1851. "We followed the dripping passage through the smoke of the powder, sometimes leaping across yawning chasms, and now crawling on hand and knees, or climbing over heaps of ore, till we reached the end of the corridor." Another visitor warned that if

the reader wishes to know what is going on at a depth of 300 feet, he must go and examine for himself, for we cannot tell, although we explored those capacious subterraneous abodes of the living. There the sound of the hammer and joyous laughs are heard as above and there are displayed the beauties of the mineral world. Acres have been excavated, and a stranger might wander for days without being able to find his way to the upper world. The traveler can form no just idea of what is going on at Gold Hill without exploring the depths below which may be done with entire safety, provided one can look dangers full in the face without trepidation.

To Porte Crayon, on the other hand, the "joyous laughs" sounded more like "inarticulate hollow moanings."

Visitors to Gold Hill agreed that the world of underground mining possessed an eeriness and novelty that challenged their powers of description. The sounds of the pump and exploding gunpowder echoed constantly, and smoke filled the shafts. Miners from Cornwall found that North Carolina's mines were cooler than those in Great Britain, but another observer noted that "the rough footing, the stooping posture . . . and the confined air were so disagreeable that I had never before known how to sympathize fully with those who are condemned to the mines." Journalists describing the scene left an overall impression of an impenetrable world that could never be explained to the casual reader. Some accounts hint of a realm that had been violated, perhaps better never entered at all. As one correspondent remarked ominously, "there is the black slate and black sand, with brimstone intermingled, in abundance. . . . The brimstone comes up with the gold—rather a suspicious circumstance, as indicating the invasion of a territory we suppose the miners did not bargain for."

Ascending to the surface could be equally hazardous. When Porte Crayon prepared to end his visit in the Gold Hill mine, the Cornish foreman Matthew Moyle offered him a choice of climbing ladders or riding in the ore bucket. "The ladders are more fatiguing, the bucket more dangerous," Crayon observed, "and several miners counseled against attempting [the bucket]. Moyle, however, encouraged [me] with the assurance that they did not lose many men that way."

Unfortunately, workers were indeed in constant physical peril. Foreman Moyle himself died suddenly soon after Crayon's visit in 1857, although the circumstances of his death were not recorded in company records or local newspapers. Accidents in the mines occurred throughout the antebellum period, especially after the commencement of deep mining in the late 1840s. Threats to the underground worker came chiefly from three sources: blasting, poor footing along intermediate levels, and falling objects within the shaft. In 1846, for example, the *Carolina Watchman* reported the death of Calvin Webster, who "had descended a shaft to set a match for blasting in doing which it is supposed he let the fire fall on the priming. He was dreadfully torn by the explosion and died within four hours after the accident." A visitor in 1850 reported two accidents within two weeks—"one man blown up, back 'most broke, and another falling in a shaft broke his nose [and] came out with it hanging down on his chin. . . ."

During the 1850s at least three other deaths resulting from underground accidents were recorded. A twenty-one-year-old slave, Alexander Holmes, fell 120 feet down a pit and broke his neck. A Cornish miner, John Waters, twenty-five years old, died when "a bucket broke loose from the rope and fell 300 feet to the bottom of the shaft where Mr. Waters was at work, striking him in its descent, [wounding] him so badly that he died two hours after the accident." The *Carolina Watchman* described another Cornishman's death with dramatic detail:

A most estimable man, John Stediford, was killed at Gold Hill in Martin and Peter's mining shaft. This pit is 220 or more feet deep descending perpendicularly. It is lined with plank. One of these 14 inches by 12 feet broke from its fastenings and descended end wise. Stediford was at work at the bottom, with his pick, stooping down. The plank made no noise in its descent but came down without touching the sides. The end of the plank struck him fairly on the back of the neck, and he was

94

Illustrator Porte Crayon found that riding on an ascending ore bucket was far less tiring than climbing a ladder to exit a deep mine shaft at Gold Hill.

whirled completely over by the tremendous blow . . . he never spoke or breathed afterwards. He was highly respected by all who knew him for the good qualities of his heart, for his industry and mining skill.

Stediford was the fourth member of his family to lose his life in a gold mine.

Ironically, the very respect accorded the Cornish in deep mines such as Gold Hill placed these men most frequently in the most dangerous situations. Their leadership even extended into the organization and regulation of the underground work force. Indeed, some historians have argued that the most enduring contributions of the Cornish miners came in the area of labor management. The traditional wage system in Cornwall allowed workers to negotiate a "setting," or contract, with employers. The contract price varied according to different ways of measuring the product—by weight or by market value. That system developed over several centuries, although many miners began to complain that it worked well only during periods of high production. Nevertheless, a careful review of the wage and hour records at Gold Hill reveals some continuity with the Cornish contract system.

Each Gold Hill worker—laborer or miner—received a monthly wage based on twenty-six work days per month. In the early 1850s, for example, Honeycutt, Culp and Company set a figure of $13 a month or 50 cents a day for common laborers. By the middle of the decade, the Gold Hill Mining Company raised that basic rate to $1.00 a day or $26.00 a month. The practice of setting monthly wages resembled the Cornish wage procedure and brought a degree of autonomy to the miner, especially during periods when several small companies operated at the same time. In addition, the wage system at Gold Hill offered an improvement over the Cornish model, since workers could be compensated for extra work—odd jobs usually performed above ground or in the mills. Shop work; cleanup; breaking ore; digging an engine pit; tending an engine, boiler, or whim; or dipping candles were jobs that could earn workers additional cash. Many workers, mostly laborers, took advantage of those opportunities. A few earned as much as thirty dollars a month over their base monthly wage. Slaves could also take on extra work, and at the same rates as white workers. That arrangement allowed ambitious common laborers and slaves to improve themselves and perhaps enhance their status within the mining community. Even without such incentives, the basic wage at Gold Hill—an average of twenty dollars per month for all workers—was considerably higher than those paid to textile or tobacco workers in North Carolina during the antebellum period.

The employment of slaves at Gold Hill increased in direct proportion to the extensive development of underground shafts. The number of slaves working for the Gold Hill Mining Company averaged around forty, or about one-third of the total work force, and most of those men worked underground. The sight of white and black workers laboring cooperatively was not unusual in the gold mines of the South. Most slave workers earned the respect of supervisors and co-workers. Crayon concluded that "negroes are . . . among the most efficient laborers," and a company report from a mine in Guilford County observed that slaves "are among our best laborers."

While numerous mining companies owned slaves outright, many mines, including Gold Hill, rented their slave labor. The Gold Hill Mining Company leased slaves from neighboring farms in Rowan County and from farmers in at least six counties in the Piedmont. The annual rental fee paid to a slave owner for the services of a slave averaged about $125, and feeding each such slave could average around $55 per year. In addition, each slave earned approximately $18 per month, along with payments for "extra work" that always seemed available around the mines. Therefore, each slave cost the company close to $400 per year.

In comparison, the average salary for native white workers was no greater than $250 per year, and their wives or children could add perhaps another $70 to $120 per year. Consequently, a company was able to purchase the labor of two "hands"—a white parent and child—for less than the labor of a single adult slave. Nevertheless, this expense did not discourage companies from depending upon slaves, who were more reliable as workers and less likely to leave the company without notice. Indeed, the poor reputation of native white workers was an ongoing concern among promoters of industry in the South. "These mining people," wrote one reporter, "are peculiarly indolent and devoid of energy, never working until forced by absolute cogency of existing circumstances to exert themselves to meet the direct wants of the time being. . . ." The general impression of contemporary observers as well as historians has been that slavery influenced white attitudes toward work. "The existence of slavery in North Carolina, as elsewhere in the South," concluded Guion Johnson in her classic *Ante-Bellum North Carolina: A Social History*, "tended to place a social stigma upon those who worked with their hands."

Regardless of ethnic origin or compensation levels, the miners and laborers of Gold Hill lived simply and rarely accumulated very much personal property or real estate. Tax records reveal that only two miners owned their own homes in the mining district. Most rented "little log cabins, daubed with clay . . . of a real primitive order, with clapboard roofs and weight poles; with a chimney at one end as wide as the whole house, [and] very few that exhibit brass nobs [*sic*] on pannelled doors, whilst there are many of rough boards with string and latch." The census of 1850 estimated about 125 dwellings in the village, including a boardinghouse and a hotel. The Gold Hill Mining Company built several tenant houses during the 1850s for their workers and slaves, who lived in groups of three and four per cabin. Even the houses of the mine managers, the Holmes and Mauney brothers, were quite modest and did not reflect great wealth or luxury.

One of the major concerns during the antebellum period at Gold Hill was the overall health of people living in the district. In the mid-1850s a prolonged "epidemic" of unspecified origin "prevailed for nearly a year, reducing the number of miners underground at times from 80 to 40, and on top in the like population. . . ." Several years later, an outbreak of smallpox caused the city of Salisbury to pass a quarantine ordinance prohibiting visitors from Gold Hill and forbidding visits by Salisbury residents to the mining district. One of the more remarkable assessments of these public health problems came from the mortality census of 1860:

The Water at Gold Hill is thrown out of the mines at the depth of some 675 hundred [*sic*] feet by means of engines at the rate of 200 Gallons per minute, compound of sulpher, copper, and copperas which is of a poisonous character, which has the effect of destroying vegetation, Fish, frogs, Snakes, and all water quadruples [quadrupeds], it also destroys the land over which it passes in time (floods), it also produces chronic diareah [*sic*] and Flux and [in] the great mineral belt running mainly from North to South embracing the counties of Guilford, Randolph, Davidson, Stanly, Rowan, Cabarrus, Union and Mecklenburg, I am told the use of the water produces the same Diseases.

Outbreaks of smallpox and typhoid fever at Gold Hill usually occurred in the spring of the year, when disease-bearing insects bred and spawned along the water sources and water-filled pits excavated by the miners. Other maladies such as flux, consumption, and diarrhea were linked to the drinking water at Gold Hill. Even before the development of germ theory by modern scientists, observers of the mining industry understood the grim consequences of industrial pollution. Descriptions of the Gold Hill district at the peak of its productivity conveyed an image of a rough, raw, and primitive society. "There is certainly nothing in the appearance of the place or its inhabitants," wrote Porte Crayon, "to remind one of its auriferous origin, but, on the contrary, a deal of dirt and shabbiness." As he entered the village, Crayon noted "heaps of red earth, broken rocks, decaying windlasses, and roofless sheds, designating the spots where men had wasted time and money in searching for the earth's most operant poison."

Despite the reports of poor health conditions, safety hazards, and occasional lawlessness, Gold Hill was best known as North Carolina's most famous gold-mining enterprise and perhaps the state's best-documented industrial community in the antebellum period. By the mid-1850s, it had become the yardstick by which all other mining properties in the South were measured. Its history, geology, corporate structure, technology, and labor management were points of reference for entrepreneurs, geologists, and journalists. A report in *DeBow's Review* in 1855, for example, flatly stated that "The Gold Hill mines of North Carolina are the richest in the Atlantic States."

The reputation of the mining district rested on a burst of productivity that accelerated after the opening of the Randolph shaft in 1855. During the period between 1854 and 1858, one-third of the total deposits at the United States branch mint in Charlotte came from Gold Hill. In seven years of operation, the Gold Hill Mining Company deposited nearly 21,500 ounces of gold worth more than $400,000. In 1999 dollars that sum would amount to approximately $7.8 million, while the actual value of the gold would now be worth only $6.235 million.

Whether mining was a profitable as well as a productive venture is less certain. Estimates of net profits ranged from $3,500 to $5,600 per month. Nevertheless, the dream of achieving long-term profits eluded the proprietors at Gold Hill. Two accounts from this period offer revealing evidence of the difficulties involved in the business of gold mining. The first report, produced by the state geologist Ebenezer Emmons in 1856, called attention to technological problems, especially in the use of Chilean mills to extract gold that was mixed in minerals "so fine, that even when rich, it requires great care and attention in grinding and panning to find it." These mills tended to flatten the fine gold flakes and make them so light that they floated away with the wasted ore when water flowed through the mill. Although Emmons proposed some alternative methods, he grudgingly acknowledged that the managers of Gold Hill "show some good sense; the amount of gold which is obtained by the methods now in use is very respectable; and if not wholly satisfactory as to method, the determination seems to be to keep the wheels in motion and save what they can. . . ."

Nonetheless, a dramatic decline in productivity in 1859 and 1860 exposed the technological deficiencies inherent in a process that recovered only one-fifth of the potential gold deposits. Despite this drop in productivity and a resulting reduction in revenue, expenses at the mine remained constant, especially in maintaining a labor force needed to "keep the wheels in motion." Payroll expenses as a percentage of gross revenues rose from 30 percent in the early 1850s to 47 percent in the mid-1850s to 90 percent by 1860.

Another report, issued by the president of the Gold Hill Mining Company in 1856, confirmed the precarious financial conditions that prevailed through-out the brief lifetime of the company. To keep Wall Street investors satisfied, the company had designed a strategy to repay the debts it incurred during the purchase of the mine in 1853 and also pay regular dividends to stockholders. At the same time, investments in mining and milling technology had to be made in order to maintain and, preferably, increase the production of gold. Three sources of capital were available to finance this strategy: deposits of gold at the Charlotte branch mint, sale of stock, and modest assessments upon stock-holders. The company tried mightily to sustain the confidence of investors and keep the mines in operation, but the depression in stocks caused by the panic of 1857 limited the amount of money available to reinvest in new technology or to provide dividends to stockholders. Faced with two years of low investor confidence and low productivity of gold, the company suspended all dividends and capital improvements, ceased all operations by the summer of 1861, and went into receivership in October of that year. A court-ordered sale of the mining property brought a high bid of $11,500 for a property that had sold for nearly $300,000 in 1853.

While the Civil War did not directly precipitate the decline of gold mining, the outbreak of hostilities in the spring of 1861 certainly contributed to the further erosion of the industry. Like denizens of many industrial communities, residents of Gold Hill tended to favor a strong federal government and an economic system that balanced agricultural and commercial interests. In February 1861 they voted three-to-one against the call for a state convention to consider secession. Once North Carolina joined the Confederacy, however, as one eyewitness noted, "Gold Hill was inundated with recruiting parties, and such was the spirit created that in less than two months, nineteen out of every twenty of the male adults were either in the service of the local or the general army."

Many Cornish miners in the district were reluctant at first to become involved in the conflict. Such neutrality was intolerable to other Gold Hill residents, who subjected their Cornish neighbors to "the not very welcome cries of 'You damned Britishers' mingled with oaths and curses of no flattering description. . . ." One miner recalled being chased by "a party of eight or ten. . . . However, after running about ten miles, I found that I had outstripped my blood thirsty pursuers and I at once climbed into a tree for the darkness of night before I would return to my lodgings." In 1861, when rumors spread that the Gold Hill militia might see action in the summer, at least four Cornishmen departed and, after a two-month journey that included rowing themselves to safety up the Potomac River, set sail for England.

While most of the miners marched off to war and the mines filled with water, the owners of the defunct Gold Hill mines found new opportunities during the war years. The North Carolina Ore Dressing Company, which included Moses and Reuben Holmes as proprietors, produced bluestone for use as building material and copperas, a sulfate of copper, for use as an astringent. So great was the need for those two items that the company could not keep up with the demand. The Holmes brothers also invested in cotton, which they sold after the war for Union greenbacks, thus reaping a huge harvest of cash. Eventually they moved to Salisbury and continued to prosper through a variety of commercial and manufacturing enterprises. They never lost their interest in mining, however, and remained closely involved in the affairs of Gold Hill until 1890. Ephriam Mauney and a few others from the pioneering days of the 1840s and 1850s continued to live in the small village, which by the end of the war contained no more than 250 people. For the next fifty years, the antebellum legend of Gold Hill as "the prince of mines" inspired numerous attempts to revive the mining industry, with the only results being an extended period of failure and frustration.

4

The Gold Hill Mining District, 1865–1915

During the thirty-five-year period that followed the Civil War, the mining district at Gold Hill languished through several poorly financed and ill-conceived ventures that produced for the most part little more than a spate of overly optimistic publicity and a series of lawsuits over ownership of various mining properties. The failure of those enterprises did not dampen the stubborn and widely held belief in the imminent rebirth of Gold Hill's mining industry. In that respect, Gold Hill was a microcosm of North Carolina's mining industry, an enterprise that struggled to fulfill the progressive philosophy that became known as the New South creed. According to that doctrine, industrial and technological development was an essential component of economic prosperity and a significant factor in the recovery of the South in the aftermath of the disastrous Civil War.

The relative success of mining during the antebellum years was a vivid memory in a town like Gold Hill and inspired a number of promoters to try to revive the South's most famous mining property. Most prominent among those mining men was Amos Howes, a New York businessman who had been elected president of the Gold Hill Mining Company in May 1861, just prior to the company's dissolution. After the war, Howes gained ownership of the property that included eight tracts totaling nearly six hundred acres. For the first five years after the war, mining activity at Howes's mines amounted to little more than "tribute" work by individual miners or small partnerships at the old waste dumps found throughout the district. Howes leased portions of the property to the miners, who worked tons of wasted ore through "horse mills" and log rockers and apparently "made a good day's work there." Such mining was seasonal. There would be long stretches of inactivity; for instance, the 1870 census indicated that "the [Gold Hill] mine is not in operation at this time."

In 1870 Howes did manage to secure enough financial backing to work the mines as deep-mining operations. With loans from Moses and Reuben Holmes and some New York speculators, he resumed work on Christmas Day, treating only "the old workings, being strings and veins that in former times were considered too poor to work," and using the old boilers, pumps, and mills from the antebellum period. Even with that primitive equipment, Howes was able to produce nearly $190,000 worth of gold over the next three and one-half years, a total that compared favorably to some of the best output when Gold Hill was called "the prince of mines."

Despite that steady production record, Howes was not able to turn a profit. His production costs—mostly labor—were very high, even though the company carried on most of its work above ground, treating the low-grade waste ores from earlier days. Howes realized that he needed to invest in some of the new milling machinery under development by inventors and engineers working in the southern gold region. Late in 1873 he came across a process developed by A. B. Crosby and his brother, Charles, that claimed a very high rate of gold recovered from sulfuret ore. Howes encouraged the Crosby brothers to move their machinery to Gold Hill and set up a mill near the Barnhardt shaft.

At the same time, a Philadelphia-based company contracted with Howes to purchase ore and utilize the Crosby milling process. That arrangement foundered after only a few months, even though the initial runs through the Crosby mill were impressive. By the end of 1874 Howes once again claimed total control of the mining properties in Gold Hill. During the ensuing year, little mining took place while Howes, the Holmes brothers, and the New York investors wrestled in Rowan County court over ownership of the mines. The court found that Howes had improperly used the same property as collateral for two different loans and that Moses and Reuben Holmes owed the New York investors twenty-five thousand dollars. Meanwhile, the Holmes brothers' former partners, Ephriam and Valentine Mauney, took the lead in a new venture. Under the Mauneys' supervision, a small force began working in the more shallow shafts and in clean-up operations. Most of that activity, however, was not significant enough to sustain steady production.

In the late 1870s the old pioneers of Gold Hill once again attempted to market their property. With the help of some North Carolina political leaders, Moses Holmes attracted widespread interest in the mines, especially from Great Britain, which had become a dominant source of venture capital. The development of the limited liability stock company and the publicity generated by mine promoters provided incentives for English investors eager to participate in the worldwide expansion of the British economy in the late nineteenth century. More than five hundred new British mining companies were incorporated between 1860 and 1901.

In February 1881 Holmes succeeded in attracting one of those firms to his mine at Gold Hill. For a price of $125,000, Gold Hill Mines Ltd. of London purchased the mining property and promptly sent eleven Cornish miners to examine the ore deposits and install new machinery. While the men received a warm reception from the residents of the village and the local press, the British company never demonstrated any ability to seriously develop the infrastructure needed for mining and milling the low-grade deposits of Gold Hill. Between 1881 and 1885 it invested about $150,000 but produced only $9,000 worth of gold. At the end of 1885 it maintained only a skeletal crew and "the ponderous pump . . . the only visible evidence of life, bending and groaning, day and night, as if trying to fetch from the dismal depths some excuse for money that is gone."

Over the next decade, Gold Hill Mines Ltd. reorganized three times under various names to try to raise the working capital needed for deep-mining operations. Company directors would dissolve an existing company and sell shares at a discount to stockholders, a common practice among British limited liability stock companies. In spite of optimistic predictions by the mine managers and the purchase of more equipment, none of these companies succeeded. They relied on traditional methods of crushing, amalgamating, and roasting gold-bearing deposits when they might have experimented more with newly emerging technologies. Because they were operating with very little working capital, however, such investments were too risky. The great distance between London and North Carolina prevented effective communication and further complicated the management of the mines. Local support for the British company, which initially had been very positive, evaporated as it became clear that its engineers could not make Gold Hill pay. Influenced by a pattern of nativist sentiment, observers of the operations at Gold Hill concluded that an American mining engineer was preferable to "foreign management." One commentary in a journal for mining engineers declared that "if one of our practical mining men can not make a mine pay, outsiders will do well to leave it alone."

In fact, the local experts at Gold Hill, veterans of the peak period of profits in the 1850s, did not fare any better than their British counterparts in turning around the fortunes of mining. Three local men tried at various times in the 1880s and 1890s to use "practical" methods to coax the fine deposits of gold from the ore. The results were always the same and always disappointing. By 1895 all companies, foreign and local, had formally abandoned their operations. The mines had filled with water and the mill, operated by a small crew, ran only three days a week. The local men reworked the old "waste" that had accumulated over fifty years and used stamp mills,

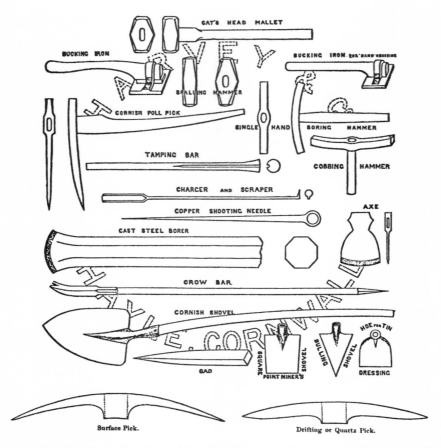

Typical hand tools used by Cornish hard-rock miners of the nineteenth century. Advertisement reproduced in Bryan Earl, *Cornish Mining: The Techniques of Metal Mining in the West of England, Past and Present* (Truro, England: Barton, 1968), 110.

log rockers lined with quicksilver riffles, and woolen blankets, which were placed at the bases of the stamp mills and washed every twenty minutes to capture any stray particles of gold. Thus, at the close of the nineteenth century, mining at Gold Hill had come full circle: a few independent miners working in small partnerships and in some cases relying upon very primitive machinery.

The cast-iron California-style stamp mills in use at Gold Hill had been installed by the British. Such mills, particularly models manufactured by the Mecklenburg Iron Works, became the technology of choice in the late

Mill buildings and head frame of Barnhardt shaft, Gold Hill, ca. 1895. From Nitze and Wilkens, *Gold Mining in North Carolina*, facing p. 60.

nineteenth century chiefly because they were able to produce larger volumes of ore than rival milling machines. Unfortunately, the low-grade quality of the ore at Gold Hill and most other southern mines required that owners supplement the stamp mills with slower, more primitive methods that at times resulted in a higher yield of gold.

The poor results obtained from the use of stamp mills did not dampen the belief of most mine owners in the healing powers of technology. During the late nineteenth century, inventors, machinists, and engineers were devising a wide variety of new gadgets and devices designed to reduce costs and increase production. Because of Gold Hill's reputation both as a gold producer and as the location of some of the most sulfuret ore in North Carolina, the district became a laboratory for several experiments that promised to restore its productive capacity. Mechanical processes, such as the one promoted by the Crosby brothers in the 1870s, attempted to remove sulfur and separate minerals such as copper from gold-bearing ore. Those processes also emphasized continuous operations that reduced the need for labor and increased the speed at which ore could be crushed, mixed with mercury, and roasted in retorts.

Other experiments utilized chemical approaches. One chemist tried steam to decompose sulfur without interfering with amalgamation. Chlorine, a highly toxic and dangerous gas, nevertheless gained acceptance as a method of extracting gold at many North Carolina mines. At least one company at Gold Hill utilized chlorination to create a water-soluble mixture from which gold could be removed quickly and at low cost. At the end of the nineteenth century, cyanide replaced chlorine as the most promising chemical reagent. Richard Eames Jr., a mining engineer born in New York City, began testing the cyanide process at Gold Hill in the 1890s. Eames treated crushed gold ore with a solution of sodium cyanide and then agitated the ore in the open air. The gold dissolved in that mixture and was later precipitated onto sheets or shavings of zinc. Heating the solution in a retort completed the process. Reportedly Eames's efforts recovered only 60 percent of the assay value of the ore, and he quickly abandoned his trials.

The use of chemicals such as chlorine and cyanide subjected workers and the environment to obvious dangers in the pursuit of profits from mineral resources. The willingness to experiment with chemicals and various machines even when they proved to be costly failures demonstrated the abiding belief of promoters of North Carolina's gold mines in the efficacy of invention and technology. Such faith appeared to be justified when the living symbol of the age of invention, Thomas A. Edison, visited the gold region in 1890.

Edison's well-known interest in ore-separation technology had developed in the 1880s, but his experiments with the ores of North Carolina were shrouded in secrecy. The news of his arrival in Charlotte in January 1890 produced intense speculation. His presence in the area absorbed the local press for several months. Newspapers closely monitored his itinerary and analyzed every pronouncement by "Professor Edison" and his assistants for some indication of the nature of his research. Rumors that Edison might buy a mining property touched off a wave of speculation that envisioned a reawakening of mining and a general boost to the entire regional economy. "The surface has not been scratched as yet," observed one report. "Let us all do our best to hasten the great time surely coming."

Most observers believed that Edison had found a miraculous new method to recover gold from refractory ores through electricity. A great sense of anticipation grew as he moved from mine to mine to confer with local engineers and send samples back to his laboratory in New Jersey. By the time he reached Gold Hill on March 4, reports of his work were bursting with enthusiasm. "Here comes the 'Wizard of Menlo Park,'" wrote the *Carolina Watchman*, "and he says he can, with his wonderful friend and servant electricity, separate the gold, even when mixed with the closest and most pestiferous of its companions. If the electric process can be done at all inexpensively the gold mines of North Carolina will boom, indeed." Another editorial echoed these sentiments with the hope for "this ancient 'Hornet's Nest' . . . that 'The Wizard' will be able to solve the problem that has been vexing the souls and emptying the purses of the gold miners of this country for half a century, and should he do so they at least will have a new saint in their calendar—Saint Thomas, surnamed Edison."

In fact, Edison's primary mineral interest was not gold but iron. He had designed a magnetic ore separator to save magnetite or black sand found in great quantities in the eastern United States. The separator consisted of a hopper shaped like an inverted cone, with a group of magnets below that attracted iron particles as they fell into one bin while waste fell into another. Edison believed, as did many of his contemporaries, that the world's supply of iron ore was depleted, and he hoped his invention would open a new field of enterprise for him much as the electric light had done in the 1880s.

Edison departed North Carolina in the summer of 1890 and later established an extraordinary milling operation near Ogdensburg, New Jersey. For several years he operated what was known as the "Ogden Baby," a giant machine capable of crushing six tons of ore in thirty seconds. He also built a model industrial village named Edison to provide housing for the mill's four hundred workers. Just as he was bringing the enterprise into full production, however, the discovery of rich deposits or iron ore in the Mesabi range of northern Minnesota dramatically increased the nation's supply of that commodity. As a result, the price of iron decreased continuously through the 1890s, forcing the Wizard of Menlo Park to close "Ogden Baby." The closure was one of the few total failures in Edison's otherwise illustrious career.

A year after Edison's whirlwind visit, a rail line that linked Salisbury and Albemarle reached Gold Hill. By that time the little mining district had become a stable, quiet farming community with occasional bursts of activity brought on by various entrepreneurs seeking to restore the glory of the antebellum period. Although these companies were short-lived, the influx of new workers and their families could increase the population of the district by several hundred people. The mines tended to be inactive during the census years of 1870, 1880, and 1890, and the population ranged from about 350 to 600 people. Even with the addition of new workers who occupied the village when the mines were running, Gold Hill's population probably never exceeded one thousand in the last decades of the nineteenth century.

Miners or laborers who took up permanent residency at Gold Hill faced long periods of unemployment. Most were fortunate to find work for six months out of a year. All of them pursued other occupations to carry them through these extended periods of inaction. Like their antebellum counterparts a few owned small plots of land and did some farming. Others operated small businesses or traveled to other communities to find temporary work. A common practice throughout the period was rewashing the great piles of gold-bearing waste ore. In such ways, the people of Gold Hill sustained themselves but did not prosper. Aside from an eleven-room "Mansion House" that one of the English companies had constructed in the 1880s as one of the finest buildings in rural Rowan County, the houses, churches, and other buildings in the village were simple and undistinguished. A visitor took note of the forty or

TOP: Street scene, town of Gold Hill. BOTTOM: typical miners' quarters at Gold Hill, ca. 1890.

fifty houses for workers, most with about five or six people per dwelling. The abandoned equipment and structures of the mining industry were also important defining features of Gold Hill's landscape.

When the mines were operating, however briefly, companies organized the work force much as antebellum companies had done. Engineers and skilled miners from Cornwall provided direction. Local laborers and miners

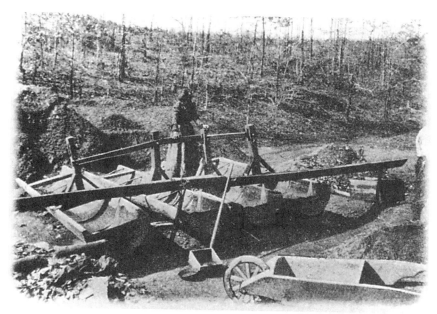

Use of log rockers to separate gold from gravel persisted at Gold Hill for sixty years.

comprised most of the crew both above and below ground. The children of these workers made up a significant portion of the work force—as much as one-third on some occasions—performing odd jobs underground, in the mill, and at the log rockers used to rework sand wastes. The only major difference in the work force prior to about 1895 was that there was little evidence of a sizable black component, probably never more than 10 percent during the entire period.

Wages compared favorably with those of the antebellum period. In the 1860s and 1870s miners earned between $30 and $40 a month and laborers between $15 and $20 a month. Carpenters, blacksmiths, and other "mechanics" could earn as much as $50 a month. Engineers received top monthly salaries of $80. Children could make as much as $10. These wages generally kept pace with the prevailing prices charged in company stores and other mercantile outlets. Prices for food and clothing remained stable throughout those years. Molasses cost around 50 cents a gallon. Bacon sold for around 12 or 13 cents a pound, while fish sold for 10 cents apiece.

The district's agricultural base provided continuity and stability in the shadow of steam engines, stamp mills, and ore wastes. Visitors investigating mining prospects made special note of the farming community that surrounded the mines at Gold Hill, making inexpensive foodstuffs and other provisions readily available to the mine workers. Others marveled at the fine meadows along the Gold Hill Road between Salisbury and Albemarle. In addition to being leading producers of hay, Gold Hill's farmers also produced wheat, corn, cotton, molasses, and fresh produce. A new mining venture might bring an infusion of economic activity; however, in most years mining was a supplement for farming. In between the excitement of companies starting up new operations, events could be summarized by the statement of one observer, who wrote: "Gold Hill is moving right along in its usual quiet way."

The tranquillity of that scene ended abruptly at the close of the nineteenth century when a new generation of mining men—armed with new machinery and new capital—tried to harness the mineral riches of Gold Hill with unprecedented energy and enthusiasm. Those projects came about in the context of a vigorous expansion of industrial and commercial activity throughout the country. In the South, those ventures generally took the form of low-wage and low-value processing industries such as cottonseed oil, turpentine, cotton yarn and coarse cloth, polished rice, fertilizers, and wood products, and extractive industries such as mining. The fact that northern capitalists controlled most of these initiatives reinforced the image of the South as a colonial and dependent region with "branch banks, branch plants, captive mines, and chain stores." The dream of an independent New South equal to the other regions of the country would remain unfulfilled during the first decades of the twentieth century.

The two entrepreneurs who dominated the Gold Hill district between 1899 and 1915 were Walter George Newman and E. B. C. Hambley. Although entirely different in their backgrounds and their methods of operation, both men reflected the pattern of the South as a colonial outpost of expansive northern interests. Newman, a flamboyant promoter of gold and copper mines at Gold Hill, attracted large sums from investors in Boston and New York. During this same period, Hambley, a Cornish mining engineer, collaborated with a Pittsburgh financier who had ties to Andrew Mellon's economic empire in a visionary proposal to develop the Yadkin River as a power source for the mines and mills at Gold Hill and other sites in the region.

Walter George Newman was born in Orange County, Virginia, in 1860. By the time he arrived in Gold Hill, he had spent parts of his adult life as a sailor, a jockey, a railway express messenger, an advertising salesman, and a self-proclaimed world traveler. With his trademark derby, umbrella, solid gold scarf pin, and white suit, he was the single most memorable character in the history of the Gold Hill mining district. Newman was part promoter and part clown, a shrewd and even inspirational leader and also a pathetic alcoholic and gambler. His greatest contribution ended up being his own legendary performance during fifteen turbulent years. Only the deafening roar of ore being crushed in iron stamp mills created as lasting an impression.

Newman went to Gold Hill in 1898 to join his brother, Joseph, a mining engineer who had occasionally worked in the district since the early 1880s. Within a year, Newman began buying all the major tracts of mining property and formed two companies—the Union Copper Mining Company and the Gold Hill Copper Mining Company. Those companies devoted most of their energies to the extraction of copper rather than gold. Although the antebellum operators of the Gold Hill mines—Moses Holmes and Ephriam Mauney— acknowledged the presence of copper, they preferred to concentrate exclusively on gold extraction. Nevertheless, the next generation of miners encountered ores of even greater sulfide content, and the cost of processing that ore to remove gold became prohibitive. As the celebrated Randolph shaft increased in depth, the copper content of the ore also increased. At the same time, the development of electricity and electrical equipment in the 1880s and 1890s made copper a more valuable commodity. By the end of the nineteenth century, the geology of Gold Hill and the growing importance of copper convinced Newman and his associates to take a fresh look at the potential of the mining district. "The famous Gold Hill mines," concluded one geologist, "would not be operated were it not for the copper contents which they carry."

Within a year, Newman produced dramatic changes in the district. The Union Copper Mining Company constructed new facilities and dwellings— more than one hundred buildings—to accommodate a work force of one thousand men. A spur from the Southern Railway ran directly to the company's mills, power plant, and shops. The underground works consisted of a dozen or more shafts, some at depths of more than two hundred feet, with hundreds of feet of tunnels and drifts. The company's plant processed more than 150 tons

Union Copper Mine complex, Gold Hill.

Interior of millhouse, Union Copper Mine.

of ore daily and shipped about fifty carloads of 30,000 pounds each to concentrating plants in New Jersey during the first months of operation. Meanwhile, the construction of the first of a projected five concentrating plants, each with a daily capacity of four hundred tons, pressed ahead.

At the Gold Hill Copper Mining Company, Newman made use of some of the infrastructure that remained on the property from previous operations. During the first half of 1900 the company invested around $35,000 in preparatory work, dewatering the major shafts at the Barnhardt and Randolph mines, and securing new power and milling equipment for copper-mining operations. Newman set up a twenty-stamp mill with five concentrating tables. The company complex also included a supply house, a machine shop, a blacksmith shop, an assay office, a powder house, a pump house, and an office. Contracts with a wide range of suppliers brought machinery and equipment from Salisbury and Charlotte, as well as from Charleston, Baltimore, Washington, Wilmington (Delaware), Paterson (New Jersey), and Harrisburg (Pennsylvania).

By the end of 1900, Newman had lost control of both companies. A shortage of cash forced him to turn operation of the Union Copper Mine over to managers from Colorado. For the next several years, they ran the mine at full capacity and produced some very rich ore. However, returns from their smelter on site and from the ore shipped to northern smelters were not consistently large enough to support the operation. Even after they adopted

Randolph shaft, Gold Hill Copper Company, ca. 1915.

new and more efficient methods, they could not turn a profit. A court-appointed receiver operated the mine from late 1906 through the beginning of 1907 when the property was sold at auction. After the price of copper fell during the panic of 1907, the company ceased operations and laid off one hundred men. The Gold Hill Copper Mining Company experienced failure within a few months into the new century. By August 1900 the U.S. Circuit Court in Flat Rock, North Carolina, appointed a receiver to run the company.

Yet Walter George Newman reappeared in Gold Hill several times to manage the mining properties at the Union and Gold Hill mines. In 1909 he secured enough cash to hire one hundred men to reopen the Union Copper Mine. "With the large whistle blowing and the small whistle and the wild cat whistle all blowing at the same time, there seems to be something doing," exclaimed the *Carolina Watchman*. By the summer, Newman had little to show for his efforts. The mine was sold in a foreclosure proceeding in September 1909. For the next decade, various reports and studies suggested possible reuses for the mine, and some production did occur from the ore wastes found throughout the property; but large-scale mining at the Union mine never resumed.

The history of the neighboring Gold Hill Copper Mine was equally brief but somewhat more colorful. After Newman relinquished the property in 1900, the succeeding managers ran the company into receivership twice more over the next eight years. Each time, Newman regained control of the operation and repeated his familiar pattern of lavish spending with little or no return in copper or gold. After 1905, with Newman promising "new life" for Gold Hill, he and his associates concentrated exclusively on gold production, but again without success. In early 1909, with lawsuits and countersuits draining whatever resources existed, the company was sold for a third and final time to northern interests for $45,000. The Gold Hill Consolidated Company, a successor firm chartered in Maine, elected Newman president but ceased operations only a few weeks after the nearby Union mine had closed. Walter George Newman drifted away from Gold Hill, presumably for good.

For four years, the mines of Gold Hill were dormant, and potential investors showed little interest. In the summer of 1913 Newman made a surprise and triumphant return to the mines and for two turbulent, tragicomic years threw himself into the business of mining with his full energy. By that time, however, his credibility with investors and local residents had eroded completely. Newman's notorious reputation reached a national audience when an investigation in 1914 by the United States Senate revealed the improper use of Senate stationery to promote his company. Although he avoided formal charges and even managed to turn a small profit at the end of 1914, he could not secure long-term financial support. The company suspended operations at the end of April 1915 and issued its final payroll on May 15. In June one mining journal reported that "A news dispatch from North Carolina now announces the appointment by the court of receivers for the Gold Hill property, which has been shut down and idle . . . and adds that Walter George Newman . . . is not at the mine and there is no one in his absence to tell of the company's assets and liabilities. It did not require a periscope of perspicacity to foresee this denouement."

Newman's repeated failures at Gold Hill reflected his instability as a person, as well as his serious inadequacies as a businessman. His erratic personal behavior attracted as much attention, as did the fortunes of his various enterprises. He craved that attention and nurtured his reputation as the best-known mining man in North Carolina. In the end, he was consumed by the celebrity he so consciously cultivated. Newman could be most generous and aspired to be a philanthropist on the order of Andrew Carnegie. Nonetheless, he had neither a plan nor resources for his donations. He built a children's park in Gold Hill and announced plans to endow a modern hospital in Salisbury, an offer he later withdrew. Numerous stories told by Gold Hill residents documented his charity toward individuals. According to those recollections, he was fond of throwing dollar bills and coins from his carriage or automobile and often sent expensive gifts to favorite employees.

Newman's propensity for free spending, entertaining, drinking, and gambling also contributed to his lusty legend. He reportedly offered one thousand dollars to anyone who could invent a new "cuss" word. He claimed to be a champion spitter and once bet that he could put out the fire of his cigar with one splash of tobacco juice at a distance of ten feet. He sponsored cockfights and reveled in "battles royal," especially among black workers, to whom he offered rounds of free drinks and a cash prize to the survivor of a group melee. He awed local citizens with his feats of strength, his womanizing, and his drunken outbursts. One particularly violent dispute with his brother, Joe, led to the latter's suicide in 1898. Newman's eccentric behavior overshadowed any positive deeds he may have achieved and certainly distracted him from the effective conduct of his business.

Newman's final days at Gold Hill are exemplary of his capacity to inspire legend. One account reported Newman arriving at Gold Hill just ahead of a carload of potential investors from New York. Newman borrowed money from local miners for paint and whitewash, then hired some workers to paint the buildings at the Gold Hill mine. When he led his prospects through the mine, these same workers donned miners' outfits in time to be seen working in the shafts. The con game worked, and Newman received twelve thousand dollars from the visitors to further develop the mine. But he immediately boarded a train to New York and never returned to Gold Hill. Nor did he repay the miners the money he had borrowed.

A second version of Newman's last day at Gold Hill involved an angry mob of miners seeking back wages of several weeks. The miners advanced upon Newman's office and cornered him on the second-floor balcony. He was unable to pacify the crowd and finally resorted to throwing bills and coins from the balcony. During the confusion that followed, Newman slipped out the back door, boarded his private train, and sped off as the miners scrambled below. The truthfulness of either account is not important except as an illustration of the mythic quality Newman had attained by the close of his career at Gold Hill. After he drifted away from the mines, he apparently wandered around the country before he ended up in a rented hotel suite in New York. He died there in 1918 at the age of fifty-eight.

While Newman focused his attention on the development of individual mining properties, Egbert Barry Cornwall Hambley envisioned the mining industry at Gold Hill as merely a small part of an ambitious regional plan to create an industrial and technological network in North Carolina's Piedmont. Hambley's plan brought traditional industries such as mining and textiles together with a new form of power technology—hydroelectricity. The successful exploitation of the Piedmont's abundant waterpower, according to Hambley, would make it possible not only to sustain industry but to allow towns and cities to grow through a dramatic expansion of urban services.

Hambley was born in Cornwall, England, and followed his father into a career of civil and mining engineering. While he was enrolled at the Royal

School of Mines in Kensington, his father died, forcing young Hambley to leave school and find employment. In January 1881, just before his nineteenth birthday, he joined Gold Hill Mines, Ltd., as a mining captain and assistant to the principal engineer. He arrived at Gold Hill in January 1882 after, according to his diary, an eight-hour buggy ride from Salisbury, which was only fourteen miles away. The village was so remote and the roads so impassable that Hambley's driver abandoned the route and took the vehicle through the woods.

"Gold Hill was once a noted mining camp," Hambley reported in his diary, "when the mines were making big returns. Now it is not an important place. There are some 600 people, mostly miners. The houses are in a terrible down condition . . . the only decent house . . . was the manager's house where I was quartered. . . . Here I was after about 15 days travel [from England] landed at my destination for how long I cannot say." Hambley remained at Gold Hill for three years and while there found more success as a member of various hunting parties than in the discouraging prospects at the mines. In 1884 he accepted a position as special engineer with John Taylor & Sons, one of England's most successful engineering firms. Hambley's assignments took him to mining regions throughout the world—India, the Gold Coast and Transvaal in Africa, Mexico, California, Spain, and Norway.

During that intensive three-year period he acquired considerable knowledge of the latest techniques of mining engineering, as well as the design of modern power plants. In 1887, at the age of twenty-six, he returned to North Carolina, attracted both by the possibilities for mining and business enterprises and the presence of Lottie Coleman, the daughter of a prominent Rowan County physician. Hambley married Miss Coleman that same year and established permanent residence in Rowan County. For the next eleven years, he served as a consulting engineer for no fewer than eight British mining companies located in North Carolina. His tireless and successful promotion of various business and industrial activities earned him widespread recognition as a leader in the Salisbury region and established him as a credible source of information about the potential for economic development.

In the late 1890s Hambley convinced several investors from New York and Pennsylvania to develop a site on the Yadkin River, seven miles from Gold Hill, for hydroelectric power. He recognized the potential of a section of the river known as the Narrows, a deep gorge running three and one-half miles before it emptied into the Falls of the Yadkin. In 1899 he organized the North Carolina Power Company with $5 million in capital stock and $2.5 million worth of bonds. At the same time, he engaged the support of George I. Whitney, a financier from Pittsburgh and a confidant of banker and industrialist Andrew W. Mellon. Whitney established the Whitney Development Company, with Hambley serving as general manager. With headquarters in the Gold Hill mining district, the company purchased two mines three miles southwest of Walter George Newman's operations and set up a gold-reduction works.

The facility at Gold Hill was only part of the Whitney company's bold and far-reaching plan to develop the resources of the central North Carolina Piedmont—a plan that included promotion of mining, manufacturing, real estate, and utilities. Additional enterprises included the Rowan Granite Works in what became Granite Quarry, the Barringer Gold Mining Company near Gold Hill, and five other mining and real-estate firms. Those companies served as the foundation for a regional network of manufacturing and power outlets designed to produce and distribute electricity as far away as Knoxville, Tennessee.

The pivotal element in the Whitney-Hambley partnership was the construction of a hydroelectric power dam at the Narrows of the Yadkin, a granite structure 35 feet high and 1,100 feet long that was designed to create 27,000 horsepower. A five-mile canal would connect the dam to a power plant along the river. The company built railroad spurs that linked its various facilities. Hundreds of workers, including miners from Gold Hill and stone masons from Sicily, arrived to build the dam out of huge blocks of granite. Company engineers laid out streets and boulevards for what was to become the model manufacturing town of Whitney, located at the construction site, and the company purchased nearly 30,000 acres of land in five counties for future development. The public response to the Whitney project was warm and enthusiastic. Local newspapers greeted each progress report with predictions that Whitney and Hambley would transform the Piedmont into the garden spot of North Carolina, comparable to the great industrial sites of New England. "The great master minds at Whitney," exulted one reporter, "are engaged in carrying out a giant scheme to grapple with and subdue elemental nature, forcing her with many inventions to lend her untamed energy, wasted for ages, to the direction of human intelligence, that much good may result of the world of man."

Despite the infusion of capital investment and an enthusiastic public, the Whitney company floundered and ultimately failed within its first decade. The initial setback came in the mines at the Gold Hill district when an accident at the Barringer mine in 1904 left eight men dead and the company in debt to families and creditors. The Barringer, the oldest underground mine in the state, never reopened. Within a year, the other mines in the district were likewise filled with water. At the dam construction site along the Yadkin River, outbreaks of typhoid fever severely depleted the labor force each summer.

E. B. C. Hambley himself contracted typhoid in the summer of 1906 and after a prolonged illness died on August 13 at the age of forty-four. His death shocked the business community of North Carolina. An editorial in the *Charlotte Observer* called Hambley's death "a most deplorable event. . . . Few

117

men have done more for [North Carolina] in a material way, and his value to it and the extent of the loss it has sustained in his death are beyond estimate." The Barringer mine disaster and Hambley's death were serious setbacks for the Whitney project. The panic of 1907 produced devastating losses for George Whitney's coal-mining companies near Pittsburgh, leading him to sell much of his business to Andrew Mellon at a huge discount. By 1910 the Whitney company filed for bankruptcy protection.

The repeated failures to revive the mining industry at Gold Hill did not surprise most knowledgeable observers. Explanations usually began and ended with the geology of the mining district. Most of the district's "free gold"—gold found in non-sulfuret ore—had been mined by the mid-1850s. Copper ore could be found, but rarely in quantities greater than 4 percent of the ore body, and the costs of mining and processing the red metal exceeded its value. These plain truths prevailed at most mines in North Carolina. The federal assayer in Charlotte in 1901 candidly summarized the situation when he wrote: "There has been almost no true mining in North Carolina and deep mining is almost unknown. . . . I suppose North Carolina is like most mining regions—the greater part of the so-called mines are mere prospect holes, and not promising; . . . I do not know of any bonanzas in North Carolina."

The belief in "bonanzas," however, fueled the dreams and ambitions of schemers like Walter George Newman and visionaries such as E. B. C. Hambley. Long after mining had ceased to be a viable enterprise, Newman and Hambley were able to persuade their absentee partners to provide the financial backing they needed for machinery and labor. They also persuaded the local citizenry and press that they were capable of restoring the mining industry to its antebellum glory. When these men failed to fulfill expectations, many analysts searched for explanations apart from the fundamental fact of geological limitations.

Newman's larger-than-life celebrity made him an easy target for those who argued that "incompetent and dishonest management and the impatience for quick returns" were pivotal factors in the demise of the mining industry at Gold Hill. The central theme of that critique called attention to the excessive investment in pumping equipment, mills, and reduction plants that characterized the mines under Newman's management. Those investments were made even before the underground ore bodies had been carefully explored and the time-consuming process of timbering the shafts had been carried out. Consequently, expensive equipment and machinery stood idle during the development phase. When Newman and his associates finally began raising hundreds of tons of ore, they decided to impress their financial backers by shipping tons of unprocessed ore to distant plants in Perth Amboy, New Jersey, even though they sustained enormous expenses in doing so.

To reduce the costs of operations at individual mines such as Gold Hill, geologists and engineers proposed the construction of a central reduction works within the region. That approach replicated the antebellum concept of centrally located ore mills to serve several mining operations. One of the more forceful proponents of a central reduction works was Richard Eames Jr., a Salisbury engineer and a veteran of both the Union and Gold Hill copper mines. Eames's proposed "metallurgical plant," to be located near the point of production, would treat all the metals contained in the ore, as well as nonmetallic material, which could be used in the manufacture of mining by-products such as sulfuric acid. "Such a plant," Eames argued, "will enable many deposits to yield profitable results . . . and will legitimize our mining industry. . . . [This] is the solution of legitimate mining in North Carolina. . . . There has been enough money squandered at the Union and Gold Hill mines to have erected two such plants."

The Eames plant was never built, and Gold Hill became synonymous with waste and incompetence. The most glaring examples of mismanagement occurred in the technological processes. Sophisticated concentrators and smelters often sat idle and rusting, while the most primitive methods of extraction were employed. In the shadow of awesome stamp mills small boys used woolen blankets spread at the end of concentrating tables to catch errant flakes of gold. Independent operators leased piles of waste ore from the major companies in the district and hired women and children to run that material through log rockers in a manner reminiscent of the antebellum period. The "best concentrator built anywhere" was unprofitable to operate and was replaced by the oldest known methods of extraction.

During the brief periods when Newman's and Hambley's mines did operate, hundreds of workers flocked to the Gold Hill mining district seeking "public work"—nonfarm work that paid cash wages. In 1900 more than 350 miners worked in the district. That concentration of workers likely made Gold Hill one of the largest employers in Rowan County, along with the Southern Railway's Spencer repair shops and the textile mills of Cannon Manufacturing Company and other firms. During periods when the mines were in the hands of receivers, small crews of fifteen served as a pump and boiler force. When Newman would periodically reopen the mines, he brought on as many as two hundred workers. Those crews consisted of four groups. A small "executive force" included a general manager, superintendent, mill foreman, assayer, and bookkeeper. A "top force" of about twenty-five workers performed odd jobs on the surface, operated the power plant, and provided a link between the mine and the mill. Skilled workers such as blacksmiths, carpenters, and machinists, as well as common laborers, water boys, cooks, and servants, were in that category. A "mill force" of about a dozen workers ran the concentrating mill and stamp mill and included ore dressers and blanket washers. The fourth and largest unit, the "underground force," consisted of as many as fifty workers, including timbermen, machine runners, miners, and laborers.

Mine-related work at Gold Hill offered local rural people the opportunity to earn cash wages and escape the hardships and vagaries of agriculture.

Many of the jobs performed by most of these workers were quite similar to tasks carried out by previous generations of miners. A repetitive, back-breaking routine dominated the daily assignments: three eight-hour shifts underground and two ten-hour shifts above ground. A small, elite corps of foremen and managers organized and directed the workers. One major difference between Gold Hill's miners of about 1900 and their pre-Civil War counterparts involved their ethnic composition. Only a handful of early-twentieth-century miners were born in foreign countries. Most of the men were born in North and South Carolina. Most of the twentieth-century underground workers were black, while white workers were assigned jobs tending machinery. That division of tasks along racial lines mirrored the prevailing Jim Crow social practices of most southern industries. The skilled workers at Gold Hill could earn more than $2 per day, while others working above ground earned $1.50 or $1.75 for their daily services. Younger workers such as water boys or "helpers" earned 50 or 75 cents per day. The under-ground foremen could earn $2 per day, but all other workers underground were paid from $1 to $1.60 a day. That wage scale represented a major difference from the antebellum period, when the miners in the shafts commanded the top pay.

Working conditions remained most precarious for the underground miner at Gold Hill. Explosives were still the chief means of clearing shafts and cutting tunnels. Accidents involving the use of explosives were common. During the

This work crew at the No. 7 shaft at Union Copper Mine included a considerable number of African Americans.

summer of 1906, for instance, at least two explosion-related accidents caused the deaths of three men and injured two others. Cave-ins from faulty timbering underground were less common but equally dangerous. Flooding caused the aforementioned accident at the Barringer mine in 1904. An extremely heavy rainfall produced a torrent that burst a pipe in the mine, quickly filling it with millions of gallons of water. Ten men had been clearing the mine at the one hundred-foot level; one of them was the company's superintendent, Tom Moyle, a descendant of a Cornish miner. Only he and a black worker, Jim Reid, escaped before the flood swept in and killed the remaining eight workers, seven of whom were African Americans. Two weeks later, search teams found the decomposed remains of the hapless miners floating four hundred feet from the shaft at the end of a tunnel.

In 1900, its peak year of activity, the Gold Hill district probably numbered around one thousand people, almost all of whom were miners or members of mining families. More than 40 percent of the population were adult males, and only 16 percent were adult females. Black workers and their families made up more than one-third of the community. More than two-thirds of the workers lived in rental houses or boarded with other families. The rental houses varied in size and quality. Although some were substantial two-story frame structures with metal roofs, the large majority were one-story shacks or duplexes

Union Copper Mine complex, ca. 1915.

measuring fifteen feet square, in which three to five miners dwelt. These company-owned houses were scattered about near the shafts in cleared fields and gave Gold Hill's townscape a bleak appearance. Very few of the makeshift dwellings survived after the mines closed. An inventory taken in 1915 enumerated only thirteen structures out of more than one hundred that had been built fifteen years earlier.

In contrast to the blighted conditions of the workers' housing, the company offices, hotel buildings, and manager's residences were imposing and impressive. The Gold Hill Copper Company's office building, for example, was a two-story structure with a drawing room, dining room, kitchen, and five bedrooms. The Union Copper Mine office was equally elaborate, and the mine manager's residence was an attractive two-story house with carpeting, kitchen appliances, curtains, and furniture, all supplied by the company. The most celebrated building in the district and perhaps one of the finest in Rowan County was the Union Mine Hotel, a large, rambling three-story building with thirty-five rooms, all supplied with steam heating and electricity.

With the mines opening and closing so frequently, Gold Hill was a transient community. There was little continuity between the mining populations of 1900, 1906, and 1915, the district's three years of greatest activity in the twentieth century. Each new period of operation brought in a new wave of workers whose presence often created an atmosphere of vice and violence. Even in its brief and episodic intervals of operation, Gold Hill developed a reputation as a wide-open mining frontier town. The roar of the stamp mill, the whistles calling a new shift, and the escapades of Walter George Newman set Gold Hill apart from the other villages of the region in the early decades of the twentieth century. Those turbulent days left indelible memories for the small permanent community that called Gold Hill home.

During periods of inactivity at the mines, the population consisted of only about 250 people, most of whom derived their livelihood as farmers or local tradesmen. The community supported the Methodist Church and managed to sustain a band, a baseball team, and a men's fraternal organization. Most residents enjoyed a satisfactory if not luxurious standard of living. Farming in North Carolina's Piedmont was, for many families, a challenging occupation that rarely offered financial security. Like many rural dwellers of that time and place, the people of Gold Hill preferred "public work." For some, the pursuit of such work led them to the growing number of textile mills and furniture factories in such nearby towns as Norwood, Concord, Lexington, or Albemarle. A few likely made superior wages at the Southern Railway's new Spencer repair shops near Salisbury, which had opened in 1896. Others supplemented their income from farming with "extra money jobs," including short stints in the mines when they were open.

The traditional complementary relationship between mining and farming so evident at Gold Hill persisted for several decades into the twentieth century. That connection endured not only at the Rowan County site but also at other gold mines in a state that had embarked on an evolution from a largely agrarian economy to an urban-centered industrial society.

5

Other Mining Activity, 1865–1915

In the two generations between the Civil War and World War I, North Carolina changed from an almost totally agricultural and rural commonwealth to a state in which long-term socioeconomic trends reflected emerging, although far from dominant, industry and urbanism. As late as 1890, less than 7 percent of North Carolina workers were employed in manufacturing, but the state underwent an industrial revolution between 1870 and 1900. The number of people residing in urban areas nearly tripled and reached almost 10 percent of the total population. Whereas in 1870 only Wilmington had possessed more than ten thousand citizens, by 1900 five more towns—four of them in or near the Piedmont—claimed that distinction. Particularly after 1880 industrialism surged ahead in the state, building on some prewar industry. Textiles, tobacco, furniture, and railroads in the Piedmont headed the list. Between 1885 and 1915, for instance, the number of textile mills and textile workers increased fivefold—to 318 mills and 51,000 men, women, and children—while textile manufacturing capacity grew at even greater rates. Native white North Carolinians from middle- and upper-class families controlled nearly all of the textile industry, for which waterpower was the clear prime mover of choice well into the 1880s. As the state's agricultural economy recovered early in the immediate post-Civil War period, then declined markedly in the 1880s and 1890s, working for wages (however small) in factories was increasingly attractive to rural Carolinians.

Gold mining, an industry that had introduced such innovations as steam power, wage labor, corporations, and foreign or northern expertise to various parts of the Piedmont as early as the 1830s, recovered from its virtual cessation during the Civil War but did not approach its prewar attainments and became an ever smaller, eventually insignificant, factor in the state's postwar economy and society. Pent-up demand engendered a short-lived spurt of production in 1866, but it was less than any prewar year's output for a generation save for the depression years. In only nine of the next fifty years did production—insofar as recorded by the federal government—equal that of 1866, and 1915 proved to be a watershed, preceding another disastrous long-term drop in output.

Yet gold mining continued sporadically, characterized by a number of prewar themes: technological continuity and change, increasing attempts to recover gold from ever poorer ore, a clear connection between mining and farming, governmental interest in spurring the industry, and the allure of the mines to outside corporate investors. For a time, various mines were active or even innovative, but the industry, largely devoid of its antebellum vigor, deteriorated as the years passed.

After the Civil War ended, however, many North Carolinians and some northern visitors were anxious and ready to rebuild the state's economy, including mining. With the defeat of the Confederacy, much of North Carolina was forced to adjust to the destructive effects of the war. Railroads, factories, bridges, roads, public buildings, private homes, and barns had been destroyed or desperately needed repair. If the economy and well-being of the state were to be returned to their prewar conditions, moneys from one source or another would be required. As one state newspaper reported, "Thousands of men stand ready to embark in agriculture, mining, manufacturing, and merchandise, but the means for the encouragement of enterprise cannot be had. . . ." In short, some North Carolinians believed that northern or foreign capital would have to be invested in their state.

Almost immediately after the war ended, northern capitalists began visiting abandoned North Carolina mines. Various journals advertised the mines' rich possibilities. One such visitor was a Dr. R. P. Stevens, who inspected several mines in the Cabarrus, Rowan, and Davidson area. In the *American Journal of Mining*, Stevens painted an optimistic picture of the mines' potential. He claimed that there was a wealth of ready gold still available and that there were numerous promising opportunities for the investment of hundreds of thousands of dollars. He described the costs of milling ore and proclaimed that "many veins will give $4 to $10 per ton profit."

Other writers elaborated on the positive attributes of North Carolina gold mines. One advertisement claimed that aspiring miners could avoid the long trek to California by purchasing land in North Carolina and cultivating it while mining in their spare time, a reiteration of the old miner-farmer theme. The most frequently cited advantages of Carolina mines were that, with slavery abolished, cheap labor was plentiful; that several minerals could be mined at once, notably gold, copper, and zinc; and that the state's abundant timber and waterpower represented inexpensive resources required in the mining process. Despite such glowing optimism, nearly ten years elapsed before North Carolina's gold mines attracted an influx of northern and foreign funds. Throughout that period various factors, including lingering resentments connected with the Civil War and its aftermath, made it difficult for many political leaders of the defeated South to embrace any overtures by northern capitalists interested in rejuvenating the state's mining industry. As one authority of the state's history has written, during "the decade of 'military rule' [1865-1876] . . . the migrating northerner with his capital was turned away by southern politics and the cold process of ostracism."

While no extensive, systematic gold mining resumed in North Carolina prior to the 1870s, miners performed some preparatory work. In 1867 water in thirty-year-old shafts at the Rudisill mine was pumped out, and by the following year the main shaft was down to two hundred feet. In Gaston (later Cleveland) County, entrepreneurs at the old Kings Mountain mine built a twenty-stamp California mill in 1867, the first installation in the state of the all-iron stamp mill. At the same time, the superintendent of the well-known North State mine in Guilford County, P. D. Barnhardt, was buying more than twenty-seven hundred dollars' worth of mining equipment and readying his mine for operations. By 1867 eighteen to twenty stamp mills had either been erected or were being built in North Carolina, and four or five of them were in operation. The Howie mine in Union County had a ten-stamp mill and in 1867 was said to be producing three hundred dollars' worth of gold per day. By 1868 the Phoenix mine in Cabarrus County had steam power and a complete ten-stamp mill, and three or four mines near Charlotte were processing ore with crushing and amalgamating equipment. Enough activity was taking place throughout the mining region by 1869 that a national mining journal took notice of the revival.

As a result of increased interest in mining, the state, federal, and local governments attempted to aid the recovering but weakened industry. The Charlotte mint reopened in March 1868, but only as an assay office. No coins were minted there, but ingots valued at from ten to twenty thousand dollars were made and sent to Philadelphia for coinage. When in 1873 the possibility arose again that the federal government might discontinue or abolish the Charlotte assay office, the state legislature asked the state's senators and representatives in Congress to make that facility a permanent operation. Within two days, Congress granted funds for the office's continuance. The assay office remained in existence—no doubt partly as a pork barrel—for forty years. In 1878 mining leaders requested the Forty-fifth Congress to survey the quality and number of southern mines, but sixteen years passed before the government undertook that task. Meanwhile, in January of that year citizens

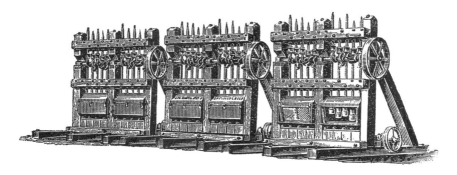

Cast-iron California stamp mills similar to the thirty-stamp model shown here began to be installed at North Carolina's gold mines shortly after the Civil War.

in Charlotte established a mining board "to consider some practicable method of advancing the mining interests of this section. . . ."

Unlike the ultimate fate of the assay office and the mining board, the state geological survey—reactivated after a lapse caused by the Civil War—proved durable and productive despite one additional expiration. Geologists George B. Hanna, J. A. Holmes, Joseph Hyde Pratt, and others published several notable reports on the state's gold deposits and mines, culminating in a long series of annual and biannual reports on the overall mining industry. Holmes, state geologist from 1891 to 1905, expanded the work of the agency to encompass broad economic development through use of natural resources such as minerals, forests, road-building materials, and water. Pratt succeeded Holmes in 1905 and further increased the diverse work of the Geological and Economic Survey, with particular emphasis on promoting improved roads for the state. In 1897, after numerous accidents in gold and coal mines, the legislature belatedly enacted legislation creating a state agency charged with inspecting and regulating mines. The law, aimed specifically at coal mines, applied to any mine with more than ten men. It authorized a state mining inspector to examine mines and keep statistics on safety, ownership, workers, and other data. The legislation established standards of ventilation in mines, specified minimum numbers of separate entrances and exits to mines, and mandated daily safety inspections.

While such efforts were being made, work under private initiative was proceeding at various mines. At Kings Mountain in 1872, the main shaft was 130 feet deep, and ore valued at fifteen dollars a ton was being extracted. Within a year, the engine shaft reached 200 feet, where a huge steplike excavation 200 feet long, 25 feet wide, and 35 feet high was carried out. Miners had extracted more than $1 million worth of gold from the mine since its first discovery. In 1875, $117,000 worth of gold reportedly was taken from the mine (a figure that appears highly inflated inasmuch as the following year the entire state's total production was only around $100,000), yet in 1876 the mine had 56,700 tons of ore with an estimated value of more than $400,000 ready to be processed. There was activity in other areas of the state as well. By 1875 considerable mining was under way again in the placer fields of the South Mountain area (Rutherford, Burke, and McDowell Counties), which lacked vein mines. In eastern North Carolina in 1875, the old Portis mine apparently experienced a fair amount of work. In 1878 J. Howard Jones attempted to reopen the well-known Silver Hill mine in Davidson County. Workers dewatered the shafts and hoisted a great deal of ore to the surface. A cave-in severely damaged the main shaft, however, and the mine, then the most extensively worked in North Carolina save for Gold Hill, closed. No significant mining occurred at Silver Hill after 1882, although decades later miners deepened the engine shaft to 876 feet during one of several intermittent periods of activity there.

Operations resumed at Gold Hill (see chapter 4) in 1870. For several years, as many as one hundred adults and children there worked old tailings. In 1874 the North Carolina Gold Amalgamating Company enlarged the operation and within a year reportedly erected a twenty-stamp mill. By 1875 there were 3 steam engines, 5 Chilean mills, 10 drag mills, 64 rockers, and a number of other devices in use. The town of Gold Hill soon had more than four hundred citizens, most of whom worked at the mine.

The renewed activity at Gold Hill and elsewhere proved that deep mining was an expensive business. Salaries had to be paid and costly equipment bought and maintained. At the Rudisill and the St. Catherine for a time during the 1870s, three shifts of miners worked on a twenty-four-hour operation. Ore diggers received $2.00 a day, while ore haulers on the surface earned $1.00 a day. The mine superintendent of Gold Hill in 1874 garnered $5.00 a day, while an engineer there was paid $2.00. An experienced miner might obtain a dollar a day. Most employees at Gold Hill, and probably at other mines, averaged about 50 to 75 cents per day. About 1880 the normal daily wage for a miner in North Carolina remained $1.00, and a foreman earned $2.00. By comparison, in Nevada such salaries at that time ranged from $4.00 to $6.00.

While salaries were a significant expense, machinery and supplies also were necessary. The price of a 180-horsepower steam engine averaged $2,500. A Blake crusher, widely used to reduce stones to the size of pebbles preparatory to their treatment in stamp mills, cost $1,200 in 1874. Other materials—such as wood, timber, iron, steel, candles, nitroglycerine powders, and quicksilver— had to be obtained. While in 1868 the average cost of sinking a shaft above water had been fifty cents a foot and underwater one dollar a foot, only eight years later one superintendent felt lucky to sink a large three-compartment

Blake-style ore and rock crusher. From contemporary advertisement.

shaft to a depth of three hundred feet for five thousand dollars. At Gold Hill in 1871 the normal cost of raising and processing ore was $13.64 per ton; that high cost required close supervision of underground mining.

As early as 1869 haste and waste already were evident in the renewed mining industry. Absentee owners often ordered expensive new mills and other machinery before physically examining mines. As a result, at many mines there was not enough prepared ore to keep a new machine in continual use. While gold mining was resumed partly by an inexperienced, new generation, much of the novel impetus resulted largely from earlier developments in the West. Miners with experience in California came to North Carolina and brought ideas and equipment. With relatively small ore bodies in the latter state, the western miners often discovered that the modern machinery, such as iron stamp mills, was less efficient than what it replaced. One local newspaper commented, "The old 'Long Tom' machine beats any patent process known. The improved machinery doesn't bother to try and get all the little specks of gold. . . ." At one leading mine about 1875, as little as 20 to 30 percent of the assay value of ore was saved, despite the use of newly developed equipment. Sometimes local mining superintendents were totally ignorant of the science of mining. One "mining engineer" from California had learned his trade by selling whiskey to western miners. Another, legitimate, engineer visiting the Kings Mountain mine in 1876 cited much inefficiency, noting that the pumps and stamp mill ran under "expensive and destructive methods." Wasteful operations, combined with inadequate supervision by unskilled, impractical managers, caused many state gold mines to fail. The fact that southern gold deposits were not as large or rich as in California or other western territories was likewise a factor. One leading mining journal reported that, unlike the West, the opportunity for very large returns was minimal. For example, between 1876 and 1879 North Carolina supposedly produced in all $435,000 worth of gold (mint figures), while in one year (1874) California alone produced more than $17 million worth.

Despite many local blunders prior to 1880, the ensuing decade saw a rise both in mining activity and the production of gold, as reported by federal officials. Between 1865 and 1900 North Carolina produced approximately $3.6 million worth of recorded gold, nearly half of it—some $1.5 million—in the 1880s, the pinnacle of postwar mining in the state. From 1880 to 1886 the state's rank as a gold producer varied from eleventh to thirteenth among all states. Official postwar output peaked in 1887 at $225,000 worth of gold, a sum equal to only about one-half of the totals for the best years of a generation earlier. Yet with national output in a typical year (1896) in excess of fifty million dollars, the Tar Heel role was minimal. A gradual diminution, with some upward blips, began in the 1890s. The census of 1880 revealed the existence of twelve active deep mines and three active placer mines. Of those placer operations, two were in Montgomery and the other was in Polk County. By 1881 the greatest part of accessible placer gold in the South Mountains, previously characterized as plentiful, had long since been exhausted. The underground mines employed 529 workers, including 309 subterranean miners, 185 surface workers, 21 administrative personnel, and 14 foremen. A decade later officials counted twenty-four active mines employing 882 men.

Table 5
North Carolina Mines Reporting to the Census of 1880

A. DEEP MINES:

County	Mine
Davidson	Conrad Hill
	Ethan Allen
	Eureka
	Silver Valley
Gaston	Kings Mountain
Guilford	Fisher and Willis
Mecklenburg	McGinn
	Rudisill
Moore	Henley Hill
Nash	Mann
Rowan	Dunn's Mountain
Stanly	Crowell

B. PLACERS:

County	Mine
Montgomery	Beaver Dam
	Sam Christian
Polk	Cochrane

The equipment in use at the mines reflected the national trend of modernization in mining, which seemed to require ever increasing amounts of capital and machinery to process ever rising tonnage of lower-grade ores. Nine of the twelve deep mines were equipped with ten hoisting steam engines, and two of those mines also employed steam-powered whims. All the mines except one used steel hoisting cables or hemp or manila rope; the McGinn mine in Mecklenburg reportedly was the only such facility in the nation that still utilized a chain. Census statisticians, relying upon incomplete data, accounted for only five operating stamp mills in the state; those mills maintained a total of seventy-five stamps. By 1885, in contrast, a Salisbury newspaper claimed that some four hundred stamps, twelve Chilean mills, and one chlorination plant were in use at forty-two active mines in North Carolina.

The presence of such equipment signaled that entrepreneurs, northern and foreign and especially British, were again investing in Tar Heel mines. Sites once abandoned lured prominent investors. Countless newspaper articles of the mid-1880s described such visitors touring the mining districts. By 1880 nine of the state's twelve deep mines and two of its placer mines were owned and run by northern men. A New York corporation with a capitalization of $1.2 million purchased the Kings Mountain in 1887. Nine years later a Pennsylvania company acquired the Rudisill for $40,000. The number of mines purchased by northern capitalists was so great that one naïve newspaper writer in 1886 exclaimed, "Our state is . . . to have her big success in mines and mining . . . the day of 'wild speculators' and humbugs is past in North Carolina."

Between 1880 and 1900 twenty-three British firms received charters to mine in North Carolina. While only seven were actually operated, the mines purchased by these companies were some of the largest and, traditionally, most successful in the state. An English syndicate bought Gold Hill (see chapter 4). Brokers in London sold stock in the Russell and Hoover Hill gold mines. British investors purchased two of the largest hydraulic mining enterprises in North Carolina. The Stanly Freehold (the old Parker placer mine, opened about 1805) in Stanly brought a price of $35,000, while in adjacent Montgomery the Sam Christian mine was acquired for $150,000. By 1888 British owners of the Sam Christian perhaps had invested more than $2.5 million in land and equipment. Unfortunately for investors, only a few of these British establishments actually paid dividends. By 1910 all but one of the twenty-three British companies were either dissolved, closed voluntarily, or had their properties seized by creditors.

Nevertheless, in 1880 North Carolina had ranked first in the Southeast in capitalization authorized by mining companies. The par value of stocks and bonds in Tar Heel mines was then $5.5 million; in Georgia, the next largest state, only $1.5 million worth of such securities was outstanding. Yet North Carolina's gold-mining role nationally was minimal: mining stock in Nevada

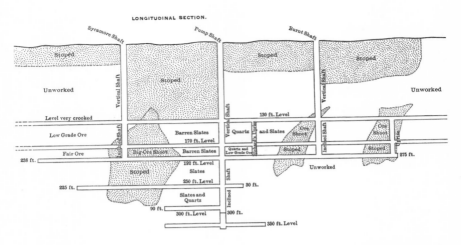

Rudisill mine, 1883, showing stoped (mined) areas and additional underground workings. From Nitze and Hanna, *Gold Deposits of North Carolina*, facing p. 127.

and California alone totaled well over $1 billion. Investors in gold mines in North Carolina received few profits. Such stock generally was regarded as of negligible worth. Still, by 1885 at least nine firms in North Carolina—including the Hoover Hill, the Phoenix, the Hunnicutt (Honeycutt), the Carolina Queen in Burke, the St. Catherine, and the Hiddenite in Alexander County—were paying at least some dividends.

During the 1880s a heightened public interest in mining and an influx of new capital resulted in renewed activity at a number of the state's leading gold mines. In Mecklenburg the three major mines continued to be the Rudisill, the St. Catherine, and the Capps. By 1883 miners at the Rudisill had reached the 350-foot level and were supplying sulfurets to a northern smelting plant, but in September 1888 the owners closed the mine after twelve years of operation. Meanwhile the St. Catherine, adjacent to the Rudisill, had been worked to 370 feet of vertical depth. In 1883 its operators purchased a ten-stamp mill to pulverize ore. The material was then treated to separate gold from pyrites, and pyrites and concentrates were sent north for smelting, despite the brief existence of at least two smelting companies in the area a few years earlier. Work was suspended in 1887 because of high operating costs. At the Capps, a few miles north, activity resumed in 1882 after four idle decades, and within two years a ten-stamp mill was erected. Apparently the miners did no underground work, inasmuch as the mill was used to process ore from surrounding dumps. By about 1885, when operations at the Capps terminated, total production there was estimated at $250,000. Nonetheless, about that time the editor of a newspaper declared: "There is more activity in the mining circles now than at any time since the war."

During the 1880s the Conrad Hill mine, located in Davidson County about six miles east of Lexington, was active. The Conrad Hill Gold and Copper Company worked the mine for those two metals. In 1880 the main shaft was down to 400 feet; two years later the mine's 130 employees worked twenty stamps, with ore averaging fifty-five dollars a ton. After copper had been extracted from the ore, the residue was treated for gold. The Conrad Hill in 1882 reportedly produced about twenty thousand dollars' worth of gold—more than any other mine in the state. The following year Conrad Hill again was a large producer: along with another mine, it yielded $49,000 worth of gold. Soon, however, the company ran into unexpected difficulties, culminating in 1886 in a bankruptcy auction.

In 1881 the only operating mine in western North Carolina was Kings Mountain, in Gaston County, which had been worked to a depth of 320 feet. A year later the mine was one of the most completely outfitted in the state. By 1883 it boasted forty stamps but produced a mere $3,500 in gold during part of the year. The ore was of a low grade (worth about $3 to $8 per ton) but, because it contained relatively few sulfates, was cheap to mill; and labor cost only fifty cents to one dollar a day per man. The mine continued to operate into the summer of 1895, when it finally closed. At that time, the mine employed twenty men, who raised forty tons of ore daily. The mine's cumulative production to that time was said to be from $750,000 to $1 million.

The North State, or McCullock, mine in Guilford County reached 325 feet in depth in 1884. A year earlier its owners had purchased a ten-stamp mill to pulverize ore from previously extracted rock. The old ore failed to provide a profit, and by 1886 the mine lay abandoned. The pumps were removed and shipped elsewhere, a common practice with costly machinery. At two other old Guilford mines—the Gardner Hill and Fentress (copper) facilities—little work occurred after 1865. Some fifteen miles south, in Randolph County, production continued at the Hoover Hill mine from 1881 to 1895.

During the early 1880s work began at the Coggins, or Appalachian, mine in Montgomery about fifteen miles north of Troy. In 1882 laborers undertook only testing work, but within a year water-powered Chilean mills were in use and the yield was four thousand dollars' worth of gold. By 1887 the Coggins had a forty-stamp mill. The mine and stamps ran until 1896, when the owners moved the stamps to another mine in Randolph County. Years later the mine was reopened for a time.

Through much of the 1880s the English owners of Gold Hill (see chapter 4) were generally unsuccessful, despite occasional high points. Mining engineer Richard Eames installed a twenty-stamp mill and dewatered the Randolph shaft to the 750-foot level, and George Crampton, a graduate of the

Royal School of Mines, subsequently supervised operations. For a brief period, air drills resounded through the mine night and day, replacing some human muscle power. Yet lack of working capital crippled the company. By 1891 the estimated value of all production since 1842 passed five million dollars, yet the financially stricken mine was inactive except for pumping to keep the water down. The following year the British company pulled out, and only spasmodic operations occurred until work ceased in 1895.

In the 1880s, despite continued serious problems at leading mines across North Carolina, several new mines began operations in the state. In Montgomery County late in the decade, so the story goes, a tenant on the Tebe Saunders farm by accident kicked nuggets out of an uprooted stump. By 1889 one hundred employees worked there, recovering in one week two thousand pennyweights of gold worth in excess of two thousand dollars at that time. By year's end, the Tebe Saunders mine purportedly yielded more than two hundred thousand dollars' worth of gold. In 1890 ownership changed three times, with the third purchaser paying one hundred thousand dollars for the property. The new owner, a New York company, planned to enlarge the enterprise, but by 1896 operations ceased. Another noted mine was the Ingram, or Crawford, discovered in 1892 some four miles southeast of Albemarle. For lack of water, the placer mine was worked only periodically. In 1894 the Crawford Gold Mining Company purchased it and built a two hundred-cubic-yard wooden tank to supply water. Richard Eames traveled from Gold Hill to supervise the enterprise. All gold at the mine was in nugget form rather than dust or grains. In April 1895 miners found an eight-pound nugget, followed in a year by a ten-pound rock. Twenty-five men processed forty-five cubic yards of ore daily at a cost of fifty cents per yard. Laborers received sixty to sixty-five cents a day. In 1896 promoters claimed that more than one hundred thousand dollars' worth of gold had been recovered, an extravagant claim likely exceeding the entire state's output. Shortly thereafter, the mine was inactive.

Prior to 1880, hydraulic mining, perfected in California by the early 1860s, was rarely seen in North Carolina. The process avoided costly underground work but demanded large outlays for dams, reservoirs, and pipelines. Experts knew that hydraulic mining would be successful in the state only at a few locations, since most Carolina gold was found in thin streaks less than three feet wide, far different from thick California gravels. One writer pointed out that "the returns—considering the risk—will be small, . . . no 'bonanza' need be expected . . . no operations can be successful unless the strictest economy is observed."

Yet in the 1880s miners began several hydraulic operations. One of the first, and probably the largest, was in Montgomery County at the Sam Christian mine, which had received only sporadic prior attention despite large ore deposits. In 1879 a new firm (capitalized at $600,000) acquired the mine

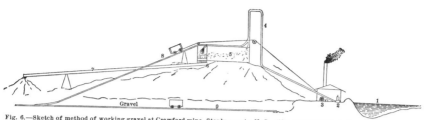

Fig. 6.—Sketch of method of working gravel at Crawford mine, Stanly county, N. C. (Not drawn to scale.) 1, reservoir; 2, pump; 3, hoisting engine; 4, stand-pipe; 5, washing-box; 6, grizzly; 7, sluices; 8, inclined plane; 9, track on bedrock.

Sketch showing how gravel was processed at the Ingram (Crawford) mine in Stanly County. From Nitze and Wilkens, *Gold Mining in North Carolina*, 92.

and its 1,286 acres. In a one-year period the mine operated for only eighty-eight days because of a shortage of water. The company constructed reservoirs and dams and planned an extensive placer operation, but accidental damage to a dam resulted in closure of the mine for several years. Mining resumed in 1887, when an English syndicate, the Sam Christian Gold Hydraulic Company, Ltd., purchased the mine for $150,000. That company naïvely projected a yearly profit of more than $300,000. Large shipments of equipment arrived, and more than a hundred men worked to install the machinery. By October 1888 the mine was ready to start operations. One observer guessed that the owners had invested more than two million dollars, but a skeptical journalist predicted poor returns for the investment. Two months later the company faced a lawsuit as a result of the discharge of gravel and other pollutants, but the Superior Court of Montgomery County refused to issue an injunction to stop the mining, which still employed dozens of people. Water for the mine came from the Yadkin River. Because the mine was 416 feet above the river, it was necessary to elevate the water. Two large Worthington pumps and five 100-horsepower boilers delivered up to 5.5 million gallons of water each day. The water was pumped three miles to the mine through a 20-inch pipe. One newspaper called the Sam Christian the biggest hydraulic establishment in the nation. The operation, which must have been extremely expensive, closed by 1893.

Another large hydraulic works was the Stanly Freehold (the old Parker) in northern Stanly County. English capitalists purchased and renamed that mine in 1887. Civil engineers planned another pipeline to bring water from the Yadkin River, and a quick migration to the village of Bilesville, optimistically renamed New London, took place. Carpenters arrived daily, men began laying a twenty-inch pipe four miles from the river to the mine, and mechanics set up machinery. By the end of 1888, New London's population was said to be four hundred people. More than a thousand men were employed, at least briefly, in

At the Stanly Freehold mine, British investors introduced hydraulic mining—the use of high-pressure water to wash away earth and rocks. Photograph from Nitze and Wilkens, *Gold Mining in North Carolina*, facing p. 54.

Stanly and Montgomery mines. The most prominent feature of New London was a gigantic 90-foot tank. Water from it ran a quarter of a mile to the mine site through a 14-inch-diameter pipe that gradually decreased to 2 inches at the nozzle. The system was equipped to provide 1.5 million gallons of water every twenty-four hours. The water washed away all dirt down to solid rock, and the dirt was sent through a long line of troughs with riffle boxes to collect gold. Large deposits of gold reportedly were found; in one six-week period miners recovered nearly seven pounds of the precious metal. Capt. Henry A. Judd, a knowledgeable English miner, managed the facility. Unlike the larger Sam Christian and most other Tar Heel mining companies, the Stanly Freehold paid dividends to its stockholders. In October 1895 an explosion occurred at the mine when two African American workers, preparing some dynamite, dropped a candle on the powder. The blast killed the two men instantly. Shortly thereafter, the Stanly Freehold ceased operations for a time.

One of the more successful deep mines of the 1880s was the Phoenix in Cabarrus County. Mining probably resumed at the Phoenix prior to 1880, as a ten-stamp mill was reported to be in operation there in 1868 and a post office had been established in 1876. By April 1881 the monthly payroll reached $2,000, stimulating local business. Superintendent Adolph Thies apparently

Mill and chlorination plant, Phoenix mine, Cabarrus County, ca. 1900. From Joseph Hyde Pratt, *The Mining Industry in North Carolina during 1906*, North Carolina Geological and Economic Survey Economic Paper No. 14 (Raleigh: E. M. Uzzell and Co., State Printers and Binders, 1907), facing p. 60.

never let a month pass without paying employees. Mining officials spent more than $4,000 for equipment from the Mecklenburg Iron Works that year. The following year fifty men processed about $20,000 worth of gold. Production rose, and in 1885 the Phoenix was one of about ten gold mines in North Carolina that paid dividends to stockholders. By 1887 the Phoenix, at a depth of 425 feet, was among the largest mines in the state and reportedly yielded $3,500 worth of gold per month. For two years the mine's annual gross output was $20,000, which gave Thies $15,000 a year to put into wages. Activity stopped in 1889 when he moved to the Haile mine in South Carolina. No additional mining was recorded at the Phoenix until 1897, when copper apparently was mined.

The true importance of the Phoenix was not the gold it furnished but the chlorination process perfected there by Thies. Experts had long known that deeper Carolina ore was so refractory that simple pulverization and amalgamation was inadequate for processing. Many productive mines had been abandoned suddenly at the water level. In the 1880s the most promising new treatment for refractory ore was chlorination, which involved use of a chemical solvent to separate gold. The technique had been developed in Europe and used commercially in Germany by 1848, reaching California ten years later.

While the procedure had many complicated steps, basically "pulverized and roasted ore was first placed in tanks and allowed to steep in chlorine gas, which drew the sulfides from the gold; the gold was then leached out of the mixture with water." The new method, successful in processing refractory ore, had several drawbacks. First, chlorination was dangerous, as chlorine gas is a deadly killer. The process was also expensive: the gas had to be purchased, stored in costly pressure tanks, and was lost after one use. Many attempts were made to adapt the method so that low-grade ores could be treated profitably; numerous patented methodologies, differing only in one or two detailed steps, appeared. The cost of chlorination was most important in the South, because ores there were not as rich or plentiful as in the West.

At the Phoenix mine in the early 1880s Adolph Thies developed a cheap chlorination process by adapting an earlier procedure to low-grade southern ores. While less than 40 percent of the assayed value of ore could be saved by previous techniques, Thies's method reputedly extracted 94 to 97 percent of the value and became known as the "Thies system." The innovative technology had several advantages: it was not patented, the cost of the plant was reasonable, and there was a high percentage of extraction. Thies's chlorination was found profitably to process ore worth only four dollars a ton; by 1898 his system was in use at many mines. Thies, a German educated at the European mining school at Lieger, had immigrated in 1860 to work in copper mines at Ducktown, Tennessee, after managing mines in Germany and South Africa. During the Civil War, he operated a lead mine in South Carolina. Thies was at the Phoenix from 1878 to 1889, then went to South Carolina to achieve his greatest success. In 1893 officials asked him to demonstrate his process at the World's Columbian Exposition. With the Phoenix the most active mine in Cabarrus County in 1885 and 1886, annual production in the county was fourteen thousand dollars and eighteen thousand dollars respectively.

Despite some new technology, during the 1890s North Carolina mines produced less than half their output of the 1880s. By mid-decade the value of annual yields had fallen to fifty thousand dollars or less, and by 1896 most mines across the state were abandoned and inaccessible. While twenty mines allegedly made deposits at the Charlotte assay office in 1897, the total amount was only $34,600. Of the twenty, few were steady producers; most merely experienced prospecting and developmental work. The major factor in the decline of gold mining in the state, and the entire South, was the low quantity and quality of remaining ore. As years passed, miners found ore increasingly more refractory and more costly to process with the technology then available. The census of 1890 notes that the cost of producing $318,000 in southern gold in 1889 was $535,000. The cost of processing $145,000 worth of Tar Heel gold was calculated at $286,000. In short, the cost of a dollar in gold was almost two dollars; obviously such mining was not profitable. In 1896 no southern mine met the western requirement of being a good mine, that is, one that paid dividends even under poor management.

Such inept leadership caused many southern mine failures. By 1895 the southern gold fields for many years had been the playground of dubious technicians, promoters, and inventors. Numerous mines had been directed by innocent amateurs or dishonest bunglers. Visitors often found poorly administered enterprises rather than efficient work. That pattern had continued so long that one expert concluded that "solicitations to engage in the mining of gold in the South are not entirely free from the danger of a commission *de lunatico enquirendo*." Another observer bluntly asserted that "ignorance, stupidity, and mismanagement" were the key reasons for failures. As a result, mines in the state and the South gained a bad reputation among investors.

If investors risked their money, miners—as always—risked life and limb in their physically difficult and dangerous occupation. Employees worked with such equipment as nitroglycerine, dynamite, blasting caps, blasting powder, and fuses. Such supplies, coupled with an unsafe, underground environment, made dangers apparent. Census officials in 1880 recorded two fatalities during 1879 and eight nonfatal accidents. The ratio of men killed or injured to the total work force was one to fifty-three. One miner in sixty-six was hurt, while one of 264 was injured fatally. From newspaper accounts one gains the impression that many unfortunate incidents occurred in or near shafts. Timbers giving way and ore buckets falling were common occurrences. Dynamite explosions killed several men, while underground cave-ins happened frequently. One grim story told of a miner who, holding a drill for someone else, carelessly looked aside and had a finger smashed. When no one would cut off the smashed finger, the miner "coolly took out his knife and cut it off himself." Such events and dangers affected the daily lives of the men. Many miners purportedly were heavy drinkers and pursued their work "with energy and a large outlay of spirits." As the *Concord Times* expressed it, "Gold is found in 36 counties in this state, Silver in 3, . . . and whiskey in all of them, and the last gets away with all the rest."

Both black and white men toiled in gold mines. In 1898 the state labor department estimated that miners earned an average of 60 cents to $1.25 for a ten-hour shift. One mining superintendent, who employed from seventy-five to three hundred African Americans, commented, "As a hammer man in the mine the Negro cannot be surpassed by any other nationality." He noted, however, that the black laborer did not "like to work with an English miner, because he has to strike through the whole shift. The English miner wants to hold the drill all the time." More times than not, experienced workers were supervisors or machinery technicians, leaving more physical labor to the blacks and some whites.

Charlotte's Mecklenburg Iron Works lightened some backbreaking labor by supplying machinery to mines throughout the South. The company had

Amalgamation table, screen, and mortar of Mecklenburg Iron Works stamp mill at Reed Gold Mine State Historic Site.

been established by 1846, and after 1859 it belonged to John Wilkes, son of miner Charles Wilkes. During the Civil War the foundry served as a Confederate navy yard. After the war, Wilkes helped begin the First National Bank of Charlotte. In 1874, with mining resuming, he devoted his whole energy to the ironworks. Soon the company made mining machinery, including steam boilers, engines, pumps, and chlorination systems. Its most famous machine was its iron stamp mill, a high-quality variation on the mill refined in California.

With the arrival of new machinery, despite decreased production and increasing problems with refractory ore in the 1890s, some men still held hope for the fading industry. In 1892 North Carolina governor Thomas M. Holt dispatched a delegation to the National Mining Congress with expectations that renewed interest in the state's gold could be rekindled. Two years later the state geologist, J. A. Holmes, announced that mining soon would reach stability. In 1896 New South spokesman Richard H. Edmunds, editor of the *Manufacturers' Record* of Baltimore, claimed that southern gold ore still offered a "good chance for solid development." Nonetheless, the industry was not rejuvenated in the twentieth century, although limited work continued sporadically, generating an average output that for a time exceeded that of the 1890s.

The first fifteen years of the twentieth century witnessed a renewed effort to modernize the industry in parts of the state. Although in 1900 only $28,500 worth of gold was produced, within five years the figure jumped fourfold. In 1915, $172,000 worth of gold was processed, the largest production in any year since 1887. The rising output resulted largely from the application of new mining and processing methods to low-grade ores previously found unprofitable, a habitual experiment in the mining industry. One such attempt—copied from the West and Alaska but unsuccessful in North Carolina—was dredging, whereby various streams in the mining districts could be worked on a large scale. By 1899 one company reportedly was mining the Uwharrie River. The following year the Catawba Placer Mining Company had acquired rights to mine along more than six miles of the Catawba River. Dredging was under way in Halifax County in 1904, and three years later miners used the technique in creeks near the old Portis mine. Yet the amount of gold produced by dredging was minimal. In 1901 workers recovered only twenty-one dollars' worth of metal with the procedure, and the following year it practically was abandoned. While U.S. mint statistics reveal that $123,900 worth of gold was mined in 1904, only $456 resulted from dredging.

The most dramatic improvement in gold processing, which created a global "rush" to low-grade ores and old tailings, was the cyanide process, which helped double annual world production. Earlier, chlorination also had offered hope of profits from low-grade ore. Chlorination, especially the Thies system, was successful at some mines, but at others the method simply did not work. Promoters claimed that the cyanide process would actually do what chlorination had only promised. Experiments with cyanide had occurred since 1844, but it was not until 1889 that a successful cyanide process was developed. J. S. MacArthur, a chemist, and two physicians—R. W. Forrest and W. Forrest— all of Scotland, patented the MacArthur and Forrest system in 1890. Basically "the pulp [slurry of ore] was treated with a weak solution of cyanide of potassium, which has a strong solvent action on gold, which subsequently was precipitated by zinc or by electrolysis." The first successful commercial treatment of low-grade ore with cyanide in the United States occurred in Utah in 1891. While miners attempted cyanidation at no fewer than five locations in North Carolina prior to 1900, none was profitable. During the early 1900s, however, with improvements in the milling of ore, several mines in the state successfully used cyanidation. By 1903 a large plant had been built at the Howie mine in Union County, and within a few years other mines, such as the Phoenix, the Iola, and the Uwharrie, were experimenting with the cyanide process.

In 1902 the U.S. Census Bureau listed fifteen producing mines in North Carolina. Those mines employed 327 workers, of whom 122 worked underground. Only eight mines operated for more than nine months that year. The authorized stock of mining companies in the state totaled $26,362,000, yet apparently none of the ventures paid dividends. Still, in 1903 the number of mines either producing or conducting developmental work increased to thirty-seven. Mines such as the Ingram/Crawford, Parker, Gold Hill, Howie, Capps, and Portis actually yielded gold. By 1905 seven placer mines and sixteen underground mines produced more than $125,000 worth of the precious metal.

About 1905 the new St. Catherine and Rudisill Gold Mining Company of New York leased both Charlotte mines whose names it bore. The Rudisill had not been worked since 1888. The company hired George E. Price, a mining engineer with South African experience. His men dewatered the Rudisill, installed a new pump and hoist, and enlarged and extended tunnels in both mines. In 1907 the Rudisill operated extensively, shipping ore to northern smelters, and the company planned to put in new machinery for crushing, amalgamation, and cyanidation of ore. That effort must have proven too costly, for by 1908 the company defaulted and the mine again was idle and offered at auction. In 1917 fire destroyed the Rudisill's hoist and other machinery.

Meanwhile, by 1903 cyanide was used successfully to treat sulfide ores at the Howie, the largest mine in Union County. A new owner, the Colossus Gold Mining and Milling Company, worked the mine extensively, then sold the facility for $241,000. By 1912 the 250 acres at the mine were owned by the Howie Mining Company. The mine, then 355 feet deep, yielded ore valued at ten to thirty dollars a ton. From 1913 to 1915 the Howie was the largest gold producer in Union County, although the value of its output averaged perhaps only three thousand dollars a year. A fire in 1916 resulted in months of repairs, and—like most other North Carolina mines—the Howie soon closed.

In 1910 the Coggins mine in Montgomery County was dewatered for the first time in twenty-four years. The main shaft was retimbered, and some crosscutting and drifting was done. The operators installed a slow Lane Chilean mill with amalgamating and concentrating equipment, and the mine became the leading producer of gold in the county. In 1911 a visiting mining engineer stated that $4,820 in gold had been recovered at the Coggins by amalgamation of 1,698 tons of ore—an average of $2.84 per ton. An additional 35 tons of concentrates assayed $49 per ton, the total value being $1,715. Early in 1912 fire destroyed the mine's equipment. The firm reorganized as the Rich Cog Mining Company and erected a new ten-stamp mill, an office, an assay office, a manager's house, and a pumping plant on the Uwharrie River. The daily capacity of the mill, which had large 1,050-pound stamps, was thirty to forty tons of ore. Soon the mine was down to 268 feet with about 1,000 feet of drifts and crosscuts. Until 1916 the mine experienced a great deal of developmental work.

The state's deepest mines—at Gold Hill—were three times as deep as the Coggins and also boasted the largest physical plant of any Tar Heel mine. Yet far more copper (for a time by design) than gold was produced at Gold Hill from 1900 to 1915. The mines there operated sporadically under the independent leadership of energetic and flamboyant promoter Walter George Newman and visionary engineer E. B. C. Hambley. During that period Gold

Hill (see chapter 4) was at times the busiest mining district in the state and on other occasions a run-down place of sparse mining activity.

Between 1900 and 1915 little mining was performed in the eastern slate geologic belt of Warren, Halifax, Franklin and Nash Counties, more than a hundred miles east of Gold Hill and the state's other chief mines. In 1900 twenty men reportedly worked near Ransom's Bridge for about six months with unknown success. The total value of gold extracted in the four counties in 1902, as recorded by state geologists, was about $2,400—less than 3 percent of the state's output. The following year the Portis mine in Franklin and the Mann-Arrington mine in Nash each produced only a few hundred dollars' worth of gold. In 1905 and 1906 combined, the Mann-Arrington yielded more than $3,000 worth of gold; never again would it produce so much. In 1911 operators installed a new plant at the Portis with a capacity of one hundred cubic yards of gravel per day. The novel excavating machinery consisted of a radial cableway able to dig with a scraper bucket in a circle sixteen hundred feet in diameter. A pumping plant delivered one thousand gallons of water per minute through a pipeline one mile in length. Costs were expected not to exceed six cents per cubic yard, but in two years the facility yielded only two thousand dollars' worth of gold. The mine closed, reopened in 1915, and then soon closed again.

Miners recovered substantially more gold in Cabarrus County at the Phoenix mine, which in 1902 produced, according to state geologists, about $1,200 worth of gold. The Miami Mining Company invested $75,000 in developmental work and opened 3,932 feet of underground shafts, drifts, and crosscuts. Workers blocked out and made ready for processing an estimated 35,000 tons of ore. The mine had a ten-stamp mill, several concentrating tables, and a cyanide plant to process tailings. Renamed the Miami, the Phoenix was worked vigorously in 1904 with cyanidation and chlorination, the latter more successful. By 1905 Cabarrus County produced more than $22,000 worth of gold annually, largely from the well-equipped Miami, with its chlorination system, ten stamps, and electric pump and generator. In 1906 the cyanide plant was inactive, inasmuch as the ore could not be worked economically owing to a 2 percent copper content. The mine was worked only four months that year before it closed. From 1908 to 1912 a small output of gold was obtained by working old ore dumps, but substantial activity soon ceased.

One of the most productive mines in North Carolina in the early twentieth century was the Iola, discovered in 1901 about eight miles southeast of Troy in Montgomery County. By 1902 the Iola Mining Company had a ten-stamp mill and furnished $15,000 worth of gold between June and October, making it the largest producer in the state at that time. The following year the company added ten more stamps and a cyanide plant to treat tailings, and the mine produced nearly $45,000 worth of gold. In 1904 the Iola was worked extensively at the 250-foot level and was again the chief producer of Montgomery's $50,460 worth of gold, joining Gold Hill and the Haile in South Carolina as the most important mines in the South at that time. The Iola was the state's largest producer of gold for the next several years, with ore valued from a few dollars to more than thirty dollars a ton. The main vein, often eight feet wide, consisted of "soft white sugary quartz." The state geological survey reported that Montgomery County yielded more than $52,000 worth of gold in 1907. The Iola's superintendent, Milton L. Jones, displayed a gold bar worth $5,000, claiming that it was the result of only fifteen days of work. Three months later he showed three more gold bricks valued at $10,000, the product of two weeks of labor.

Early in 1908 new machinery arrived at the mine, but the owners apparently over-equipped the facility. A new 200-horsepower boiler furnished steam for the entire mine, where even underground workings were illuminated by electricity. The operators added forty stamps—twenty from an old mine and twenty from the Mecklenburg Iron Works—and expected to process $12,000 worth of gold monthly. The Iola's cumulative output passed $300,000 in eight years, but profits were marginal. In August 1908 the Iola Mining Company, with liabilities perhaps exceeding assets, was reorganized as the Candor Mines Company. The Iola produced little gold in 1909, inasmuch as the surface plant evidently was being remodeled. The facility operated for six months in 1910 before being destroyed by fire. In 1911 the company constructed a new plant with a battery of five 1,750-pound Allis-Chalmers stamps—the heaviest stamps in the United States, twenty times heavier than stamps initially utilized at Charlotte about 1830—and a capacity of fifty tons per day. The mill also used cyanide, along with other up-to-date techniques and technologies. Treatment cost per ton of ore was estimated at $1.64. Only seven employees worked in the millhouse: two millmen earned $2.50 each, two "solution men" were paid $1.85 each, two mill helpers received $1.65 each, and a "filter man" was entitled to $2.00. The mine operated two twelve-hour shifts, and labor for the millhouse cost only $14 per day. The following year the Iola produced the bulk of the $149,000 worth of reported Montgomery County gold, making the mine the largest gold producer east of the Black Hills. In 1913 the Iola's output decreased slightly, and after that date state officials received no further reports of production. Late in 1914 the owners of an adjacent mine—itself barely active—purchased the Iola. Operations at both mines ended by 1916.

At the end of 1915 gold production in North Carolina plummeted suddenly and dramatically from a level of a few thousand ounces annually to a sparse several hundred ounces per year. The state's diminished officially reported output in 1916 was about equal to the recorded product of 1827. In the sixteen years after 1916, cumulative production tallied by government

In the early twentieth century, the Howie mine (*top*) and the Iola mine (*bottom*), among others, employed the cyanide process to recover gold. Photo at top courtesy North Carolina Geological Survey; at bottom from Joseph Hyde Pratt, *The Mining Industry in North Carolina during 1911 and 1912*, Geological and Economic Paper No. 34 (Raleigh: E. M. Uzzell and Co., State Printers and Binders, 1914), facing p. 15.

geologists was barely half that of 1915 alone. By 1918 not a single deep gold mine was operating in the state.

Several factors contributed to the precipitous decline. To begin with, few miners were willing to acknowledge publicly the fundamental and enduring problem: an obvious lack of sulfur-free or low-sulfur ore able to be extracted and processed economically. Moreover, the sudden closing in April 1915 of Walter George Newman's Gold Hill mine in Rowan, a county that alone accounted for more than one-fourth of the gold produced in North Carolina at that time, surely sullied the state's already disreputable reputation among potential investors in gold mines. Between 1915 and 1916 Montgomery County, home of the Iola mine, saw the value of its reported gold production fall from $90,324 to $4,408. Specific records of various key mines are not available to help explain the huge decline. Although virtually all of the twenty-three British companies formed between 1880 and 1900 to mine gold in North Carolina were defunct by late 1910, it was undoubtedly Britain's involvement since late 1914 in World War I that drew the attention of financiers in England and America away from gold mining in the state. The conflict quickly made investing in war production much more necessary, strategic, and profitable than continuing to pour capital into such a risky enterprise as mining. Even within North Carolina, the overall production of minerals—in contrast to that of gold—rose dramatically between 1915 and 1916 and again in 1917, although the state was home to a number of other dynamic industries (such as textiles) of major significance to a wartime economy.

Meanwhile, North Carolina had changed radically since 1865. For one thing, it was abundantly obvious by 1915 (yet hardly a secret for two generations before that year) that what was then perceived as the state's easily recoverable and reasonably profitable gold had been exhausted. Since the end of the Civil War, gold mining had been a small and diminishing factor in the state's economy. More importantly, while agriculture (so long a partner of sorts to mining) still greatly exceeded industry in providing employment, the pace of change to industrialism was beginning to accelerate with the rising prospects for invigorated Piedmont industries such as textiles, tobacco, and furniture manufacturing. Thus, for most North Carolinians of the twentieth century, gold mining in their state would be, if anything, a memory, often faded and not always pleasant, or perhaps a romantic dream. While not even a near doubling of the price of gold in dollars two decades later would revive the failed industry (for the bulk of the high-grade gold was indeed gone), some fascinating and enduring aspects of North Carolina's evolving mining heritage were yet to emerge in the mid- to late twentieth century.

Legacies: The Heritage of Gold Mining, 1915-1999

In a few locations, North Carolina's gold mining industry continued to function after 1915, by which time Gold Hill and other major properties had closed. Among those mines, the Coggins near Eldorado in Montgomery County was the most productive in the 1910s and 1920s. The Rich Cog Mining Company had reached the 550-foot level by 1920 and later erected a fifty-stamp mill powered by electricity, using both amalgamation with quicksilver and the cyanide process to capture the precious metal. Despite this sizable investment, the assay value of the ore samples could not justify further development, and the mine closed by 1930.

The Great Depression rekindled a brief flurry of activity in the gold region. Such factors as rising gold prices (from $20.67 to $35.00 an ounce), low labor costs, and a new process known as "flotation" (a method of separating minerals through a controlled combination of water, oil, and chemicals) encouraged a few noteworthy developments. At the Rudisill mine in Mecklenburg County, a company invested $75,000 in the mid-1930s and produced $130,000 worth of ore over three years. At the old Howie mine in Union County, a Canadian company in the early 1930s erected a cyanide plant with a one-hundred-ton daily capacity. The company continued mining operations until an order from the War Production Board in 1942 limited gold production. (In the early 1960s a High Point company remodeled the plant at the Howie mine and there produced some $150,000 worth of gold—actually from ore taken from the Star mine in Montgomery County—over a four-year period before shutting down.)

At the celebrated Gold Hill mines, there were occasional but unsuccessful attempts to revive the industry. Test runs of ore through a ten-stamp mill in 1925 produced modest returns. In 1930 the Rowan Mining Company, with several descendants of Gold Hill miners as officers, attempted to operate the ore-washing plant using piles of wasted ore as raw material. Unfortunately, those miners did not inherit the good fortune of their ancestors, and the

Small stamp mill in use in Cabarrus County during the Great Depression.

company disbanded without establishing any record of gold production. Perhaps the saddest story associated with gold fever there concerned C. R. Hays, a mining engineer, who took up residence at the old Gold Hill hotel and office after World War II and tried to produce gold from the Randolph shaft. For two decades he lived alone amid stacks of records from former companies and a large brood of dogs, possibly as many as fifty. In 1969 a fire killed Hays and the dogs and destroyed many of the records. The Carolina gold rush had sputtered to a dramatic and tragic end.

Vestiges of the gold mining industry are found throughout the Piedmont region, and several notable efforts to preserve the heritage of mining have occurred. Gold Hill is now a tiny rural settlement of some one hundred people. A highway historical marker reminds motorists along U.S. Highway 52 that at one time the Gold Hill mining district was the most productive in the state. The Methodist church still holds regular services in the sanctuary built about 1855 and maintains a cemetery that contains the graves of Cornish miners and their families. In 1992 local citizens established a new organization known as the Historic Gold Hill and Mines Foundation "to attain, restore, maintain, and preserve the mining town of Gold Hill and the mines for the continuation and perpetuation of the tradition upon which the town and surrounding area was established." Mauney's Store, the old jail, and other buildings are now open to visitors, and a community park, constructed near the Barnhardt and Miller shafts, is now the setting for annual festivals and special events.

North Carolina has preserved its mining heritage in several ways. In addition to the sign at Gold Hill, highway historical markers recognize the Bechtler mint, the Portis and Reed mines, St. Joseph's Catholic Church in Gaston County (built in 1843 for Irish immigrant miners), and the Charlotte branch mint. Mines in that city—notably the Rudisill and St. Catherine—and the Barringer mine in Montgomery County have been approved for recognition by such markers. In Guilford County, near Jamestown, the McCullock gold mill, erected in 1832 to house steam engines that drove Chilean mills, has been rebuilt, but not as a true historic site. The complex, now known as Castle McCullock, features some recent additions, including facilities for weddings, corporate social functions, and panning for gold and gemstones. Tourists can also pan for gold at other places, including the Cotton Patch Gold Mine in New London. In Charlotte, the Mint Museum of Art occupies the building (now relocated and altered) that served as the United States branch mint from 1837 to 1861 and as a federal assay office until 1913. Some of these sites also are listed on the National Register of Historic Places. Such properties include the aforementioned Bechtler mint and the McCullock gold mill. Additional National Register-listed properties in North Carolina with connections to gold mining include the Gardner House (with the Gardner Hill mine site) in Guilford County, the Kindley farm and mine in Randolph County, and the Morrison House and Pioneer Mills mine in Cabarrus County.

One of the unique landmarks of the late mining era is the mansion built by E. B. C. Hambley at 508 South Fulton Street in Salisbury. Hambley commissioned architect Charles C. Hook of Charlotte to design the house as both a residence and a lavish showpiece to entertain prospective investors in his industrial and engineering projects. The house consists of three stories and a basement and is constructed entirely of granite quarried from Hambley's property in Rowan County. The grounds of the estate are as impressive as the residence itself. A large carriage house included servants' bedrooms, an area for vehicles, and stalls for horses. Both the entrance and exit to the property have large iron gates, and a third gate leads straight to the steps of the front porch. In the side yard, Hambley maintained a tennis court. Hambley died within three years of moving into his mansion, although his family occupied the estate until 1917. For most of the twentieth century, the house and grounds have been faithfully preserved by two generations of the Wallace family, and the Hambley-Wallace House is a prominent component of Salisbury's National Register Historic District.

The Reed mine in Cabarrus County became a National Historic Landmark (the highest level of recognition offered by the National Park Service) in 1966 and a state historic site in December 1971 when the heirs of Armin Kelly donated to the state of North Carolina seventy acres containing the most significant remains of the mining area. The state purchased the remaining 753

Salisbury mansion completed in 1903 for visionary industrialist E. B. C. Hambley.

acres from the family at a price well below appraised value. The historic site, administered by the state Division of Archives and History, opened in April 1977 with a new visitor center and more than four hundred feet of restored underground tunnels. At the dedication ceremony, Gov. James B. Hunt Jr. observed that "here at this site, we can learn something about a people who . . . met the challenges of boom and bust. They discovered and profited from a rare and precious resource. When that resource grew more and more scarce, they learned a new way of life. We face that same prospect today as we learn a new way of life, dealing with resources that grow more and more scarce." Reed Gold Mine is now open all year free to the public with a color orientation film, special events, exhibits on mining history and technology, guided underground tours, a restored and operating stamp mill, picnic grounds, and numerous trails. More than sixty thousand visitors come to the site annually, drawn by the opportunity to pan for gold along Little Meadow Creek and learn about America's first gold rush.

The North Carolina Geological Survey is another activity of state government that reflects the influence of the gold-mining industry. In early 1999 that agency was staffed with thirteen geologists, a technician, and three additional employees. In the twentieth century the survey spawned state efforts to describe, protect, and develop natural resources, greatly expanding on its traditional role of the mid-nineteenth century. Late in that century the survey had emphasized the state's mineral and timber resources. In 1905 the organization was rechartered as the Geological and Economic Survey with authority to, among other powers, examine mineral, forest, and fishery resources; study soils and road-building materials; and examine water supplies and waterpower sites. In 1925 another state government reorganization created a Department of Conservation and Development, which incorporated the geological survey and its functions. The new agency was charged with promoting commerce and industry and soon included a forestry division.

Meanwhile, a powerful State Highway Commission had been created in 1921 to oversee construction of a modern statewide road system. By the end of the 1990s the geological survey (after additional bureaucratic shifting) was part of the Land Resources Division of the Department of Environment and Natural Resources. Within that department, other divisions—dealing with issues such as coastal management, marine fisheries, pollution control, waste management, water quality and resources, forest resources, and soil and water conservation—address concerns identified almost a century earlier by the geological survey. Recruiting and developing industry are now responsibilities of the Department of Commerce. At the present time, the North Carolina Geological Survey, institutional ancestor of many of the agencies listed above, continues to conduct its professional studies of the state's mineral resources, to add to its lengthy list of publications, and to engage in geological mapping of the state. Of particular note are the survey's topographical and digital orthographic mapping and its extensive use and provision of digitized and computerized data. The impact of the geological survey on the development of North Carolina's resources has been most significant and represents a commitment by the state to diversify and to move from a mostly agricultural economy to one that is highly industrialized.

The emergence of the Piedmont region as a center of industrial activity in the twentieth century is attributable in part to the presence of the mining industry in the nineteenth century. Mining, after all, predated even railroads in attracting the first wave of investment capital for non-agricultural ventures in North Carolina. The promotion of mining by the press and by government presaged the supportive roles each institution would play in the future quest for industrial development. The use of up-to-date technology in a backward area—best exemplified by the steam engines and stamp mills set up in Charlotte about 1830—introduced a key concept of industrialization to the region. Another part of the new industrial equation was the notion of working for wages in a mine or plant according to a fixed schedule rather than on a farm as desired or needed. The growth of small manufacturing suppliers and railroads (several state supported) provided a foundation for the industrial infrastructure that would be crucial to the success of the state's traditional industries—textiles, tobacco, and furniture. Although mining clearly did not survive as a viable industry past the Civil War, the industry did contribute to a framework that allowed other industrial activity to flourish.

Perhaps the best example of the connection between mining and modern industrialization is the story of Badin, a small company town in Stanly County just a few miles from the Gold Hill mining district. In many respects, Badin is a direct descendant of the ambitious but failed plans of George Whitney and E. B. C. Hambley described in chapter 4. The Whitney company folded in 1910. In 1912 the Southern Aluminum Company, a subsidiary of the French firm L'Aluminum Française, purchased the former Whitney property along the Yadkin River. By that time, industrialist James B. Duke had already demonstrated the value of a system of hydroelectric plants (which subsequently evolved into Duke Power Company) on the Catawba River as a major source of power for industry. The French were likewise interested in obtaining inexpensive electrical power; they sought to produce aluminum, which had become an essential component of the electrical and building industries since Charles Martin Hall patented the process for its production in 1886.

Southern Aluminum abandoned the original Whitney dam site and announced plans to build its dam, power plant, and production facilities directly at the Narrows, a few miles downstream. By the spring of 1913 the company had cleared ten acres of land, poured footings, and erected steel columns. Engineers planned a company town to include workers' housing, a clubhouse, and a modern water and sewer system. The town, named Badin after the company's president, Adrien Badin, incorporated contemporary landscape design and town planning. By the outbreak of World War I in August 1914, Southern Aluminum had completed two bypass tunnels and several building foundations, as well as a number of buildings in Badin, less than two miles away. Construction ended when key company employees, who served as reservists in the French army, departed Badin by early 1915. More important, Southern Aluminum found its lines of credit in Europe redirected to support the war effort. President Badin turned to northern bankers and investment houses for assistance but found no support.

At that point, the Badin story could have ended in failure much like other projects to harness the natural resources of North Carolina. One American company, however, did express interest in the sagging fortunes of the French firm. The Aluminum Company of America (Alcoa), based in Pittsburgh, had emerged as the predominant national producer. Anticipating spectacular wartime profits, the company could not pass up the opportunity to purchase a potential rival at a bargain price. Southern Aluminum sold out to Alcoa in November 1915 at a loss of one million dollars. Thereafter, Alcoa controlled a major source of cheap electrical power at a site within reasonable distance of its southern bauxite mines. Early in 1916 an Alcoa subsidiary began work to complete the dam begun by the Southern Aluminum Company.

The Narrows Dam was completed on June 17, 1917, creating Badin Lake, and a month later began generating power—nearly 125,000 horsepower—to run the plant in Badin, at which one thousand workers produced pig aluminum. "Not only North Carolina but the entire South will be benefited by this great development," observed the *Manufacturers' Record* of Baltimore. "The completion of the plant will give to the South leadership in the aluminum industry . . . [and] mark a very important event in the broadening of Southern industrial development, and especially in the manufacture of the finer class of goods requiring skilled labor." Over the next fifty years, Alcoa constructed three more dams along the Yadkin River, and Badin became a major component of one of America's most successful manufacturing enterprises. Some four hundred workers still produce aluminum ingots at Alcoa's Badin Works.

It is indeed a long journey from the primitive steam-powered Chilean mills at the gold mines of the nineteenth century to the massive dams along the Yadkin River that energize the giant smelters at Badin. The contrast, however, should not obscure the important connections between gold mining and the emergence of what has become known as the Piedmont Industrial Crescent of North Carolina. The entrepreneurs at the Reed mine, in the Gold Hill mining district, and at dozens of other mines faced the basic challenges that confront any new industry. They harnessed crude machinery to exploit the natural resources of the region, formed companies and raised money to finance their operations, assembled and organized large numbers of workers, and earned the support and attention of government and the press. They instilled a belief in progress as an inevitable and desirable condition and in technology as the instrument of that progress. Despite their frustrations and failures, that faith remained unshaken and provided the bedrock for industrial development throughout the twentieth century. The Narrows Dam at Badin, along with the mills and factories of the Piedmont, are the lineal descendants of the miners and farmers who created one of North Carolina's first substantive industries.

At the same time, the manner in which the mining industry in North Carolina developed also contributed to a unique combination of rural and urban values, attitudes, and appearances that are typical of the Piedmont region. North Carolina is now one of the most populous states in the nation, yet it remains one of the most rural. The industrial landscape of the state reflects the powerful presence of agriculture in a way reminiscent of the enterprising farmers of the nineteenth century who leased their land to the "gold seekers." That notable pattern of industrial geography is also a legacy of the Carolina gold rush.

The belief in progress through economic development is still a driving force in North Carolina. For at least the past thirty years, a modern "gold rush" has been taking place, with Charlotte once again at its forefront. Indeed, Charlotte has become a national banking and financial center. The outcome of this latest push toward progress, two centuries after Conrad Reed's discovery along Little Meadow Creek, can be seen as a fulfillment of many aspirations of the miners and farmers of his generation. Whether the agrarian values, character, and history of the region will survive in harmony with that extraordinary growth is a central question at the dawn of a new century.

Will gold mining ever revive in North Carolina on a large scale? Over the years, professional geologists and mineral companies have occasionally conducted exploration and testing of land in the state deemed likely to contain gold. Surprisingly, the largest producer of gold by far in the Southeast has been the open-pit Ridgeway mine in *South* Carolina, a facility opened in 1988 and slated to close in late 1999 after having produced 1.5 million ounces of gold. Ridgeway, employing new heap-leaching technology (primarily a chemical process involving the application of cyanide to dissolve gold), has catapulted South Carolina well ahead of North Carolina and Georgia in cumulative gold production. Ridgeway's technology made recovery of extremely minute amounts of gold per ton from vast amounts of low-grade ore economically feasible for a decade. Yet, in 1999 neither North Carolina nor Georgia has a counterpart to Ridgeway.

Whether a combination of requisite factors such as suitable ores, a higher price for gold and other favorable economic conditions, available land, adequate environmental safeguards, and new technology will rejuvenate mining in North Carolina remains in doubt. Even when the price of gold peaked at some $800 an ounce about 1980, mining did not revive in the state, and the metal's value in 1999 dollars (diminished in purchasing power by some 100 percent since 1980) presently appears destined to remain in the $300 range. Nevertheless, it seems certain that enthusiasts and hobbyists will pan for gold in North Carolina for years to come and that many others in the Tar Heel State will continue to appreciate the rich cultural heritage of the precious metal.

Two hundred years after Conrad Reed's chance discovery of gold in Little Meadow Creek, Reed Gold Mine State Historic Site preserves and brings to perpetual life the state's intriguing gold-mining heritage.

Glossary

Adit: In underground mining, a horizontal entry driven into deeper zones of a mine so that broken material can be removed by gravity

Amalgamation: The process in which mercury is used to separate gold from an ore. An ore containing gold is crushed in a mill and then passed over metal plates coated with mercury. The mercury absorbs the gold, forming an amalgam. In placer mining, mercury can be placed in a pan, sluice, or rocker to amalgamate with gold. The amalgam is then heated in a retort to separate the gold from the mercury.

Arrastra: A crushing mill for grinding ore beneath granite stones (suspended from arms fastened to a central shaft) and dragged around on a flat, circular base of laid stones

Assay: A chemical test or analysis to determine the proportions of metals in an ore. Careful assays are very precise and can reveal the efficiency of gold recovery by a mining company.

Auriferous: Containing or yielding gold

Belt: A region having distinct geological characteristics, such as a dominant type of rock

Blake jaw crusher: An adjustable machine for crushing rocks to various sizes preparatory to their treatment in a stamp mill. The crusher superseded the breaking of ore by hand with hammers.

Boiler: A closed tank, often iron and cylindrical, in which water is heated to form steam to power a steam engine or steam pump

California stamp mill: A refined stamp mill (developed in California in the 1850s) with all key working parts made of cast iron rather than wood and iron, as in earlier stamp mills. The machine featured other improvements as well.

Carolina slate belt: A geological region of North Carolina, ten to sixty miles wide, extending southwestward from Person County to South Carolina and containing a significant portion of the state's best-known gold mines

Charlotte belt: A geological region of North Carolina some fifteen to thirty miles wide, with gold deposits concentrated in Guilford, Davidson, Rowan, Cabarrus, and Mecklenburg Counties. The Charlotte belt lies west of the Carolina slate belt.

Chilean mill: A mill for crushing gold, usually with two stone wheels five or six feet in diameter set on edge, that rotated around a shaft set in a circular stone base containing ore, water, and mercury. The heavy wheels, often made of granite, pulverized the ore.

Chlorination: A method of treating refractory ore in which pulverized and roasted ore was placed in pressure tanks with poisonous chlorine gas

Clean-up: Cleaning parts of a mill, such as the mortar of a stamp mill, when the mill is stopped, to recover gold left in the mill. An arrastra was cleaned by taking up the floor rocks.

Cobber: An above-ground worker who broke ore with a hammer to separate the worthless rock from the better ore, usually before the ore was further processed in a Chilean mill or another mill

Concentrating table: A flat table (often set to catch the wet pulp from a stamp mill) with parallel riffle bars along which ore slurry ran as the table vibrated in a back-and-forth motion. Water carried away the lighter sand and waste; heavier material was classified according to its specific gravity.

Concentration: The separation of heavier minerals, such as gold, from lighter materials based on their differing specific gravities. Heavier minerals tended to settle in the bottom of a container (such as a pan) and not travel as far (or wash over the side of a pan) as lighter substances of similar volume.

Cornish pump: A submersible steam-powered pump (invented in Cornwall) used to remove water from deep (up to hundreds of feet) mines. Heavy wooden pump rods extended the entire depth of the pump shafts.

Cornwall: A county in southwestern Britain and a center of underground mining technology by about 1800. Much tin was mined in Cornwall.

Country rock: The rock enclosing or traversed by a mineral deposit; also, the rock intruded by and surrounding an igneous intrusion

Crosscut: In underground mining, a horizontal tunnel (often perpendicular to the general direction of veins of ore) used to connect drifts

Cyanidation: The process in which a solution of potassium cyanide is passed through crushed ore to remove gold. Cyanidation is not used when the ore contains copper.

Drag-stone mill. *See* Arrastra

Dredging: The process of using a large floating machine for scooping up or excavating material from the bottom of a body of water, raising the material to the surface, and processing the material to remove the gold

Drill: A bar of cast steel about 1½ inches in diameter and 3 or 4 feet long. One end was flat for striking by a hammer, and the other was shaped like a chisel with a flared edge. Miners pounded drills into underground rock walls.

Drift: A horizontal tunnel that extends through a body of ore.

Engine shaft: A shaft in a deep mine over which an engine sat. The engine often ran pumps to remove water from the mine and hoists for moving men, equipment, and ore in the shaft.

Fault: A surface or zone of rock fracture along which there has been displacement. Such displacement, a slipping movement of one large mass of rock relative to an adjacent surface, may range from a few inches to many miles.

Flotation: A process of mineral separation in which water, oil, and chemicals are combined to make a froth of air bubbles to which certain minerals adhere and can be collected in a trough

Hydraulic mining: A mining method used for processing placer deposits where gravels are excavated and swept away into sluiceways by powerful jets of water

Kibble: A large bucket, made of copper or iron, in which ore and men can be hoisted from a mine

Level: A gallery stope driven on a lode at a uniform distance below the surface. Levels were often driven every thirty to fifty feet (for instance, "the fifty-foot level," "the one hundred-foot level") below the surface.

Lode deposit: A mineral deposit consisting of a zone of veins; also, a mineral deposit in consolidated rock as opposed to placer deposits

Long tom: A sluicelike trough, perhaps twelve feet long, that processed placer gold somewhat like a cradle rocker but at a faster speed. One man might work a cradle rocker, whereas two men normally worked a long tom.

Mercury: A heavy, silver-colored metal that is liquid at ordinary temperatures and combines with minute particles of gold to form an amalgam, from which gold may be recovered

Millhouse: A mine building containing machinery such as stamp mills and concentrating tables for crushing or processing ore

Native gold (copper): Any element (such as gold or copper) found un-combined with other elements

Ore: The naturally occurring material from which a mineral or minerals of value can be extracted economically

Pennyweight: A unit of measurement equal to 20 grains or 1.55 grams of gold. *See* Troy weight

Placer deposit: A surficial mineral deposit formed by mechanical concentration of mineral particles from weathered debris. Placers are formed by gravitational separation of heavy from light minerals by means of water or air.

Pyrite: A compound of sulfur and a metal, such as tin or copper. Iron pyrites resemble gold visually and are known as "fool's gold."

Quartz: A very hard mineral composed of silica, commonly found as a whitish vein material that may contain metals such as gold

Quicksilver. *See* Mercury

Reduction: A chemical reaction in which oxygen is removed from a compound

Refractory ore: Gold ore associated with copper or iron pyrites, resulting in more difficulty in separating the precious metal from the pyritic material

Retort: A closed container, often iron, for heating an amalgam of gold and mercury to drive off the mercury as a gas (which is then recoverable by condensation) and leave behind the gold

Riffles: Narrow slots, grooves, or small raised bars to catch and hold particles of gold in a rocker, long tom, sluice, or concentrating table. Mercury was often put in the riffles.

Roasting: Heating gold ore to attempt to drive off the sulfur, a process common in nineteenth-century efforts to deal with refractory ore

Rocker: A device used for concentrating gold in small-scale placer mining operations. The rocker (often a box, a vertical half of a barrel, or half of a hollowed-out tree) is usually operated by hand and is used by shoveling gravel into a hopper, bailing water into the hopper, and rocking the device from side to side to wash the gravel and concentrate the heavier gold.

Saprolite: Soft, earthy decomposed rock formed in place by chemical weathering of igneous and metamorphic rocks, in which many of the structural features of the original material are visible

Shaft: A vertical or steeply inclined opening sunk from the surface of the ground into or near an ore body

Shaking (bumping) table: An ineffective predecessor of the concentrating table that combined some actions of the sluice and rocker

Sluice: A narrow inclined trough used in placer operations to collect gold. The sluice contains riffles in the bottom that provide collecting sites for the gold, while lighter materials are washed along and out the end of the trough.

Smelting: The process of melting ores in blast or reverberatory furnaces to obtain metals

Specific gravity: A number that expresses the ratio between the weight of a mineral and the weight of an equal volume of water at 4°C. If a mineral has a specific gravity of 2, a given specimen of that mineral weighs twice as much as the same volume of water. Specific gravity is frequently helpful in identifying minerals. Gold has a specific gravity of about nineteen.

Stamp mill: A large machine for pounding pieces of ore into a fine gravel to separate gold. The stamps (on the bottoms of heavy stems) rise and fall to crush ore in a box called a mortar.

Stirring bowl: A device used in the 1850s to stir gold slurry produced by a stamp mill in hopes of amalgamating gold particles with mercury in the bowl

Steam engine: An engine operated by steam from an external boiler. The expanding steam moves a sliding piston in a cylinder, providing reciprocal motion that can also be converted to rotary motion. A gasoline or diesel engine, in contrast, uses internal combustion inside the cylinder.

Stope: In underground mining, the area (a chamber or room) from which the ore is removed. A stope is made larger as more ore is extracted and moved to the surface.

Surficial: Lying in or near the earth's surface

Tailings: Milled particles of residue left after processing of ore and removal of gold by a mining machine or company. Sometimes a second group of miners could profitably rework tailings from an inefficient initial effort.

Timbering: Heavy wooden frameworks and supports utilized in some underground mines, particularly to guard against falling rock in stopes and in shafts used for pumping water and raising ore

Trestle: A framework of timber that can be used to support a pipe or sluice carrying water across a valley, gap, or gorge

Tribute work: Mining in which miners' pay is a portion of the ore or of the value of the gold they produce

Troy weight: A system of weight used for precious metals and gems. 24 grains equal 1 pennyweight (1.55 grams); 20 pennyweights equal 1 ounce (31.1035 grams); 12 ounces (5,760 grains) equal 1 pound (373.24 grams). A pound troy equals a bit more than four-fifths of an ordinary (avoirdupois) pound.

Vein: A thin, sheet-like igneous intrusion or mineral filling in a fracture or crevice in country rock

Waste: Broken country rock removed in mining. Waste piles were often found around the mouths of shafts or the entries to adits.

Whim: A large vertical drum, often powered by a horse, around which a rope could be wound or unwound to raise or lower an ore bucket within a shaft below

Winze: In underground mining, a vertical or steeply inclined passage driven downward to connect one level to another level

Worthington pump: A steam-powered pump patented in 1841 with its own steam cylinder that pumped water independent of any outside support other than a boiler. Submersible Worthington pumps did not require the surface steam engines or heavy, cumbersome pump rods needed by Cornish pumps.

(Some definitions have been adapted, courtesy of the North Carolina Geological Survey, from P. Albert Carpenter, *Gold in North Carolina*.)

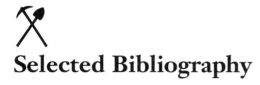

Selected Bibliography

Books and Pamphlets

Agricola, Georgius (Georg Bauer). *De Re Metallica.* Translated and edited by Herbert C. Hoover and Lou Henry Hoover. New York: Dover Publications, 1950.

Aitchison, Leslie. *A History of Metals.* 2 vols. New York: Interscience Publishers, 1960.

Alexander, John B. *The History of Mecklenburg County from 1740 to 1900.* Charlotte: Observer Printing House, 1902.

André, George G. *Mining Machinery, a Descriptive Treatise . . . .* 2 vols. London: E. and F. N. Spon, 1877-1879.

Atkins, Job. *The Practical Miner's Own Book and Guide.* Richmond: J. W. Randolph, 1860.

Barfield, Rodney, and Keith Strawn. *The Bechtlers and Their Coinage: North Carolina Mint Masters of Pioneer Gold.* Raleigh: Division of Archives and History, Department of Cultural Resources, 1980.

Barton, Denys B. *Historic Cornish Mining Scenes Underground.* Truro, England: Truro Bookshop, 1967.

Battle, Kemp P., ed. *Diary of a Geological Tour by Dr. Elisha Mitchell in 1827 and 1828.* Chapel Hill: University of North Carolina Press, 1905.

Birdsall, Clair M. *United States Branch Mint at Charlotte, North Carolina: Its History and Coinage.* Easley, S.C.: Southern Historical Press, 1988.

Blythe, Le Gette, and Charles R. Brockmann. *Hornet's Nest: The Story of Charlotte and Mecklenburg County.* Charlotte: McNally, 1961.

Brawley, James S. *The Rowan Story, 1753-1953: A Narrative History of Rowan County, North Carolina.* Salisbury, N.C.: Rowan Printing Company, 1953.

Bryson, Herman J. *Gold Deposits in North Carolina.* Raleigh: North Carolina Department of Conservation and Development (Bulletin 38), 1936.

Budge, John. *The Practical Miner's Guide . . . .* 2d ed. London: Longmans, 1845.

Burt, Roger, ed. *Cornish Mining.* New York: A. M. Kelley, 1969.

Carpenter, P. Albert. *Gold in North Carolina.* Raleigh: North Carolina Department of Environmental, Health, and Natural Resources N.C. Geological Survey (Information Circular 29), 1993.

_____. *Metallic Mineral Deposits of the Carolina Slate Belt, North Carolina*. Raleigh: North Carolina Department of Natural and Economic Resources (Bulletin 84), 1976.

Charlotte, North Carolina, Mining Board. *Statistics of Mines and Minerals in North Carolina* . . . . Charlotte: Observer Printing House, 1878.

Earl, Bryan. *Cornish Mining: The Techniques of Metal Mining in the West of England, Past and Present*. Truro, England: D. B. Barton, 1968.

Emmons, Ebenezer. *Geological Report on the Midland Counties of North Carolina*. New York: George P. Putnam and Co., 1856.

Featherstonhaugh, George W. *Excursion through the Slave States, from Washington on the Potomac to the Frontier of Mexico*. 2 vols. London: John Murray, 1844.

Foster, James T. *A Brief Sketch of the Early Discoveries of Gold Mines and Mining in North Carolina down to the Present Period*. Greensboro: J. S. Hampton and Company, 1883.

Freeman, Berry Bright. *Bechtler's Gold*. Spindale, N.C.: Spindale Press, 1958.

Genth, Friedrich A. *Mineral Resources of North Carolina*. Philadelphia: [Franklin Institute], 1871.

Griffin, Clarence. *The Bechtlers and Bechtler Coinage; and, Gold Mining in North Carolina, 1814-1830*. Forest City, N.C.: Forest City Courier, 1929.

Jenkins, Alfred K. H. *The Cornish Miner: An Account of his Life Above and Underground from Early Times*. 2d rev. ed. London: Allen and Unwin, 1948.

Johnston, S. C. *Description of Reed Gold Mine*. N.p., 1882.

Kasson, John F. *Civilizing the Machine: Technology and Republican Values in America, 1776-1900*. New York: Grossman Publishers, 1976.

Kerr, Washington C. *Report of the Geological Survey of North Carolina*. Raleigh: J. Turner, 1875.

_____, and George B. Hanna. "Ores of North Carolina." Chapter 2 of *Geology of North Carolina*. Raleigh: Edwards and Broughton, 1888.

Knapp, Richard F. *Golden Promise in the Piedmont: The Story of John Reed's Mine*. Rev. ed. Raleigh: Division of Archives and History, Department of Cultural Resources, 1999.

_____, comp. *North Carolina Gold: A Selected Bibliography of Mining History, Technology, and the Reed Gold Mine*. Concord: Gold History Corporation, 1978.

Laney, Francis B. *The Gold Hill Mining District of North Carolina*. Raleigh: North Carolina Geological and Economic Survey (Bulletin 21), 1910.

_____, and Katherine Hill Wood. *Bibliography of North Carolina Geology, Mineralogy, and Geography*. Raleigh: E. M. Uzzell and Company, 1909.

Lock, Charles G. *Practical Gold-Mining* . . . . New York: E. and F. N. Spon, 1889.

Mumford, Lewis. *Technics and Civilization*. New York: Harcourt, Brace, and World, 1934.

Nitze, Henry B. C., and George B. Hanna. *Gold Deposits of North Carolina.* Winston, N.C.: M. I. and J. C. Stewart (N.C. Geological Survey Bulletin 3), 1896.

Nitze, Henry B. C., and H. A. J. Wilkens. *Gold Mining in North Carolina and Adjacent South Appalachian Regions.* Raleigh: Guy V. Barnes (N.C. Geological Survey Bulletin 10), 1897.

Olmsted, Denison. *Report on the Geology of North Carolina.* 3 vols. Raleigh: J. Gales and Sons, 1824-1827.

Pardee, J. T. *Preliminary Report on Gold Deposits in North Carolina and South Carolina.* [Washington: U.S. Geological Survey], 1935.

Pardee, J. T., and C. F. Park Jr. *Gold Deposits of the Southern Piedmont.* Washington, D.C.: Government Printing Office (U.S. Geological Survey Professional Paper 213), 1948.

Paul, Rodman W. *California Gold: The Beginning of Mining in the Far West.* Lincoln: University of Nebraska Press, 1947; Bison Books edition, 1969.

_____. *Mining Frontiers of the Far West, 1848-1880.* New York: Holt, Rinehart, and Winston, 1963.

Pittman, Clyde C. *Death of a Gold Mine; or The True Story of an Eye Witness Who Saw the Explosion at Haile Gold Mine, South Carolina . . . .* Great Falls, S.C. [1972].

Pogue, Joseph E. *Cid Mining District of Davidson County, North Carolina.* Raleigh: Edwards and Broughton (N.C. Geological Survey Bulletin 22), 1910.

Poovey, Ruth. *Burke County Gold Rush.* N.p.: the author[?], 1967.

Pratt, Joseph H. *The Mining Industry in North Carolina during 1899.* Bound as Chapter 6 of the *Annual Report* of the North Carolina Bureau of Labor and Printing. Raleigh: Edwards and Broughton, 1900. There are numerous subsequent reports in the series, published for the North Carolina Geological Survey.

Pursell, Carroll W., Jr. *Early Stationary Steam Engines in America.* Washington, D.C.: Smithsonian Institution Press, 1969.

Reid, Jeffrey C. *A Geochemical Atlas of North Carolina.* Raleigh: North Carolina Geological Survey (Bulletin 93), 1991.

Rickard, Thomas A. *Man and Metals: A History of Mining with Relation to the Development of Civilization.* New York: McGraw-Hill, 1932.

Roberts, Bruce. *The Carolina Gold Rush.* Charlotte: McNally and Loftin, 1971.

Rohrbough, Malcolm J. *Days of Gold: The California Gold Rush and the American Nation.* Berkeley: University of California Press, 1997.

Ross, Malcolm. *Machine Age in the Hills.* New York: Macmillan, 1933.

Rowe, John. *The Hard-Rock Men: Cornish Immigrants and the North American Mining Frontier.* New York: Barnes and Noble, 1974.

Schmidbauer, Hubert, ed. *Gold: Progress in Chemistry, Biochemistry, and Technology.* New York: Wiley, 1999.

163

Schwalm, Mark A. *A Hessian Immigrant Finds Gold: The Story of John Reed*. Stanfield, N.C.: Reed Gold Mine, 1996.

Spence, Clark C. *British Investment and the American Mining Frontier, 1860-1901*. Ithaca: Cornell University Press, 1958.

Starobin, Robert S. *Industrial Slavery in the Old South*. New York: Oxford University Press, 1970.

Stautzenberger, Anthony Joseph. *The Establishment of the Charlotte Branch Mint: A Documented History*. Austin, Tex.: the author, 1976.

Wheeler, John H. *Historical Sketches of North Carolina, from 1584 to 1851*. Philadelphia: Lippincott, Grambo and Co., 1851.

Winter, Douglas. *Charlotte Mint Gold Coins, 1838-1861: A Numismatic History and Analysis*. N.p.: Bowers and Merena Galleries[?], 1987.

Young, Otis E., Jr. *Western Mining*. Norman: University of Oklahoma Press, 1970.

Articles

Ayres, Stephen. "A Description of the Region in North Carolina Where Gold Has Been Found." *Medical Repository* 10 (1807): 150.

California History 77 (1998). Numbers 1 and 4 are special issues that include many new articles for the sesquicentennial of the California gold rush.

Blosser, Susan Sokol. "Calvin J. Cowles's Gap Creek Mine: A Case Study of Mine Speculation in the Gilded Age." *North Carolina Historical Review* 51 (October 1974): 379-400.

Bridges, Daisy W. "Carolina Gold and the U.S. Branch Mint in Charlotte." *Antiques* 106 (December 1974): 1041-1046.

Craig, James R., and J. Donald Rimstidt. "Gold Production History of the United States." *Ore Geology Reviews* (1998).

Crosby, William O. "Ore Deposits of the Eastern Gold Belt of North Carolina." *Technology Quarterly* 20 (1907): 280-286.

Dickson, James. "An Essay on the Gold Region of the United States." *Transactions of the Geological Society of Pennsylvania* 1 (1835): 16-32.

Egenhoff, Elisabeth L. "The Cornish Pump." (California Division of Mines and Geology) *Mineral Information Service* 20 (June, August 1967): 59-70, 91-97.

Ellery, J. G. "The Property of the Catawba Mining Company in McDowell County, North Carolina." *Mining Magazine* 3 (July 1854): 15-25.

Ellet, William H. "Gold Mining by the Hydraulic Method in North Carolina and Georgia." *Mining Magazine* 10 (1858): 27-30.

Featherstonhaugh, Thomas. "A Private Mint in North Carolina." *Publications of the Southern History Association* 10 (March 1906): 67-77.

Forret, Jeffrey P. "Slave Labor in North Carolina's Antebellum Gold Mines." *North Carolina Historical Review* 76 (April 1999): 135-162.

Glass, Brent D. "The Miner's World: Life and Labor at Gold Hill." *North Carolina Historical Review* 62 (October 1985): 420-447.

_____. "'Poor Men with Rude Machinery': The Formative Years of the Gold Hill Mining District, 1842-1853." *North Carolina Historical Review* 61 (January 1984): 1-35.

"Gold and Silver Produced by the Mines of America from 1492 to 1848." *Mining Magazine* 1 (October 1853): 365-373.

Green, Fletcher M. "Georgia's Forgotten Industry: Gold Mining." *Georgia Historical Quarterly* 19 (June, September 1935): 93-111, 210-228.

_____. "Gold Mining: A Forgotten Industry of Ante-Bellum North Carolina." *North Carolina Historical Review* 14 (January, April 1937): 1-19, 135-155.

_____. "Gold Mining in Ante-Bellum Virginia." *Virginia Magazine of History and Biography* 45 (July, October 1937): 227-235, 357-366.

Gutman, Herbert G. "Work, Culture, and Society in Industrializing America, 1815-1919." *American Historical Review* 78 (June 1973): 531-588.

Hewitt, Kimberley. "Not a Baby nor a Devil." *Golden Gazette* [newsletter of Reed Gold Mine] 13 (spring/summer 1996): 6.

Highsmith, Patrick. "The Evolution of Gold Mining in the United States from East to West (and then East Again?)." *Golden Gazette* 15 (spring/summer 1998): 1, 3, 6-11.

Hines, Elizabeth. "Cousin Jacks and the Tarheel Gold Boom: Cornish Miners in North Carolina, 1830-1880." *North Carolina Geographer* 5 (winter 1997): 1-10.

_____. "McCulloch's Rock Engine House: An Antebellum Cornish-Style Gold Ore Mill near Jamestown, North Carolina." *Material Culture* 27 (1995): 1-28.

_____, and Michael Smith. "Gold Mining in North Carolina." *Snapshots of the Carolinas* (Washington, D.C.: Association of American Geographers, 1996.

Holmes, G. Fred. "Effect of the Increase of Gold Throughout the World." *DeBow's Review* 21 (August 1856): 103-121.

Jackson, Charles T. "Report on the Conrad Hill Gold Mine, Davidson County, North Carolina." *Mining Magazine* 2 (February 1854): 190-191.

Kerr, Washington C. "The Gold Gravels of North Carolina: Their Structure and Origin." *Transactions of the American Institute of Mining Engineers* 8 (1880): 462-466.

_____. "Our Mineral Wealth." *South Atlantic* 2 (August, September, October 1878): 289-299, 470-471, 484-495.

Kral, Steve. "Ridgeway: Successfully Mining Low-Grade Ore." *Mining Engineering* 41 (December 1989): 1182.

Ledoux, Albert R. "The Union Copper Mines, Gold Hill, North Carolina." *Engineering and Mining Journal* 69 (1900): 167-170.

Leeds, Stephen P. "Gold Ores and their Working." *Mining Magazine* 7 (July-August, October, November, December 1856): 23-32, 265-275, 344-356, 445-453.

_____. "Notes on the Gold Regions of North and South Carolina." *Mining Magazine* 2 (January and April 1854): 27-34, 357-369.

_____. "The Rudisel Gold and Copper Mine of North Carolina." *Mining Magazine* 2 (May 1854): 516-518.

Lyon, Edward W. "The Progress of Gold Mining in North Carolina." *Engineering and Mining Journal* 87 (1909): 293-297.

Megraw, Herbert A. "Cyanidation in the South." *Engineering and Mining Journal* 79 (1905): 705-707.

"Mining in Wall Street." *Mining Magazine* 4 (May-June 1855): 370-375.

"More Gold Picked up in North Carolina." *Medical Repository* 8 (1805): 439-440.

"Native Gold Discovered in North Carolina." *Medical Repository* 7 (1804): 307.

Nitze, Henry B. C. "Gold Mining in the Southern States." *Engineering Magazine* 10 (February 1896): 821-844.

_____, and Henry A. J. Wilkens. "The Present Condition of Gold Mining in the Southern Appalachian States." *Transactions of the American Institute of Mining Engineers* 25 (1895): 661-796, 1016-1027.

Olmsted, Denison. "On the Gold Mines of North Carolina." *American Journal of Science* 9 (1825): 5-15.

_____. "Report on the Geology of North Carolina . . . ." *Southern Review* 1 (February 1828): 235-261.

Palmer, Walter W., and Thomas C. Buckley. "Statement of the McCullock Copper and Gold Mining Company of Guilford County, North Carolina." *Mining Magazine* 4 (April 1855): 282-286.

Partz, August. "Examinations and Explorations of the Gold-Bearing Belts of the Atlantic States: The Reid Mines, North Carolina." *Mining Magazine* 3 (August 1854): 161-168.

Pearce, T. H. "The Portis Diggings: A Gold Mining Operation which Flashed, Flourished, Faltered, and Finally Failed 100 Years Later." *The State* 39 (April 1972): 10-12.

Peck, Jacob. "Geological and Mineralogical Account of the Mining Districts in the State of Georgia, the Western Part of North Carolina . . . with a map." *American Journal of Science* 23 (1833): 1-10.

Phifer, Edward W. "Champagne at Brindletown: The Story of the Burke County Gold Rush, 1829-1833." *North Carolina Historical Review* 40 (October 1963): 489-500.

Pratt, Joseph H. "Coggins (Appalachian) Gold Mine." *Journal of the Elisha Mitchell Scientific Society* 30 (March 1915): 165-178.

———, and A. A. Steel. "Recent Changes in Gold Mining in North Carolina that have Favorably Affected this Industry." *Journal of the Elisha Mitchell Scientific Society* 23 (1907): 108-133.

"Progress of Finding Gold in North Carolina." *Medical Repository* 12 (1809): 192-193.

"Projected Branch Mint of North Carolina." *American Journal of Science* 20 (July 1831): 400-404.

Roske, Ralph J. "The World Impact of the California Gold Rush, 1849-1857." *Arizona and the West* 5 (1963): 187-232.

Rothe, Charles E. "Remarks on the Gold of North Carolina." *American Journal of Science and Arts* 13 (1828): 201-217.

Shepard, Charles U. "Report on Sumner, Hipp, Fulwood, and Lemons Mines of North Carolina." *Mining Magazine* 1(December 1853): 591-597.

Shinn, James F. "Discovery of Gold in North Carolina." *Trinity Archive* 6 (1893): 335.

"The Silver Hill Mine, North Carolina." *Mining Magazine* (2d ser.) 1 (1860): 368-371.

Smith, Franklin L. "Notices of Some Facts Connected with the Gold of a Portion of North Carolina." *American Journal of Science* 32 (1837): 130-133.

Stevens, R. P. "Gold in North Carolina." *American Journal of Mining* 1 (1866): 313-314.

Strother, David H. (Porte Crayon). "North Carolina Illustrated: The Gold Region." *Harper's New Monthly Magazine* 15 (August 1857): 289-300.

Talbot, Frederick A. "Edison's Latest Invention: A Revolution in Iron-Making." *Chamber's Journal* (September 1898): 598.

Thies, Adolph, and William B. Phillips. "The Thies Process of Treating the Low-grade Auriferous Sulphides at the Haile Gold Mine, Lancaster County, South Carolina." *Transactions of the American Institute of Mining Engineers* 19 (1890): 601-614.

Thornton, W[illiam]. "Letter from W. Thornton, Esq. to the members of the North Carolina Gold Mine Company." *London, Edinburgh, and Dublin Philosophical Magazine* 27 (1807): 261-264.

Tischendorf, Alfred P. "North Carolina and the British Investor, 1880-1910." *North Carolina Historical Review* 32 (October 1955): 512-518.

Vance, Lee J. "The Gold Fields of the South." *Godey's Magazine* 131 (November 1895): 529.

Verplanck, G[ulian] C. "Report (made by G. C. Verplanck) of the Select Committee for the Purpose of Inquiring into the Expediency of Establishing Assay Offices within the Gold Districts of North and South Carolina and Georgia." *American Quarterly Review* 9 (March 1832): 66-102.

Weed, Walter H. "Copper in North Carolina." *Mining Industry* 10 (1902): 184-185.

Wheeler, John H. "Gold Mines of North Carolina." *American Almanac* (1841): 211-217.

Wilkes, J. Frank. "Gold Mining in the South." *Proceedings of the Engineering Association of the South* 19 (1908): 1-15.

Young, Otis E., Jr. "The Southern Gold Rush, 1828-1836." *Journal of Southern History* 48 (August 1982): 373-392. Incomplete on North Carolina gold.

_____. "The Spanish Tradition in Gold and Silver Mining." *Arizona and the West* 7 (winter 1965): 299-314.

Reports and Prospectuses on Mines

Baltimore and North Carolina Copper and Gold Mine Company. *Charter and By-laws.* . . . Baltimore: Hamilton and Company, Printers, 1883.

Bishop, W. L. *Report on Gold Veins of Burke and Caldwell Counties.* N.p., n.d.

Blake, William P. *Report upon the Property of the Valley River Gold Company, Cherokee County, North Carolina.* Boston: n.p., 1860.

[Cherry, Cummings]. *Geological Report, Gap Creek Mine, North Carolina.* [Pittsburgh: C. and J. Cherry, 1870].

Clingman, Thomas L. *Gold Hill Mine in Rowan County, North Carolina.* Washington, D.C.: McGill and Witherow, Printers, 1875.

Conrad Hill Gold and Copper Company. *Prospectus.* Baltimore: The Sun, 1881.

Cram, Thomas J. *Discussion of the Problem of Probable Profit to be Expected from the Gold and Mercury Amalgamating Mill . . . at Gold Hill Mine.* . . . Philadelphia: Collins, 1874.

_____. *Report upon the Mine and Mills, with Estimates for the Use of the "North Carolina Gold Amalgamating Company."* Philadelphia: Collins, 1874.

Credner, Hermann. *Report on Certain Mineral Lands in Cabarrus and Mecklenburg Counties, North Carolina.* Translated by Adelbert and Raymond. New York: Adelbert and Raymond, 1866.

Dickeson, Montroville M. *Report of the Geological Survey and Condition of the Rhea Mine in the County of Mecklenburg, North Carolina.* Philadelphia: J. B. Chandler, 1860.

_____. *Report of the Geological Survey and Condition of the Twin Mine in the County of Guilford, North Carolina.* Philadelphia: J. B. Chandler, 1860.

Eights, James. *A Report relating to the Fisher Hill Mining Company.* New York: William S. Dorr, 1856.

_____. *A Report relating to the Fisher Hill and Puckett mines in Guilford County, North Carolina.* N.p., 1854.

Franklin Gold Mining Company. *Charter, with Amendments and Descriptions of their Mines.* New York: W. M. Mercein and Son, 1835.

Gibson Hill Gold and Copper Mine. *Reports on the Gibson Hill Gold and Copper Mine of North Carolina*. Baltimore: J. F. Wiley, printer, 1860.

Gipperich, Frederick. *Report on the Gold Mines of the Philadelphia and North Carolina Mining and Smelting Company*. Philadelphia: John H. Schwacke, 1847.

Gold Hill Copper Company. *Status of the Gold Hill Copper Company*. New York: Gold Hill Copper Co., 1902.

[Gold Hill Mining Company]. *Report of the Gold Hill Mining Company: January 21, 1856*. New York: Nathan Lane and Company, 1856.

Hodge, James T. "Report to the President and Directors of the Vanderburg Mining Company." In *Tetra-Chordon: A Pot Pourri of Rhymes and Prose*, by William Furniss, pp. 117-125. New York: American News Company, 1874.

Iola Mining Company. *Prospectus of the Iola Mining Company*. Baltimore: n.p., [1904].

Jackson, Charles T. *Report on the McCullock Copper and Gold Mining Company*. New York: McSpedon and Baker, 1853.

King's Mountain Mining Company. *Information in regard to the Property of the King's Mountain Mining Company, near Charlotte, North Carolina*. Philadelphia: Allen, Lane, and Schott, 1877.

Kropff, Frederick C. *Report on the Lewis Mine in Union County, North Carolina*. Philadelphia: John C. Clark, 1849.

Leeds, Stephen P., and August D. Partz. *Charter and By-Laws of the Karriker Gold and Copper Company*. Jersey City: J. Raymond, 1855.

North Carolina Gold-Mining and Bullion Co., New York. *The Gold Fields of North Carolina*. New York, n.p., [1891].

Pioneer Mills Mine Company. *Report of the Superintendent of the Pioneer Mills Mine, Cabarrus County, N.C., December 24, 1855*. Albany, N.Y.: Joel Munsell, 1856.

[Rhymer Gold Mining Company]. *Prospectus and By-laws of the Rhymer Gold Mining Company*. New York: W. H. Arthur, 1854.

[Rowan Gold and Copper Mining Company]. *Prospectus, Reports of Geologists of the Rowan Gold and Copper Mining Company*. Baltimore: J. F. Wiley, 1860.

Rudisell Gold Mining Company. *Prospectus*. Baltimore: John D. Toy, 1853.

Shepard, Charles U. *Description of Gold and Copper Mines at Gold Hill, Rowan County, North Carolina*. N.p., [1853].

Taylor, Richard C. *Report on the Washington Silver Mine in Davidson County, North Carolina, with an Appendix containing Assays of the Ores, Returns of Silver and Gold Produced and Statements of the Affairs of the Washington Mining Company*. Philadelphia: E. G. Dorsey, 1845.

Thornton, William. *North Carolina Gold-Mine Company*. [Washington, D.C.: n.p., 1806].

Tyson, Phillip T. *Report on the Gold Deposits and Works of the Manteo Mining Company in North Carolina*. Baltimore: John D. Toy, 1853.

_____. *Report on the Gold Deposits and Works of the Perseverance Mining Company in North Carolina*. Baltimore: John D. Toy, 1853.

[Ward Gold-Mine Company]. *Prospectus of the Ward Gold-Mine Company*. New York: R. C. Root and Anthony, [1854].

Zinc and Silver Mining Company. *A Statement of the Condition and Prospects of the Zinc and Silver Hill Mine in Davidson County, N.C.: with Returns of the Gold and Silver from the United States Mint, Illustative Diagrams, and Assays of the Ores*. New York: Baker, Godwin, and Co., 1854.

Newspapers and Journals

Several journals, notably the *Mining Magazine*, and to a lesser extent the *American Institute of Mining Engineers Transactions*, the *American Journal of Mining*, *DeBow's Review*, and the *Manufacturers' Record* (Baltimore), contain much scattered information on gold mining in North Carolina.

Catawba Journal (Charlotte). January 4, 1824-April 29, 1828.

Concord Register. November 5, 1875-May 8, 1885.

Concord Standard. January 14, 1888-December 29, 1898.

Concord Times. November 19, 1885-December 30, 1897.

Daily Concord Standard. January 13, 1893-December 31, 1898.

Miners' and Farmers' Journal (Charlotte). September 27, 1830-June 19, 1835.

North Carolina Herald (Salisbury). October 8, 1885-July 22, 1896.

North Carolina Spectator and Western Advertiser (Rutherfordton). February 19, 1830-February 28, 1835.

Western Carolinian (Salisbury). January 13, 1820-December 30, 1833.

Yadkin and Catawba Journal (Salisbury). May 20, 1828-December 15, 1829.

Federal Published Documents

U.S. Congress. House. *Assay Offices, Gold Districts North Carolina and Georgia*. H. Rept. 82, 21st Cong., 2d sess, 1831.

_____. *Assay Offices, Gold Districts, North Carolina, Georgia, etc. Report [39] to Accompany H.R. 84*, 22d Cong., 1st sess., 1831.

_____. *Assay Offices—Gold Regions, South, Report [391] to Accompany H.R. 407*, 23d Cong., 1st sess., 1834.

U.S. Congress. Senate. *Report concerning Coin and Bullion*, by Secretary of the Treasury Levi Woodbury. S. Doc 290, 26th Cong., 1st sess., 1840.

————. Committee on Privileges and Elections. *Stationery in Promoting Gold Hill Consolidated Company*. S. Rept. 688, 63d Cong, 2d sess., 1913.

U.S. Department of the Interior. Bureau of the Census. *Eleventh Census of the United States, 1890: Report on Mineral Industries in the United States*, vol. 14.

————. *Tenth Census of the United States, 1880: Statistics and Technology of the Precious Metals*, vol. 13.

————. *Twelfth Census of the United States, 1900: Special Reports, Mines and Quarries*, 1902.

U.S. Department of the Interior. Geological Survey. *Sixteenth Annual Report*. "Gold Fields of the Southern Appalachians," by George F. Becker. Pp. 251-331. Washington, D.C.: Government Printing Office, 1895.

North Carolina Published Documents

N.C. Bureau of Labor Statistics. Inspector of Mines. *Annual Report* (1897). Raleigh, 1898. The report for 1898 is also useful.

N.C. General Assembly. *An act to Provide for the Regulation and Inspection of Mines. N.C. Public Laws*, 1897, c. 251.

————. *An Act to Incorporate the Gold Hill Mining Company. N.C. Session Laws*, 1852-1853. Similar acts exist for other companies listed in table 2.

————. "Memorial from Ephriam Mauney of Gold Hill, North Carolina." December 20, 1858.

————. Committee on a Bill to Incorporate the Mecklenburg Gold Mining Company. *Report*. Raleigh: Lawrence and Lemay, 1830.

Unpublished Materials

Chapel Hill, North Carolina. University of North Carolina. Southern Historical Collection: Archibald D. Alston Papers, Waightstill Avery Papers, Daniel M. Barringer Papers, Battle Family Papers, Bryan and Leventhorpe Family Papers, Burwell Family Papers, William P. Bynum Papers, Mrs. Charles A. Cannon Papers, Karl B. Cline Papers, Calvin J. Cowles Papers, Roswell Elmer Diary, George Phifer Erwin Papers, Fisher Family Papers, Leonidas C. Glenn Papers, John Gluyas Papers, Gold Hill Mining Company Records, Ralph Gorrell Papers, William A. Hoke Papers, Lenoir Family Papers, Joseph A. Linn Papers, William L. Long Papers, Robert H. Morrison Papers, North Carolina Geological Survey Papers, Silver Hill Mining Company Ledger, Speculation Land Company Records, Vein Mountain Mining Company Records, University of North Carolina Papers, Washington Mine Account Book.

Charlotte, North Carolina. Public Library of Charlotte and Mecklenburg County. James Parks McCombs Papers.

Durham, North Carolina. Duke University. Duke University Library. Manuscript Department: William H. Bailey Sr. Papers, Bissell and Barker Account, William Blanding Journal, Campbell Family Papers, Alonzo G. Beardsley Papers, Benjamin P. Elliott Papers, John Fox Papers, Gillingham-Stith Family Papers, William A. Graham Papers, Edwin Clark Gregory and Lee S. Overman Papers, Jesse Hedrick Letters, William W. Holden Papers, D. T. McEachin Account Book, Archibald M. McIntyre Papers, Pleasant C. Saunders Account Books, John Belknap Smith Papers, Charles L. Van Noppen Papers, Lewis Ward Papers, Washington Mining Company Ledgers, Charles Wilkes Papers, Worth Family Papers.

Greenville, North Carolina. East Carolina University. Manuscript Department: Barnhardt Family Papers, Mauney Family Papers, North Carolina Geological Survey Collection.

Nashville, Tennessee. Tennessee State Library and Archives: Jones Family Papers.

Raleigh, North Carolina. State Archives: North Carolina Supreme Court, Original Case Records: *George Reid v. George Barnhart and others*, also reported as 54 N.C. (1 Jones Eq.) 142 (1853). Private Collections: Brown Family and W. Vance Brown Papers, V. P. Clark Papers, Atlas Cochran Papers, Calvin J. Cowles Papers, Edmund Deberry Papers, Richard M. Eames Papers, Gold Hill Copper Company Ledger, Gold Hill Mining Company Papers, John M. and Ruth Hodges Papers, William A. Hoke Papers, Mecklenburg Iron Works Records, Edward W. Phifer Jr. Collection, John Scott Papers, Silver Hill Mining Company Records, James E. Smoot Papers, David L. Swain Papers, Union Copper Mining Company Papers, Richard D. White Collection, Calvin H. Wiley Papers.

Salisbury, N.C. Rowan County Public Library: McCubbins Collection, Heilig Family Papers, McMakin Family Papers, Mauney Family Papers, Union Copper Mine Papers.

Federal Records

Third Census of the United States, 1810: Cabarrus County, North Carolina, Population Schedule.

Fourth Census of the United States, 1820: Cabarrus County, North Carolina, Population Schedule.

Fifth Census of the United States, 1830: Cabarrus and Mecklenburg Counties, North Carolina, Population Schedules.

Sixth Census of the United States, 1840: Cabarrus, Mecklenburg, Montgomery, and Rowan Counties, North Carolina, Population Schedules.

Seventh Census of the United States, 1850. Cabarrus and Rowan Counties, North Carolina: Agricultural, Mortality, Population, Slave, and Social Statistics Schedules. North Carolina, Industrial Schedules.

Eighth Census of the United States, 1860. Cabarrus and Rowan Counties, North Carolina: Mortality, Population, Slave, and Social Statistics Schedules. North Carolina: Industrial Schedules.

Ninth Census of the United States, 1870. Rowan County, North Carolina: Agricultural, and Population Schedules. North Carolina, Industrial Schedules.

Tenth Census of the United States, 1880. Rowan County, North Carolina: Agricultural, and Population Schedules. North Carolina, Manufacturing Schedules.

Twelfth Census of the United States, 1900. Cabarrus and Rowan Counties, North Carolina, Population Schedules.

Records of the Bureau of the Mint, National Archives Record Group 104: Register of Gold Bullion, 1795-1836 (A.G. 104.113), 2 vols.; Charlotte Branch Mint, Register of Gold Bullion Received from Depositors, December 1837-May 1861 (RG 104.390), 2 vols. Other records from the Charlotte mint are preserved at the National Archives and, on microfilm, at the Mint Museum of Art, Charlotte.

Theses, Dissertations, and Reports

Brown, Henry S., and Mary F. Hoffman. "Gold Mining on the Rudisill Lode and the Development of Charlotte, N.C." August 1978. Prepared for the city of Charlotte.

Forret, Jeffrey Paul. " '. . . Promises to be Very Rich': The Development of the Gold Mining Industry in the Agrarian Society of Western North Carolina, 1825-1837." Master's thesis, University of North Carolina at Charlotte, 1998.

Glass, Brent D. "King Midas and Old Rip: The Gold Hill Mining District of North Carolina." Ph.D. dissertation, University of North Carolina at Chapel Hill, 1980.

Knapp, Richard F. "A Preliminary Report on Mining Technology and Machinery at the Reed Gold Mine and Other Gold Mines in North Carolina." 1973. Copy at University of North Carolina library.

_____, and George Stinagle. "A Preliminary Report on Gold Mining in North Carolina with Particular Emphasis on the Reed Gold Mine." 1976. Copy at University of North Carolina library.

Suttlemyre, Charles Greer, Jr. "Gold Mining in North Carolina, 1799-1860." Master's thesis, Western Carolina University, Cullowhee, 1970.

Database

Mason, George T., and Raymond E. Arndt. U.S. Geological Survey Digital Data Series DDS-26 (1996).

Index

A

C

D

Daniel and Company mine (Randolph County), 42t

Davidson, William: quoted, 29

Davidson County, N.C.: farmers from, market produce at Gold Hill, 82; gold discovered in, 14; gold fields in, relatively late to be explored, 74; mines and mining in, 7, 18, 27, 35, 36t, 130t; opportunities for investment in, publicized, 83

Deep River Gold Mine (Guilford County), 38

Deep River mine (Guilford County), 32

"Double-jacking," 87

Drag-stone mill. *See* Arrastra

Dredging (as mining technique), 141

Drifts, 87

Drilling, 86-87; pictured, 87

Drunkenness (among miners), 22, 139

Duke, James B., 152

Duke Power Company, 152

Dunn and Alexander mine (Mecklenburg County), 27

Dunn mine (Mecklenburg County): early creek mining at, 10, 11; location of, shown on map, 9

Dunn's Mountain mine (Rowan County), 130t

Dutch Buffalo Creek, 49

E

Eames, Richard, Jr., 106, 119, 133, 134

Earnhardt, Phillip, 77

Earnhardt family, 74

Earnhardt mine (Gold Hill mining district), 85

Earnhardt shaft (Gold Hill mine), 76, 78

Eastern (N.C.) gold region, 7

Eastern slate geologic belt, 7, 144

Edison, Thomas: visits gold region of N.C., 106-107

Edmunds, Richard H.: quoted, 140

Electric-powered mining machinery, 144, 147

Emmons, Ebenezer, 61, 91; quoted, 39, 99

Emmons mine (Davidson County), 41

Erwin mine (Burke County), 36t

Ethan Allen mine (Davidson County), 130t

Eureka mine (Davidson County), 130t

Excelsior Gold Mining Company, 37t, 40

Explosions. *See* Mine explosions

Explosives. *See* Blasting

F

Farmers: in area that became known as Gold Hill, 74; engage in mining, 11, 12, 14, 31

Farming: relative importance of in N.C., 18

Female workers. *See* Women

Fentress (copper) mine (Guilford County), 133; location of, shown on map, 9

Fisher, Charles, 18, 29; cited, 28; quoted, 3

Fisher Hill mine (Guilford County): location of, shown on map, 9

Fisher Hill Mining Company, 37t; installs steam engine and Chilean mills, 40

Fisher and Willis mine (Guilford county), 130t

Flooding. *See* Mining accidents

"Flotation" (method of separating minerals), 147

Martin, Samuel, 16

Mauney, Ephraim, 77, 84, 97, 100, 101, 111

Mauney, Valentine, 77, 84, 97, 101

Mauney's Store (Gold Hill), 148

Meadow Creek, 49

Mecklenburg County, N.C., 12; devoid of active mines in 1850, 35, by 1860, 42; exaggerated stories concerning gold in, 17, 27; gold discovered in, 11; mines and mining in, 7, 14, 31, 76, 130t; social conditions in, 1830, 22

Mecklenburg Gold and Copper Company, 40

Mecklenburg Gold Mining Company: incorporated, 18; mills ore from Reed mine, 55; new leaders to reorganize, 32; operates Capps and other mines, 26

Mecklenburg Iron Works: mining equipment made by, 68, 104, 137, 139-140, 145, pictured, 140

Medical Repository (periodical): publicizes presence of gold in N.C., 17

Mellon, Andrew, 110, 118

Mercury, 128; used in amalgamation process to retrieve gold, 52, 147, in Gold Hill mining district, 78, 80, 90, 104, 105, at Reed mine, 60-61

Metallurgy, 41

Methodist Church: at Gold Hill, 83, 123

Mezger, C. A., 66, 67

Miami (formerly Phoenix) mine, 144

Miami Mining Company, 144

Miller shaft (Gold Hill mine), 148

Mine explosions, 1, 3, 57, 94, 120-121, 136, 139. *See also* Blasting

Miners' and Farmers' Journal (Charlotte): denies nativist resentment of foreigners, 19; establishment of, symbolic of

close relationship between agriculture and mining, 2; masthead of, pictured, 17; prints technical articles on mining, 23; publicizes presence of gold in N.C., 17; quoted, 26

Miners and mine workers: deaths of, resulting from accidents, 94-95, 121, 139; demographic composition of, not precisely known, 20; living conditions of, described, 97; numbers of, in Mecklenburg County (1850), reported, 20; often regarded as poor or undependable employees, 97; pictured, 10, 13, 16, 20; typical lives of, described, 22-23; wages earned by, 23, 128, 139; working conditions of, 93-94, 139

Mining accidents, 1, 94-95, 117, 120-121, 136, 139

Mining equipment: costs associated with, 23

Mining industry (N.C.): and agriculture, 2, 3-4, 74-75, 123, 153; attempts by government to aid, 126-127; attempts to modernize (early twentieth century), described, 140-141; attracts foreign experts, foremen, and laborers, 19; becomes socioeconomic factor in N.C. in decade after 1825, 13; begins evolution from creek beds to hillsides, 14; benefits of, extolled, 28; briefly leads textile industry in attracting capital, 18; British investors in, 131; characterized by haphazard operations, 10, 12, 14, by inept leadership, 138-139; continues to function in some N.C. locations after 1915, 147-148; contributes to rise of Piedmont as center of industrial activity in N.C., 151; costs of engaging in, 23; declines sharply in late 1850s, early 1860s, 42, 43; in early 1900s, 141-143; efforts to preserve heritage of, 148-149; in 1850, 35; European experts in,

O

2/02